HANDBOOK

OF

MEDIÆVAL

GEOGRAPHY AND HISTORY.

BY

WILHELM PÜTZ,

PRINCIPAL TUTOR AT THE GYMNASIUM OF DÜREN.

TRANSLATED FROM THE GERMAN,

BY THE

REV. R. B. PAUL, M. A.,

VICAR OF ST. AUGUSTINE'S, BRISTOL, AND LATE FELLOW
OF EXETER COLLEGE, OXFORD.

NEW-YORK:
D. APPLETON & COMPANY, 200 BROADWAY.
PHILADELPHIA:
GEO. S. APPLETON, 164 CHESNUT-STREET.
1850.

PREFACE

BY THE AMERICAN EDITOR.

The characteristics of this volume are the same as those of the first: precision, condensation, and luminous arrangement. It is precisely what it pretends to be—a manual, a sure and conscientious guide for the student through the crooks and tangles of mediæval history. Many things of course are omitted; many rather indicated than developed;—but all the great principles of this extensive period are carefully laid down, and the most important facts skilfully grouped around them. There is no period of history for which it is more difficult to prepare a work like this, and none for which it is so much needed. The leading facts are well established, but they are scattered over an immense space; the principles are ascertained, but their development was slow, unequal, and interrupted. There is a general breaking up of a great body, and a parcelling of it out among small tribes, concerning whom we have only a few general data, and are left to analogy and conjecture for the details. Then come successive attempts at organization, each more or less independent, and all very imperfect. At last, modern Europe begins slowly to emerge from the chaos, but still under forms which the most diligent historian cannot always comprehend. To reduce such materials to a clear and definite form is a task of no small difficulty, and in which even partial success deserves great praise. It is not too much to say, that it has never been so well done within a compass so easily mastered, as in the little volume which is now offered to the public.

In the English edition there were no references. It would have been easy to supply this want by a long list of the sources of mdiæval history, which the student into whose hands this volume will fall would never have taken the trouble to read. I have preferred giving a reference for each section to works which are accessible to all, and where more copious indications will be found by those who wish to push their inquiries further. For greater convenience it is printed collectively in the Appendix.

GEO. W. GREENE.

Brown University, March 5, 1850.

CONTENTS.

INTRODUCTION.

THE MIDDLE AGES.

HANDBOOK

OF

GEOGRAPHY AND HISTORY.

PART II.—THE MIDDLE AGES.

INTRODUCTION.

1. Germany before the Migrations.

§ 1. *Geography of Germany in the First Century after Christ.*

B o u n d a r i e s. The Roman provinces on the left bank 1
of the Rhine, with some important stations on the right A
bank, were protected partly by fortresses, partly by lines
of pallisades and a rampart (vallum Romanum) which extended from Ratisbon on the Danube (across the Mayn
and Lahn) to Neuwied on the Rhine. All the territory
southward and westward of this frontier belonged to the
Roman empire, and was divided into G e r m a n i a Superior
or Prima (from Bâsle to Mainz), and G e r m a n i a Inferior
or Secunda (from Mainz to the country of the Batăvi).
The rest of Germany (between the Rhine, Danube, Elbe, B
and North Sea) was occupied by independent native
tribes.

S o i l a n d P r o d u c t s. According to the Roman writers, 2
Cæsar and Tacitus, the soil of Germany in their time was little better than a succession of steppes, morasses, and wild tracts of woodland; one of which, called the Hercynian forest, was reported to be sixty days' journey in extent. Hence the coldness of the climate, and the numerous animals, which now exist only in northern latitudes, such

2) as rein-deer, elks, uruses, and bears. Their horses were
A neither handsome nor swift; the neat cattle numerous, but
small. Fruit trees and every description of metal, except
iron, were unknown. The only sorts of grain cultivated
were oats and barley.

Tribes.

3 a) *The Western Germans.* 1. The Catti (Chassians or
B Hessians) in the Hercynian forest. 2. The Frisii on
the north-western coast, from the mouths of the Rhine
to the Ems. Smaller tribes: the Usipĕtes and Tenctĕri
on the Lower Rhine, the Sigambri [or Sicambri] on the
Sieg.

4 b) *The Northern Germans.* 1. The Chauci from the
Ems to the Elbe; and southward of these, 2. The Cherusci, between the Weser and the Elbe.

5 c) The *Suevi* (or Hermiones) a general name given by
C Tacitus to all the nations in the interior of Germany. Of
these tribes three are especially mentioned by the historian
as forming a confederacy, political and religious; viz. 1.
The Senones, between the Elbe, the Oder, and the Spree,
with the Langobardi, or Longobardi, on the left bank of
the Elbe. 2. A confederacy of seven Suevic tribes between
the Lower Elbe and the Baltic, who worshipped the goddess Hertha, in a sacred grove on an island of the ocean
D (Femern or Rügen?). 3. The Lygii, on the Upper Oder.
Besides these, there belonged to the Suevic stock: 1. In
the north-east, the Gothones, between the Warthe and the
Vistula; and the Æstiæi (Esthonians), at the mouth of the
Vistula, on the amber coast. 2. In the south, the Hermunduri on the Upper Danube, the Marcomanni in Bohemia, the Quadi in Moravia. The language of these
various tribes, no less than the peculiarities of their personal appearance, (the bold blue eye, golden hair, lofty
stature, and fair complexion,) are a sufficient indication
of their common descent from a distinct and unmixed
race.

§ 2. *Religion, Manners, and Customs in the First Century of the Christian Æra.*

Religion. The Supreme Being was worshipped by 6
the Germans under the names of Wodan (= Odin) and A
Thor (the god of thunder). Sacrifices were offered to these deities in groves and forests, and auguries drawn from the neighing and snorting of the white horses which were kept in honour of them. They believed in a future state of martial existence in Walhalla [Valhalla]. When a warrior died, his arms, and in the case of chieftains, his horse, were burnt at the grave.

Political Constitution. There was a distinction 7
between freemen and serfs. Every member of the former B
class enjoyed the privilege of being present in arms and taking part in the great national councils, which assembled regularly on the new and full moons, under the presidence of the elders or priests, for the purpose of deciding all important state questions, electing officers, and trying criminals. The assent of the assembly was expressed by a clattering of spears, and their disapprobation by a murmur. In these assemblies young men were solemnly declared capable of bearing arms. Their princes were chosen out of the most distinguished families, and their dukes or leaders from among the bravest warriors. The power of both these officers was limited.

War. Their arms consisted of a short spear, called *frame* 8
[*framea*], and a shield of painted wood. Their order of C
battle was in the form of a wedge, surrounded on three sides with a barricade of carriages, which sheltered the wives and children of the combatants. Before and during the engagement a battle-hymn was chanted by the bards. If the first attack was unsuccessful, they retired to their barricades, and renewed the fight, which was often won through the assistance afforded them by their wives and children.

Manners and customs. The ancient Germans had 9
no towns, nor even connected villages; but lived in de- D
tached wooden huts, thatched with straw, which were generally erected near the centre of their common field. A number of these huts formed a *mark*, several marks a *zent*, and several zents a *gau*. Their ordinary dress in summer was a tunic, of wool for the men, and linen for the women;

(9) and in winter, a coat of skins. Next to war, the chief
A business of their lives was the chase; the cultivation of the
soil, as well as all other manual labor, being left to their
wives, children, and serfs. The Germans were fond of
games of hazard, and passed a considerable portion of their
time in banquets and drinking matches; during which the
sword or war-dance was performed for the amusement of
the company, by naked youths, and the most important
affairs were frequently discussed. Chastity, a religious
observance of their conjugal obligations, and unbounded
hospitality, were the distinguishing virtues of this rude
B people. Atonement might be made for all crimes, including
even murder itself, by the payment of a fine, consisting of
a certain number of heads of cattle.

§ 3. *History of the Germans to the Period of the Migrations.*

A. The German tribes.

10 It seems probable that the coasts of the Baltic were
known from the remotest antiquity to Phœnician and Greek
traders in amber; but the first distinct accounts which we
have of the Germans commence with the invasion of the
Roman territory by separate tribes. Half German clans,
for instance, from the Alps, joined the Gauls in their expedition against Rome; and the Bastarnæ formed an alliance
C with Perseus. But the most fearful invasion was that of the
Cimbri and Teutŏnes (B.C. 113), who seem to have advanced
upon Norĭcum from two distinct points. For their war
with the Romans, see part i. 3, § 79. The next migration
was that of the Marcomanni, under one of their princes
named Ariovistus, who marched to the assistance of the
Sequăni against their enemies, the Edui (B.C. 72); and
after defeating them, continued to pour fresh troops into
Gaul, until he was finally overthrown by Cæsar at Vesontio
(Besançon) (58), and compelled to recross the Rhine.
D After an obstinate struggle, the Belgic Germans (Nervii,
Aduatici, and Eburones) were subdued by Cæsar, who
crossed the Rhine twice without any result, extinguished
an insurrection of the Belgæ under Ambiorix, prince of
the Eburones, took Germans into his pay, and with their
assistance quelled an insurrection of the Gauls under
Vercingetorix, completed the subjugation of Gaul, and
gained the decisive victory of Pharsălus. Augustus

formed a body-guard of Germans. His step-sons, Drusus (10)
and Tiberius, conquered all the nations between the Alps A
and the Danube. In order to subdue, also, the Low-German tribes, who were perpetually invading Roman Gaul, Drusus took whole German clans into his pay, built a fleet on the Rhine, which he united with the Yssel by means of the fossa Drusi, undertook four expeditions into Germany (B.C. 12—9), erected fortresses for the defence of the Roman territory (50? on the Rhine), and advanced as far as the Elbe.

B. The two first unions of German tribes.— B
The empire of the Marcomanni and confederacy of the Cherusci.

1. War of these two confederacies against Rome.

After the death of his brother, Tiberius continued the 11
war in Germany, and threatened *Marbod*, the founder of the Marcomannic empire, which comprised all the *Suevic tribes* between the Elbe and Danube (the Marcomanni, Hermunduri, Langobardi, and Senones); but in consequence of the simultaneous revolt of Pannonia and Dalmatia, he was compelled to grant peace on favorable terms.
Although the Low-German tribes had been rather gained C
over by promises and alliances than actually overcome, the Romans nevertheless considered themselves masters of all the country between the Rhine and the Elbe. The unjust severity of their governor, L. Quinctilius *Varus*, in compelling the Germans to adopt the Roman language, laws, and system of taxation, occasioned a *confederation* of the *Low-German* tribes (Cherusci, Bructeri, and Marsi), under the command of *Herman* (son of a prince of the Cherusci named Siegmar), who had been educated at Rome.
In spite of the warning given him by the traitor Segestus D
(afterwards Herman's father-in-law), Varus, crediting the intelligence of a revolt on the Ems, suffered himself to be enticed into the *Teutoburgian forest*, where he was attacked by Herman [Arminius], and after losing three Roman legions, threw himself on his own sword (A.D. 9). On receiving intelligence of this disaster, Augustus disbanded his German body-guard, and compelled all the German residents to quit Rome. In the years 14—16, three campaigns in Germany, (principally against the Che-

(11) rusci, Bructeri, Marsi, and Catti,) were undertaken by
A Germanicus, the son of Drusus, who buried the bones of those who had fallen in the Teutoburgian forest, and defeated Herman at Idistaviss [Idistavisus Campus], on the Weser. On the homeward voyage a part of his fleet was wrecked in a gale of wind, and Germanicus himself was recalled by Tiberius, before he had succeeded in re-establishing the Roman supremacy in Germany.

2. War between the two confederacies.

12 The bravest of the Suevic tribes, the Langobardi and
B Senones, renounced their allegiance to Marbod, and joined the Cheruscan league; whilst, on the other hand, Hinkmar, the uncle of Herman, who envied his nephew's reputation, went over to the side of Marbod. The result of these secessions was a double intestine war. 1. Between the chiefs of the Cherusci. 2. Between the Cheruscan confederacy and the Marcomannic empire (A.D. 19). After sustaining a defeat, Marbod was expelled from his kingdom by a Gothonian named Catwald; and Herman, who was suspected of aiming at absolute power, was assassinated by his own relations (A.D. 22?).

3. The Batavian war of liberation (69).

13 After the dissolution of these two confederacies, the
C domestic feuds of the Germans were fostered by the Romans so effectually as to prevent, for a century and a half, the formation of any fresh leagues. An attempt, it is true, was made by the Batăvi (exasperated by Cl. Civilis) to unite several German tribes (Bructeri, Tencteri, Catti, Usipetes, Mattiaci, and, at a later period, the Trieri, Lingones, and Ubii) for a war of liberation; but after sustaining several defeats, most of the clans were induced, either by bribery or by the fair promises of the Romans, to withdraw from the confederacy.

4. The Marcomannic war, 166—180.

14 Whilst the Romans were occupied with a war against
D the Parthians, their provinces on the southern Danube were invaded by several clans, among whom we hear, for the first time, of the Vandals and Alans. The emperor Marcus Aurelius, after undertaking nine campaigns against these barbarians, died at Vienna, in the midst of his preparations for the tenth. His son Commodus, who wished to remain at Rome, granted peace to the Marcomanni,

Quadi, &c., on condition of their furnishing a yearly con- (14)
tingent. A

C. More extensive confederacies in the W. and E.

a. *In Western Germany.* 1. The Alemanni, a general 15
name for the union (commenced by the Hermunduri) of
the hitherto distinct Suevic tribes in the south-west, from
the Mayn to the Alps. 2. The Franks, an appellation B
indicating a similar union of Low-German clans, most of which had belonged to the Cheruscan league, but excluding the Cheruscans themselves. 3. The Saxons, whose name and confederation extended southwards, from the Cimbrian Peninsula, their original settlement, to the frontiers of the Cheruscan territory.

b. *In Eastern Germany* were also three confederacies: the Vandal, Gothic, and Alanic.

These confederacies, the origin of which might be traced 16
partly to the combination of different tribes against the C
Romans, and partly to the extension of the feudal system, availed themselves of the confusion occasioned throughout the Roman empire, by the frequent change of rulers, to raise the standard of revolt on their respective frontiers. (About 250.) Whilst the Rhenish border was distracted by the invasions of the Alemanni and Franks, the Goths appeared in Illyria and Thrace, and, in conjunction with the Heruli, carried on piratical warfare against the coasts and islands of the Archipelago, until the restoration of the ancient boundaries of the Roman empire by Aurelian, and the re-establishment by Probus, after many struggles, of the frontier wall between the Rhine and Danube. A great number
of Germans were, at the same time, transplanted into the D
Roman provinces. (Return to Germany of the Franks, who had been removed to the shores of the Pontus Euxinus.) After the death of Probus the frontier wall disappeared; the Alemanni became masters of the Upper Rhine, and extended their conquests into Vindelicia and Rhœti, whilst the Franks took possession of the Batavian islands, and forced their way through Belgium into Gaul. These encroachments were met, on the part of the Romans, by the establishment of additional settlements of German auxiliaries in their frontier provinces. At the head of these mercenaries Cæsar Julianus defeated, near Strasburg,

(16) a body of Alemanni who had invaded Gaul, and five times
A pursued the Germans across the frontier into their own territory. Notwithstanding this check, the Alemanni soon afterwards recrossed the Rhine and Danube, and were again expelled from Gaul by Valentinian I.; a portion of those who had crossed the Danube being permitted to hold fiefs on the banks of the Po.

II. The Migrations.

§ 4. *Destruction of the Gothic Empire by the Huns.*

17 The two branches of the Gothic empire had extended in
B the fourth century ever the whole of north-eastern Europe; the Western Gothic [or that of the *Visigoths*] occupying all the territory between the Lower Danube and the Dniester (including what is now Moldavia, Wallachia, and Podolia), and the Eastern Gothic [that of the *Ostrogoths*] extending from the Baltic to the Black Sea. The former of these empires was governed by an aged monarch named Hermanric, the latter by Athanaric.

18 The Goths were the first German tribe who embraced
C Christianity, according to the teaching of the heresiarch Arius. At the council of Nicæa, in 325, there appeared a Gothic bishop, Theophilus, whose successor, Ulphilas, translated the four Gospels into the Gothic dialect.

19 The Huns, who originally inhabited that part of eastern Asia which lies northwards of China, had rendered themselves formidable to the Chinese empire long before their appearance in Europe; and in the third century before Christ, the great wall of China had been erected as a bar-
D rier against them. At a later period the Hunnish empire was divided into two kingdoms, the northern of which was overthrown by a Tartaric clan, the Sienpi. The most warlike of their tribes, however, moved westwards, and, between the Volga and the Don, encountered the Alani (about 375), a portion of whom retreated before them, whilst the remainder surrendered, and were incorporated into their army. Reinforced by these new auxiliaries, the Huns assailed both the kingdoms of the Goths, who besought the emperor Valens to grant them lands on the right

bank of the Danube. Only a portion of the West Goths, (19)
[Visigoths] the Thervingians, were permitted to settle in A
Mœsia. These were soon goaded into revolt by the severity
of the Roman governors; and calling in the Huns and Alani
as auxiliaries, they crossed the Hæmus into Thrace, attacked
Valens (378) near Adrianople, and compelled him to take
refuge in a hut, where he was accidentally burnt to death.
His successor, Theodosius, beat back the Goths, who were
advancing on Constantinople, and concluded a peace, by the
terms of which, the West Goths were permitted to settle in
Mœsia and Dacia, and their allies, the Eastern Goths [Os-
trogoths], in Asia Minor, on condition of their furnishing a
contingent of mercenary troops, under their own commanders. The Eastern emperor, Arcadius, having neg- B
lected to pay the stipulated wages to these auxiliaries, the
West Goths chose Alaric to be their king, and invaded
Greece, which they were compelled to evacuate on the
approach of Stilico, who advanced with a fleet to the relief
of Peloponnesus. Alaric was invested with the prefec-
ture of the East-Roman province of Illyricum.

§ 5. *General Immigration of the Barbarians into the Countries of the West.*

From Illyria, Alaric, at the head of the Visigoths, 20
entered Italy in the year 403, but was twice defeated by C
Stilico, at Pollentia and Verōna.

Soon after this invasion (406), several German clans ap- 21
peared in Italy under the command of their prince, Radagais. At the siege of Florence most of them either died of starvation or were taken prisoners and sold as slaves. A few cut their way through the enemy's army, and escaped into Gaul.

It was, however, towards the west, that the grand move- 22
ment took place from the interior of Germany. The Bur- D
gundians established themselves in eastern Gaul, on the
Upper Rhine (407), whilst the Alani and Suevi entered
Spain by the passes of the Pyrenees, and spread themselves
over the Peninsula, the Vandals and Suevi occupying
the western portion (Galicia), the Alani settling in Lusitania and Carthagena, and a division of the Vandals taking
possession of the district called after them, Andalusia.

(22) The Tarraconian province seems to have been the only
A portion of the Peninsula which remained in the hands of the Romans.

23 After the assassination of Stilico, Alaric, disgusted at the non-payment of the subsidies granted by Honorius, invested Rome, and was only induced to spare the city by the promise of an enormous ransom. His overtures of peace having been rejected by the court of Ravenna, Alaric appeared a second time before Rome, in the year 400 ; but again raised the siege, and marched to Ravenna; then returned to Rome for the third time in 410, took the city by treachery (Aug. 24), and punished the inhabitants by allow-
B ing six (?) days' pillage to his soldiers. He died at Consentia, on the march into Lower Italy, and was buried in the channel of the river Busentinus. His successor, Athaulf, concluded a peace with Honorius, and led the Visigoths into Gaul in 412, and into Spain in 414. His successor, Wallia, overthrew the Suevi, Vandals, and Alani, who had entered the country a short time before; then recrossed the Pyrenees, and took possession of the districts ceded to him by Honorius in Aquitania (from Toulouse along the Garonne to the sea, called also Septimania), and chose Toulouse for the capital of his empire, which now extended a considerable distance on each side of the Pyrenees.

24 The Vandals and Alani, in the year 429, accepted
C an invitation from the Roman lieutenant, Bonifacius (who had fallen into disgrace at the court of his empress), and invaded the northern coast of Africa, where their king, Geiseric [Genseric], after the capture of Hippo and Carthage, founded the Vandalic empire, with Carthage for its capital. This empire comprehended also the islands of the western Mediterranean.

25 Ever since the abandonment of Britain by the Roman
D legions, the island had been ravaged by hordes of Picts and Scots. After applying in vain for protection to the Romans, the inhabitants invited the Saxons, Angles, and Jutlanders, who landed in the year 449, under the command of Hengist and Horsa, expelled the Picts, and settled in the island, where they gradually formed seven Anglo-Saxon kingdoms; viz. Kent, Sussex, Wessex, Essex, Northumberland, East-Anglia, and Mercia. The Britons retired into

Wales and Cornwall, or emigrated to the opposite coast of (25)
Armorica (Bretagne).

§ 6. *Dissolution of the Hunnish Empire.*

The Huns, who, after the subjugation of the Eastern Goths 26
[Ostrogoths], had been wandering for fifty years about A
Southern Russia, Poland, and Hungary, again became formidable under the command of their king, Attila, or Etzel
(the scourge of God), who reigned in conjunction with his
brother Bleda, from 434 to 444, and alone from 444 to 453.
The Roman emperors of the east and west having united for
the purpose of rescuing Africa from the Vandals, Geiseric
persuaded Attila to invade the eastern empire. After thrice B
defeating Theodosius II., Attila appeared before Constantinople; but being unacquainted with the art of attacking
fortified places, he contented himself with exacting a yearly
tribute, in addition to the payment already guaranteed by
Arcadius, and compelling the emperor to cede a district of
Thrace. Then he entered Gaul at the head of 700,000 men,
but was defeated on the Catalaunian plain, at Châlons
sur Marne (451), by the united forces of the West Goths
under their king Theodoric, and the Romans under their
general Aëtius. In this engagement, the most sanguinary, C
perhaps, that ever occurred in Europe (106,000 slain), Germans were opposed to each other, some of them serving in the
Roman army, and others in that of the Huns. King Theodoric was slain. The following year (452) Attila demanded
in marriage Honoria, sister of Valentinian III., requiring
half the empire as her dowry. This proposal being rejected,
he suddenly entered Italy, sacked Aquileia, and plundered
all the cities of Lombardy, the inhabitants of which fled in
great numbers to the islands in the lagunes of the Adriatic,
where they founded the city of Venice. The Romans, D
headed by their pope, Leo I., petitioned for peace, which
was granted by Attila. After his death, in the following
year (453), his empire, which had extended from the Rhine
to the eastern bank of the Volga, rapidly crumbled away;
the nations which had hitherto been subject to the Huns
driving them back to the shores of the Black Sea, and
forming kingdoms of their own, the Gepidæ in Dacia, the
East Goths in Pannonia, and, at a later period, in Thrace.

§ 7. *Dissolution of the Western Roman Empire.*

27 The progress of the Germanic tribes was favored by the
A intestine confusion of the Western Roman empire, the capital of which was plundered for fourteen days by the Vandals, in 455, and its sceptre wielded by a Suevian named Ricimer, in the name of a succession of puppets, who bore the title of emperor. The West Goths [Visigoths] extended their empire in Gaul to the Loire, the Rhone, and the Ocean, and put an end to the Roman dominion in Spain, where there remained only the little kingdom of the Suevi, in Galicia and Lusitania. The Burgundians spread still more widely in south-eastern, and the Franks in central Gaul. Two attempts of the Romans to reconquer Africa
B were rendered abortive by Geiseric, who annihilated their fleet. Finally, Adoăcer, who had entered the Roman service as a mercenary, at the head of a band composed of Heruleans, Rugians, &c., and had been refused a third of the lands in Italy, put an end to the empire of the West by deposing the emperor Romulus Augustulus, and was proclaimed king of Italy by his German mercenaries, in 476. The Roman possessions in Gaul were retained for a time by Syagrius, who was finally defeated by Chlodwig [Clovis], at Soissons, and compelled to evacuate the province in the year 486.

THE MIDDLE AGES.

First Period.

From the Dissolution of the Western Empire to the Accession of the Carlovingians and Abbasides, 476—752 (750).

A. The West.

§ 8. *Empires in Italy.*

I. The Italian empire established by German 28
mercenaries under Odoacer (476—490). A
Theodoric, king of the Eastern Goths [Ostrogoths], who had embraced the tenets of Arianism during his residence as a hostage at Constantinople, and subsequently taken service in the armies of the eastern empire, proposed to the emperor Zeno a plan for reconquering Italy with his Goths. This proposal being accepted, Theodoric fought his way through the territories of the Gepidæ, and defeated Odoacer in three engagements (on the Isonzo, the Adige, and the Adda). Odoacer, after sustaining a siege for three years in the strongly-fortified city of Ravenna, surrendered, and was put to death with his family and followers, in 493.

II. Empire of the Ostrogoths in Italy, 490— B
554.

Theodoric the Great (490—526) was recognized as king 29
of Italy by Anastasius, the successor of Zeno. This sovereign not only strengthened his newly-established throne by wise laws and institutions, but extended his empire beyond the boundaries of Italy, over the countries between the Alps and the Danube, as well as Illyricum, and finally over Provence. Imperial residence—Ravenna, and sometimes Verona or Bern (hence his German name of Dietrich of
Bern). Prosperity of Italy, in consequence of his toleration C
of the Catholics; encouragement of agriculture and com-

(29) merce; embellishment of the cities, drainage, and cultiva-
A tion of the Pontine marshes, &c. He succeeded, also, in
maintaining peace among the German princes, most of
whom were his relations. His brother-in-law, Chlodwig
(Clovis), king of the Franks, the only sovereign who offered
resistance, was compelled to lay down his arms. The Visigothic throne was secured to Amalaric, a minor, the grandson of Theodoric, who undertook the office of guardian.
Theodoric died in 526, of remorse, it is said, on account of
the (perhaps) unjust execution of the learned senator Boë-
thius (who was suspected of having negotiated with the
B eastern emperor, Justinian, for the liberation of Italy from
the Goths), and his father-in-law, Symmachus. Theodoric
was succeeded by his daughter, Amalasuntha, who governed in the name of her son, Athalaric, a minor, and, after
his untimely death, shared the throne with her cousin, The-
odotus, by whom she was murdered. Under pretence of
avenging her death, Justinian revived those claims to the
sovereignty of Italy which had never been entirely abandoned by the eastern court. Hence arose the **eighteen
years' war.** The Byzantine general, **Belisarius,** soon made
himself master of Sicily and Italy; but these advantages
were lost, in consequence of his being twice recalled, the
C Goths, under their leader Totila, reconquering the territory which had been wrested from them. Germans (Heru-
lians and Langobardi) now fought as mercenaries against
Germans, under **Narses,** who was victorious at Taginæ, in
Etruria, where Totilas was slain. In this war Rome was
taken for the fifth time; and the heroic king, Tejas, found,
like his brave predecessor, Totila, a soldier's grave on the
field of battle. A portion of the Goths capitulated, on condition of being permitted to depart in peace; whilst the
remainder, who had invited two German princes to enter
Italy at the head of the Franks and Alemanni, were overthrown, together with their allies, by Narses in 554, and
D compelled to submit to the conqueror. Italy became a
province of the eastern empire, and was governed by
exarchs resident at Ravenna, of whom Narses was the first.

III. **Byzantine dominion in Italy.**

In the year 568 the Langobardi entered Italy, and, after
30 a succession of battles, compelled the Romans to relinquish
their sovereignty over the whole of Italy, (which they had

exercised for fourteen years), and confine themselves to the (30)
territories strictly comprehended within their exarchate,— A
Rome, Naples, and southern Italy, to which was added the
name of Calabria, although they had lost that province.

IV. **Empire of the Langobardi.** 568—774.

On their return from Italy, the Langobardi, who had 31
assisted Narses against the Ostrogoths, overthrew (under
the command of their king **Alboin,** and with the aid of the
Avari) the empire of the Gepidæ, whose name, from this
time, merges in those of the neighboring tribes. Leaving
Pannonia to the Avari, the Langobardi returned to Italy,
by the invitation, as they pretended, of the disgraced general, Narses, and with the aid of 20,000 Saxons, and some
other hordes, wrested from the Byzantines the whole of
Upper Italy, which thenceforward was named from them,
Lombardy. Pavia, after a siege of three years, surrendered B
to the conquerors, and was made the capital of their kingdom. After the assassination of Alboin (at the instigation
of his wife Rosamond), the empire was extended southwards by his successor, Kleph, so as to comprehend almost
the whole of Italy, with the exception of a few strips of
land on the coast. The southern division formed the duchy
of Benevento. Kleph having been also assassinated, an
interregnum of ten years succeeded, during which the
country was governed by thirty-six dukes, among whom
the most powerful were those of Friuli and Benevento. At C
the end of this period it was found necessary to restore the
office of king, and Anthari, the son of Kleph, was raised to
the throne. The wife of this sovereign, a Bavarian Catholic named Theodolinda, commenced the conversion of
the Arian Lombards to the orthodox faith. Under succeeding kings, the eastern and western coasts of northern
Italy fell into the hands of the Langobardi, who confined
the exarchate within the limits of Calabria and the district
around Naples, and even laid claim to the sovereignty of
Rome and its territory. In his terror at this demonstration, D
Pope Stephen III. applied for aid to Pepin the Short [Pepin
le Bref], king of the Franks, whom he had himself anointed.
After two campaigns in Italy, Pepin compelled the Langobardi to cede to the Pope that portion of the coast of the
Adriatic which had most recently fallen into their hands,
and thus laid the foundation of his temporal power. The

(31) interference of the Franks in disputes between the Pope and
A the Lombards, occasioned the incorporation of the Langobardic empire into that of the Franks, in the year 774.

§ 9. *Empire of the Vandals in Africa*, 429—534.

32 Extent of the empire. *a.* In Africa: the whole northern line of coast, from the Atlantic Ocean to Cyrenaica, comprehending the ancient Roman provinces of Mauritania, Numidia, Africa Propria, and the district of the Syrtes. *b.* Out of Africa: the islands of Sardinia and Corsica, the Balearic and Pityusian islands, and Sicily (at first the whole island, but subsequently [493] only the north-western part).

33 History. For the establishment of the empire by Gei-
B seric, see § 5. The Roman emperor, Valentinian III.,
having fallen by the hand of Maximus, his widow, Eudoxia,
who had been compelled to marry the assassin, implores
the assistance of Geiseric, who lands on the coast of Italy,
and plunders Rome for fourteen days, in the year 455.
Maximus is slain; Eudoxia, with her treasures and a crowd
of prisoners, conveyed to Carthage; and all the Italian
islands ceded to the conqueror. In order to clear the
Mediterranean of Vandal pirates, a fleet of 1113 sail is
equipped, by the united exertions of the two emperors,
C and despatched to Carthage. This fleet is attacked in the
night by Geiseric, and the ships partly destroyed and partly
dispersed (468). The decline of the Vandal empire, which
commenced with the death of its founder, was accelerated
by the frequent attacks of the Barbary tribes, and the persecution carried on against the Catholics, of which Geiseric,
himself an Arian, had set the example. Availing himself
of this position of affairs, Justinian, the Byzantine emperor,
despatched a fleet to the coast of Africa, under the command of his general, Belisarius, who found the throne occupied by Gelimer, the last of the Vandal kings, and suc-
D cessor of the deposed sovereign, Hilderic. After an engagement, in which the Vandals were defeated, Carthage
surrendered, without offering any resistance; and soon
afterwards the whole Vandal army was routed, and their
country entirely subdued (534). Gelimer, after gracing
the triumphal entry of Belisarius into Constantinople, re-

ceived an allotment of land in Asia Minor; the bravest of (33)
the Vandals were enrolled in the Roman cavalry, and the A
remainder absorbed into the mass of African tributaries.

§ 10. *Empire of the Suevi in Spain,* 409—585.

The whole of Bœtica, together with the Carthaginian pro- 34
vince, had been occupied since the departure of the Vandals by the Suevi, who had settled in Galicia on their first arrival in Spain. Their first Christian (Catholic) sovereign, Rechiar, was attacked in consequence of his frequent inroads into the Roman province Tarraconensis, by Theodoric II., king of the Visigoths, defeated at Paramo, on
the river Obrego, and executed. The empire of the Suevi B
seemed now at an end; but the remnant of the nation having assembled in a remote corner of Galicia, a new king was chosen, and their former piratical practices resumed. This independent Suevic kingdom, being distracted by political struggles, was finally incorporated into the Visigothic empire, in the year 585.

§ 11. *Empire of the Visigoths,* 419—712.

Extent of the empire. *a.* In *Gaul.* At first (419), 35
Aquitania Secunda; subsequently (439), the whole country C
bordering on the Mediterranean, from the Rhone to the Pyrenees, at a later period styled exclusively Septimania; from the time of Euric (475), the country between the Rhone, the Loire, and the Ocean. After the battle of Vouglé (507), only the extreme southern part of their Gallic empire remained in the hands of the Visigoths; and even of this a portion was wrested from them by the Franks, in
531. *b.* In *Spain.* At first only the country between the D
Pyrenees, the Mediterranean, and the Ebro; from the time of Euric, the whole of Spain, with the exception of the Suevic kingdom and the territory of the Vasci in the north; from the time of Leuwigild, the whole of Spain, with the exception, at first, of some maritime cities in the south, and a part of the northern district; at a later period, Ceuta, in Africa, with its territory.

History. Wallia, the founder of the Visigothic 36
empire (see § 5), was succeeded by Theodoric I., who

(36) defeated a Roman army, extended his empire as far as the
A Rhone, and fell in the battle of the Catalaunian fields.
Theodoric II. subdued the greater part of the Suevic
empire. His successor, Euric, extended his empire in
Gaul to the Rhone, the Loire, and the Ocean; expelled the
Romans from Spain, and compiled a catalogue of the legal
usages of the Goths. His violent persecution of the Catholics compelled them to form an alliance with the half-con-
verted Frankish king, Chlodwig [Clovis], who, under pretence of rooting out the Arian heresy, attacked Alaric II.,
son and successor of Euric, slew him with his own hand in
the battle of Vouglé, near Poitiers (507), and stripped
the Visigoths of all their possessions in Gaul, except a
B portion of Septimania. During the minority of his son and
successor, Amalric, the Visigothic empire was united, for
fourteen years, to his own dominions, by Theodoric, king
of the Ostrogoths. After the death of Amalric, who was
slain during a war occasioned by his ill-treatment of his
wife, Clotilda, a daughter of Chlodwig, the imperial residence was transferred to Toledo, in 531.

37 The Visigothic empire was still surther circumscribed
by the Byzantines, who invaded the country on the invitation of Athanagild (an insurgent, and subsequently king),
C and conquered the whole southern line of coast. For this
loss they were in some measure indemnified by the subjugation of the rebellious Cantabrians and Vasci, and the
conquest of the Suevic empire, by Leuwigild, who also
compelled the Byzantines to restore several of the cities
which they had taken.

38 After the establishment of a natural boundary-line, by
the expulsion of the Greeks from Spain (624), the attention
of the Visigothic kings was directed rather to the consolidation of their own power, than the extension of their terri-
D tories. The only foreign conquest during this period was
a portion of Mauritania. Notwithstanding the amalga-
mation of the Visigoths and Romans, in consequence of
intermarriages, the adoption of the Catholic religion by the
former, and the establishment of a common code of laws,
the succession to the throne occasioned perpetual disputes,
for the settlement of which the Arabians were at last invited over from Africa. On receiving this invitation, Musa
immediately despatched an army into Spain, under the

command of his lieutenant, Tarek, who overthrew Roderic, (38)
the last of the Visigothic kings, at Xeres de la Fron- A
tera, after a struggle which lasted nine days (711). Musa
soon afterwards followed his lieutenant into Spain, and the
greater part of the Peninsula was already in their hands,
when the two generals were suddenly recalled by a command of their caliph. After their departure, the Pyrenæan
Peninsula was divided into—1. Arabian Spain, governed
by lieutenants of the caliphs of Bagdad, until the establishment (756) of an independent kingdom at Cordŏva, by
Abderrahman, the last Ommaijade. 2. The Christian
kingdom of Asturia, where a remnant of the beaten Visigoths maintained themselves against the Arabians.

§ 12. *Empire of the Burgundians in Gaul,* 407—533.

The Burgundians (probably the people named by Taci- 39
tus, Burii) first appeared in the first century, in the neigh- B
bourhood of the Vistula. They seem to have been a
branch of the great Suevic stock. The loss of a battle
against the Gepidæ (about 250) having compelled them to
retire westward, they settled on the Upper Rhine, in the
neighbourhood of the Alemanni; and, at a later period,
received allotments of land from the Romans in Germania
Superior (Alsace). Thence they spread southwards, over
parts of Helvetia, Savoy, Dauphiné, Lyonnois, and Franche-
Compté. At the head of the nation was a high-priest, who C
held his office for life (Sinist). Their kings (Hendinos),
who resided sometimes at Geneva and sometimes at Lyons,
were set aside for failure in war, or on account of personal deformity. Disputed successions occasioned the
introduction of Frankish kings (of Paris, Soissons, and
Metz), who conquered the kingdom and divided it
among themselves in the year 533 (?). The Burgun- D
dians were compelled to pay tribute and render military
service to the conqueror, but retained their own laws and
customs.

§ 13. *Empire of the Franks under the Merovingians.*

Since the middle of the first century, bands of Frankish 40
warriors had been accustomed to cross the Rhine; at first

(40) for the mere purpose of plunder, and subsequently in the
A hope of obtaining settlements; which they acquired partly
by force of arms and partly as rewards for their services in
the Roman army. These Frankish settlers in Gaul are
divided into two principal branches: the Salii, between
the Scheld and Meuse; and Ripuarii, probably between
the Meuse, Moselle, and Rhine. Their clans lived independently of one another, each under its own chief, until the
time of Chlodwig [Clovis], the grandson of Merovæus,
or Merwig, who succeeded his father as king of the Franks
B in 481. This monarch put an end to the Roman supremacy
in Gaul by the overthrow of their governor, Syagrius, at
Soissons, in 486; and, in conjunction with the Frankish
king, Siegbert, who resided at Cologne (?), subdued a portion of the Alemanni (probably only those who dwelt on
the left bank of the Rhine, between the Moselle and Alsace)
in a battle fought (perhaps) near Tolbiacum or Zülpich.
Having embraced the Catholic religion, in fulfilment of a
vow made during the battle, Chlodwig caused himself to
be anointed and crowned king of the Franks by Remigius,
C bishop of Rheims. After subduing the Armorici in Brittany,
he marched against his southern neighbours, the Burgundians and Visigoths; who were reduced to the condition
of tributaries, after sustaining a defeat at Dijon in 500,
but speedily recovered their independence. Under pretence of expelling the Arian heretics from Gaul, Chlodwig
again attacked them, and after obtaining a decisive victory
at Vouglé, on the Vienne, near Poictiers, where he slew
their king, Alaric II., with his own hand (507), deprived
them of all their possessions in Gaul, except the southern
portion. After this war Chlodwig transferred his residence
D to Paris. All the Frankish clans were at length united into
one kingdom, their petty sovereigns (Siegbert of Cologne,
Chararich of Belgium, and Ragnachar of Cambrai) having
been previously removed by assassination. After the death
of Chlodwig, in 511, the empire was divided among his
four sons, Dietrich [Thierry], Clodomer, Childebert, and
Clotar [Clothaire], who fixed their respective residences at
Metz, Orleans, Paris, and Soissons. The king of Metz overthrew the Thuringian and Burgundian empires about the
year 533, and shared the Burgundian territory with the kings
of Paris and Soissons, who had assisted him in its conquest.

The empire of the Franks was still further enlarged when (40)
the Ostrogoths, in order to prevent the formation of an A
alliance between the Franks and Byzantines, ceded to the former the Ostrogothic territories in Gaul (Provence) and the Alemannic settlements in Rhœtia. The Bavarians, also, were incorporated into the empire, retaining their own duke.

The empire of the Franks was reunited under Clotar I. 41
[Clothaire], the youngest of Chlodwig's sons, who survived all his brothers and their descendants. After his death the monarchy, which had been consolidated for three years (558—561), was again divided into four kingdoms, by his four sons, an arrangement which remained until the death of Charibert, king of Paris, in 569, when the number was reduced to three: viz.

a. Austrasia, or the eastern empire, comprehending B
the north-eastern portion of Gaul, with parts of southern Gaul; and, in Germany, the territory of the Franconians, Thuringia, and the duchies of Bavaria and Alemannia, or Swabia. Capital—Metz.

b. Neustria, or the western empire, also Soissons, comprising the whole of north-western Gaul, from the Waal to the Loire, and a part of Aquitania. Capital—Soissons.

c. Burgundy, or the southern empire, containing be- C
sides the ancient Burgundian territory, the former kingdom of Orleans (as well as Sundgau, Alsace, Thurgau, and parts of Aquitania and Provence). Capital—Orleans.

Paris continued to be the common capital of the three 42
kingdoms.

The history of Clotar's [Clothaire's] successors is a cata- 43
logue of intestine disturbances, treasons, and murders, occasioned principally by the rivalry of the two queens Brunehilde (who murdered ten kings and princes of the blood royal) and Fredegunde. The empire was a second time united by Clotar [Clothaire] II. in 613.

The Frankish empire under the administra- D
tion of the majores domus, 613—752.

In the reign of Clotar [Clothaire] II. we first hear of three 44
majores domus, i. e. heads of the royal household (gasindi); who acted also as chief stewards of the royal demesnes and fiefs (see § 14); viz. one in Austrasia, one in Neustria, and one in Burgundy. The major domus of Austrasia, Pepin of

(44) Landen, of a distinguished house in Lüttich, or Liege, in-
A duced Clotar II. to cede Austrasia (in 622) to his elder
son, Dagobert, who, after the death of his father and his
younger brothers, united the Frankish monarchy
for the third time (631). Pepin became major domus
of the whole empire, from which, however, the Austrasians
soon afterwards separated themselves, under Dagobert I.
As few of his successors attained the age, and none possessed the vigour, of manhood, the sceptre of the Frankish
monarchy was in reality wielded by their majores domus.
One of these officers, named Pepin of Heristal, a
grandson of Pepin of Landen, after his victory at Testri,
in 687, became sole major domus of France, with the title
B of duke and prince of the Franks. After his death, in 714,
the succession to the office was disputed among his sons for
ten years, and finally decided in favour of Charles Martel, who reduced the rebellious dukes of the tributary
nations Alemannia, Bavaria, and Thuringia, defeated the
Arabians (who had invaded France) between Tours and
Poictiers, in 732, and subdued the Frieses and a portion
of the Saxons. His sons Carloman and Pepin the Short
[Pepin le Bref] held the office conjointly, until the retire-
ment of Carloman into a convent (Monte Cassino), when
C the entire administration of the kingdom devolved on
Pepin. Having secured the respect of the nobles and
people by his bravery in the Saxon and Bavarian wars,
and conciliated the clergy by the support which he afforded
to Archbishop Bonifacius, in his plans for the reformation
of the Church, Pepin, with the consent of Pope Zacharias,
summoned a general assembly of the empire, which met at
Soissons, and deposed the incapable king, Childeric III.,
who retired into a convent. Pepin was then chosen king of
the Franks, and anointed by Bonifacius in the year 752.

§ 14. *Religion, Manners, and Customs of the West, particularly of the Frankish Empire.*

1. Religion.

45 a. *Introduction of Christianity.* It is worthy of remark,
D that Arianism was adopted only by those German tribes
who had previously been worshippers of Odin,—the East
and West Goths, Vandals, and Lombards; whilst, on the

other hand, no trace can be found of such a worship among (45)
the disciples of Catholicism,—the Frieses, Franks, Ale- A
manni, Thuringians, Burgundians, and Suevi. At a later period, the West Goths [or Visigoths] and Lombards were persuaded by their kings to renounce Arianism, and embrace the Catholic faith. At the commencement of this period the Germans were still heathens, and their religion nearly the same as that described by Tacitus. (Comp. § 2.) It would seem, however, that the pure adoration of nature which they originally professed, degenerated, after a time, into idolatry (e. g. the Irminsul), in consequence of their intercourse with civilized nations; and eventually into a sort of *Fetish*
worship. Although Chlodwig and his followers embraced B
Christianity after their victory over the Alemanni, an example which was gradually followed by the remainder of the Frankish nation, no attempt was made either by that monarch or his immediate successors, to convert their tributaries in Germany,—the Alemanni, Bavarians, and Thuringians. The Burgundians, soon after their settlement in Gaul, embraced the Catholic religion. In the reign of Dagobert I., some efforts were made by the Frankish bishops for the propagation of the Gospel; but the work was still more effectually performed by missionaries from
Ireland. The Alemanni were converted by Columban and C
his disciple, Gallus, and some attempts were made by Kilian in Thuringia; but the conversion of the Germans is principally due to Winfried [Winifred] of Wessex, afterwards called Bonifacius, and the "Apostle of Germany" (717—754), who preached to the Frieses and Catti, or Hessians (destruction of the sacred oak at Geismar), founded churches, convents and schools; established new bishoprics, which were immediately subject to the see of Rome; held the first synods in Germany; and after filling the office of bishop (723) and archbishop (732) without any settled diocese, was finally appointed archbishop of Mainz [Mayence] (745), and suffered martyrdom among the Frieses in 754.

b. *The Monastic Life*, considered independently of those 46
ascetic institutions (the Pythagorean obligation, the Essenes, D
&c.), which existed previously to the Christian æra, seems to have originated with those holy men who were compelled to lead secluded lives by the persecutions to which they were exposed as professors of Christianity. A con-

(46) siderable number of these solitaries (monachi), who had
A taken refuge in the Egyptian desert, established themselves in huts round the dwelling of St. Anthony (about 305), whose disciple, Pachomius, assembled them on the island Tabenna, in the Nile, within the walls of a single building, denominated Cœnobium, or Monasterium, under the presidency of a chief (abbas, hence the term "abbot"). From Egypt these Cœnobites rapidly spread over the neighbouring districts, as well as over Europe. In the west a new form was given to this institution by St. Benedict, of Nursia (480—543). His "rule," framed originally for the convent (claustrum) founded by him on Monte Cassino, near Naples, was gradually adopted in all the western
B monasteries. It required that all who entered a monastery should, at the expiration of their novitiate, solemnly promise to pass the remainder of their lives in the convent, and take the threefold vow of poverty, chastity, and obedience. From the sixth to the ninth century, the cultivation of the soil, and the introduction of Christianity among the German and Sclavonic tribes, made rapid progress, in consequence of the activity and intelligence of the monks.

47 c. *Relation of the Church to the State.* As the king was considered the protector of the Church within his own dominions, and the emperor its supreme defender, it followed, of course, that the excommunication of the Church and the
C ban of the empire were inseparable. The most capricious inroads on the privileges of the Church were made by the emperor and kings; in the collation, for instance, to episcopal sees, which the king or queen sometimes bestowed even on laymen; and in the confirmation, by the eastern emperor, of the pope's election. The jurisdiction conceded to the bishops, which at first had been restricted to ecclesiastical causes, extended itself gradually to all matters in which the duties of religion or of conscience were involved. The heaviest ecclesiastical punishment was excommunication.

48 2. Political constitution.

D *Origin and Development of the German States.*—The warlike enterprises of the ancient German nations were of two sorts: 1. Those in which all the freemen capable of bearing arms served under the command of a duke chosen from one of the principal families. These were, generally

speaking, defensive wars. 2. Expeditions or forays, under- (48)
taken by an army composed of vassals (Gasindi, Leudes), A
for purposes of plunder and conquest. Their leader was
either the proposer of the expedition, or a warrior chosen
for the occasion. A third of the land belonging to the
countries which they conquered was claimed by the conquerors (e. g. Odoacer and Theodoric the Great), or sometimes two-thirds (the Burgundians, Suevi, West Goths, and
possibly Vandals), but rarely the whole (the Langobardi
and Anglo-Saxons). The conqueror established a settlement in the conquered country. The leader retained his
office as lord or captain of his followers, even after the
conquest was completed; and after his death his nearest
relation was elected to fill the vacant throne. Thus the B
German monarchies were at once hereditary and elective.
The election was followed by the elevation of the successful candidate on a shield. The king always appeared in
public surrounded by the chiefs who composed the nobility
of his kingdom. This order comprehended, *a*. The dukes
and counts, or leaders of the divisions and sub-divisions of
the clansmen, who, as the king's lieutenants, exercised the
functions of commanders and judges, and were at the
same time invested with the four offices which existed at
every German court, viz.: Marshall, Chamberlain, Butler,
and Sewer. *b*. After the introduction of Christianity the C
order included also the superior clergy, namely, the Abbots, Bishops, and Archbishops. The power of the kings
consisted in their prerogative of calling out the army and
of pronouncing judgment on offenders. Their dependence in some sort on the Roman Emperors, in whose
service many of them had fought their way to the throne,
was manifested by the eagerness with which some of them
(Chlodwig, Theodoric the Great) sought the title of Roman Patricius or Consul; and by the fact that they generally considered themselves, at least with reference to their
Roman subjects, as the Emperor's lieutenants. The influ- D
ence of Rome was also seen in the etiquette of their
courts, as well as in their civic and provincial administration, and the retention of the Roman code for the clergy
and the Roman population.

b. *The feudal system.* The territory obtained by
conquest was divided by the king among his followers

(49) (Gasindi), each receiving an allotment termed Allodium,
A as an hereditary freehold which he was permitted to
sub-divide at his pleasure. In this division, the king himself received a larger allotment than the members of his
suite, and was therefore in a condition to confer on some of
his faithful followers (Vassen or Vassals), leasehold estates
(termed fiefs, allodia, or beneficia), tenable for life, on
condition of their swearing fidelity to the sovereign and
engaging to render military service when called on. Thus
the whole body of allodial proprietors were gradually
B reduced to the condition of vassals. The chief of these
vassals was the major domus (regiæ), who, as the king's
first lieutenant, led the serfs to battle, disposed of the
royal patronage, and sometimes (in Austrasia), represented
the king on the judgment-seat, in the place of the Comes
Palatii, who was subject to his authority. At first, the
fiefs were not hereditary, but this privilege was gradually
either granted by the kings or usurped by the vassals.
As the feudal lord was bound to protect his vassals, many
of the small proprietors, conscious of their own weakness,
made over their allodes to some powerful neighbor, from
whom they received them back as fiefs (feudum oblatum).
Thus many of the allodes were converted into feudal
C estates. At the same time their military system under-
went a revolution correspondent to the political changes
which had been effected among the Franks, Anglo-Saxons,
Lombards, and many other Germanic tribes. The army
was now composed partly of independent inhabitants of
separate Gaus, under the command of their Count, and
partly of vassals under their feudal Lords. The former
were called out, by a decree of the people, to defend the
lands in their own immediate neighborhood—the latter
served in campaigns of every description in obedience to
the sovereign's command. Among the Franks, the army
was annually reviewed in the Field of Mars.

50 c. *Legislation.* Until the middle of the fifth century
D the German tribes possessed only unwritten laws; in the
three next centuries, written *leges* were introduced amongst
the united nations of the Frankish empire (Salii, Ripuarii,
Alemanni, Bavarians, Burgundians, &c.), as well as
among the West Goths, Lombards, and Anglo-Saxons.
All these codes, with the exception of the Anglo-Saxon,

were drawn up in Latin, and seem to have been the work (50)
of deliberative councils, or the result of compacts made A
between the king and his people. Among the Eastern and Western Goths and Burgundians we find a statute book published by the king, and containing simply Roman laws (edictum Theodoricianum, breviarium Alaricianum, lex Romano Burgundionum). These statutes, especially the lex Salia, are almost exclusively penal. As a general rule none but serfs could be punished with death, or undergo corporal chastisement; the freeman was allowed to compound for his violations of the law by the payment of a fine (compositio); if unable to discharge the penalty, he
became the slave of the injured party. Even murder could B
be expiated by the payment of a pecuniary compensation (reckoned in solidis or shillings) to the relations of the deceased. Their courts of justice were of three sorts. 1. The Gau-Court; held by the Count, assisted by Schöffen, or jurymen chosen from the freemen. 2. Palatine courts, in which the lord of an exempt district (immunitas), assisted by his dependents, decided questions within the jurisdiction of his court. 3. Feudal courts, in which the feudal lord settled the disputes of his vassals, of whom a certain number acted as his assessors. There were four sorts of
proof:—1. Documentary (rare). 2. Witnesses. 3. The C
oath of the prosecutor and his consacramentales. 4. The Ordeal, which consisted of the trial by fire (red-hot iron, ploughshares, coals, logs of wood, gloves, &c.), the trial by boiling or cold water, and the judicial combat, or duel between the accused and his accuser.

III. Manners and Customs.

The advantages which *agriculture* derived from the 51
assiduous cultivation of their estates by the free proprietors, and subsequently by the monks, were in some degree neutralized by the manner in which the land was parcelled out into large farms, and by the general employment of bonds-
men. The same circumstances and the absence of cities, D
were also obstacles to the advancement of *manufacturing industry: commercial enterprise* was checked by numerous imposts and by the insecurity of the roads; and lastly, Christianity, in consequence of the universal and deeply-rooted depravity and ferocity of manners, scarcely exer-

(51) cised any beneficial influence over the people until the
A commencement of the succeeding period.

52 IV. Scientific knowledge was almost exclusively in the hands of the secular clergy and monks. Their system of education comprised the seven liberal arts, as they were called, or the Trivium (i. e. the study of classical literature, rhetoric, and dialectics), and Quadrivium (arithmetic, geometry, astronomy, and music). The best educational establishments were in England, at Cambridge, York, and Canterbury, from which learned men were from time to time sent out to enlighten the neighboring continent. Among these the most remark-
B able were the Venerable Bede, Boniface, and Alcuin. The *literature* of this period contains only works in the Latin language. The most important are Boëthii consolatio philosophiæ, the philosophical and historical writings of Cassiodorus, extracts by Jornandes from the history of the Goths by Cassiodorus, Frankish ecclesiastical history by Gregory of Tours, Spanish by Isidorus, and English by the Venerable Bede, who introduced the Christian mode of reckoning time into the West.

V. Art.

53 The transition from the ancient to the modern style of
C architecture, is seen in the old Gothic style among the Ostrogoths, and in the tasteless architecture of Lombardy, which was adopted, with a mixture of the Byzantine in all the other German states. First specimens of Christian painting.

B. The East.

§ 15. *The Eastern Roman (or Byzantine) Empire,* 395—867.

54 Extent of the empire: Since the year 395, from
D the Ionian (and at a later period from the Adriatic) Sea in the West, the Tigranocerta on the Tigris, Circesium on the Euphrates and the Arabian Desert in the East; and from the Danube and the Black Sea in the North, to Ethiopia and the Libyan Desert in the South. To this Empire was added the kingdom of the Vandals in 534, the whole of Italy in 554—568, and at a later period the Exarchate

(the limits of which became daily more restricted), and a (54
few cities on the southern coast of Spain. In the seventh A
century the empire lost all its Asiatic possessions with the exception of Asia Minor; in the seventh and eighth, Africa, the islands of Sardinia and Corsica, Dalmatia, and the right bank of the Lower Danube; and in the ninth, Sicily, Candia, and Cyprus. Military division of the empire into twenty-nine Themata.

History.

1. Period of the rise of the empire—from the year 395 to the death of Justinian in 565.

(1.) Arcadius (395—408), who had received for his 55
portion the larger (eastern) half, at the division of the empire B
by his father Theodosius (com. B. i. 3, § 111), was governed at the commencement of his reign by a Gaul named Ruffinus, then by the Eunuch Eutropius, at a later period by Gainas a Goth, and finally by his avaricious consort Eudoxia. The Huns, who had invaded the Asiatic provinces, were conciliated by the payment of a tribute, and Alaric, leader of the Western Goths, induced to withdraw his forces from Macedonia and Greece by a grant of the præfecture of Eastern Illyricum. (2.) His son and successor, Theodosius I. (under the guardianship of his sister Pulcheria), was twice compelled to increase the yearly payment to the Huns (the last time to 2100
pounds of gold). On the other hand, when the Byzantines C
and Persians divided between them the kingdom of Armenia, Theodosius received the western part (and of the western empire, Pannonia, Dalmatia, and Noricum). The codex Theodosianus was the first published digest of laws. Theodosius was succeeded by (3.) Pulcheria and her paramour Marcian, who, after the dissolution of the Hunnish empire, added to the southern Danube provinces several nations (e. g. the Eastern Goths), formerly subject to the
Huns. (4.) Leo I. (Macella), the first emperor crowned D
by the Patriarch of Constantinople, engaged unsuccessfully in an expedition against the Vandals (see § 9). The Ostrogothic Prince, Theodoric (who had been placed in his hands as the pledge of an alliance which he had purchased from that nation), was educated at Constantinople, and became the conqueror of Italy under the auspices of (5.) Zeno, the successor of Leo (comp. § 8).

(55) (6.) Anastasius, after the first invasion of the Bulgarians,
A protected his capital by a long wall, which extended from
the Black Sea to the sea of Marmora. (7.) Justin I., a
Thracian peasant, was first appointed commander-in-chief
of the body-guard, and then raised to the imperial throne,
which he shared with his nephew.

56 (8.) Justinian, 527—565, who became sole emperor
at the end of four months. Theodora, the wife of this
emperor, a woman of debauched character, who had
formerly been an actress, exercised an influence which
her profligate and cruel disposition rendered exceedingly
injurious to the interests of the empire. His first and
greatest work was the Improvement of the Roman
Code by (a.) the Codex Justinianus (12 B.), a digest of
Roman law, prepared by ten distinguished lawyers, under
B the superintendence of Tribonian. This work was soon
found defective, and at the end of six years there appeared
a new and improved edition. b. The Institutiones, a
manual of Roman law. c. The Pandectæ, or Digesta, a
collection of the most important interpretations and decisions,
from the writings of forty distinguished jurists.
d. The Novellæ, or supplement, containing some laws of
Justinian, and others of succeeding reigns. The tranquillity
of the empire was disturbed by the Nika, an insurrection
in the Hippodrome at Constantinople, occasioned by the
arrogance of the blue faction (which was favored by the
emperor), and suppressed (in 532) by the butchery of
C 30,000 of the green. The imperial palace, which had been
injured, and the church of St. Sophia, which was burnt
in this insurrection, were both restored in a style of
greater magnificence. Having secured his northern frontier
by a chain of more than eighty fortresses, extending from
the Save to the mouth of the Danube, and the eastern
partly by entrenchments and alliances, and partly by
putting an end (by a bought peace) to the Persian war,*
which had broken out in the reign of Justin, Justinian un-
D dertook the restoration of the Roman empire. In
pursuance of this object the empire of the Vandals was destroyed
by Belisarius; and after a war, begun by that general
and terminated by Narses at the end of eighteen years,

* In this war, the Persian general, Narses, went over to the Byzantines, and Belisarius gained his first laurels.

the Ostrogothic empire, already weakened by intestine (56)
divisions, became subject to Justinian. The conquests of A
Belisarius in Africa and Italy, excited jealousy and appre-
hension in the mind of the Persian king Chosroës (or Nushir-
wan), who renewed the war (partly at the instigation of the
Ostrogoths), invaded Syria, burnt Antiochia, and was
threatening Palestine, when the appearance of Belisarius
in the east compelled him to retreat. After long negotiations, which were interrupted by a dispute respecting the
possession of the eastern shores of the Black Sea, peace
was concluded, the ancient frontier line being restored, and
Chosroës renouncing all claim to the disputed territories in
consideration of an annual tribute. Conquest of the B
southern coast of Spain (see § 11). The constant wars in
this reign, terminated in some instances by a disgraceful
peace, and the enormous sums expended in the erection of
costly buildings, soon exhausted the exchequer which
Anastasius had left full, and involved the empire in debt,
nothwithstanding the attempts made to meet the expenditure
by the imposition of oppressive taxes, and the sale of
public offices and government monopolies.

II. *Period of the decline of the empire from 565 to the accession of the Macedonian Emperors in 867.*

In the reign of Justinian's immediate successor (his 57
nephew, Justin II.), began the conquests of the Lombards C
in Italy (comp. § 8. IV.), and a renewal of the wars with
Persia, which occupied almost without intermission the
four succeeding emperors, the last of whom *Heraclīus*
(610—641), lost Syria, Palestine, Egypt, and Asia Minor
to the Persians, who were in the act of encamping under
the walls of his capital, when the suburbs were plundered
by the Avars, whose empire at that time extended from
the Volga to the Saale and Ems—northward to the Car-
pathian mountains, and southward to the Danube. In this D
extremity, the emperor would have fled to Carthage, but
at the intercession of the Patriarch he abandoned his inten-
tion, landed with an army in Syria, and after three campaigns, and a victory at Nineveh (627), recovered the
four countries which had been wrested from him by the
Persians. Soon afterwards, however, Syria, Palestine,
Phœnicia, and Egypt, fell into the hands of the Ara-

(57) bians, and the southern coast of Spain into those of
A the Visigoths. Under his successors the limits of the
empire were still further circumscribed, in the west by
the Lombards, who were continually enlarging their
Italian dominions at the expense of the Exarchate (see
§ 8. III.), in the north by repeated invasions of the Bulgarians, who made themselves masters of Mœsia, and in
the east and south by the Arabians. These last not only
subdued the islands of Cyprus and Rhodes, Armenia, the
whole northern coast of Africa, and (in the ninth century)
Crete, Sicily, and Sardinia, but even ventured to attack
Constantinople itself, which they besieged every summer
from 670 to 678, and again from 717 to 718, but were
B each time repulsed by the Greek fire. Whilst the provinces were thus falling, one after another, into the hands
of the neighboring powers, the empire itself was convulsed
by the disputes of political and religious parties. Successive emperors were hurled from the throne, deprived of
sight, maimed, shut up in convents, or put to death, sometimes through the intrigues of ambitious consorts and their
paramours, sometimes by their own sons, their ministers,
or the victorious generals of their armies. The religious
feuds were for the most part occasioned by dogmatic
differences, such for example as (1.) The controversy respecting the distinction between the divine and human
natures of our Lord, pronounced to be an orthodox doctrine
C by the council of Chalcedon, 451. This dispute not only
occasioned the separation of the Monophysites from the Catholic church, but was even productive of schisms among
those heretics themselves. An attempt of the Emperor
Heraclius to reconcile the contending dogmatists by a
declaration that two natures were indeed united in the
person of our Lord, but that both had been actuated by
only one will, served merely to augment the number of
heresies by the addition of the Monotheletes, (2.) who were
condemned by a council held at Constantinople in the year
D 680. A remnant of these heretics formed the sect of the
Maronites. (3.) The iconoclastic controversy, which
lasted more than a hundred years, was occasioned by a
decree of the Emperor Leo III. (Isauricus), commanding
(in 726) the removal from the churches of all images,
except that of our Saviour. Notwithstanding the vehe-

ment opposition of the monks and the pope, this de- (57)
cree was carried into effect, and the images either dashed A
in pieces or burnt. The worship of images having been condemned as heretical by the seventh œcumenical council (held at Constantinople in 754), their destruction was carried on with augmented zeal by succeeding emperors until the reign of Irene, when it was interrupted for awhile, to be renewed in the following reign. Their restoration was at last effected by Theodora, the guardian of her son Michael III. The degradation of the Patri- B
arch of Constantinople by this emperor, prepared the way for the separation of the Greek and Roman churches. He was assassinated on account of his acts of ferocious cruelty, by his favorite, Basilius the Macedonian, in the year 867. (4.) The persecution of the sect of the Paulicians, who eventually, with the aid of the Arabians, ravaged Asia Minor, and waged war successfully against Michael III.

Political constitution, arts, sciences, &c.

1. The *constitution* which the Roman empire had re- 58
ceived from Constantine the Great (see B. i. 3. § 110), was preserved in its integrity, the emperors continuing to enjoy unlimited power. They were crowned and anointed by C
the Patriarch of Constantinople, assumed the title of Roman Emperors, and sought to conceal their real weakness by the adoption of sounding titles, a gorgeous costume, and a rigid court ceremonial. The senate, it is true, still remained, but without authority or political influence; the only deliberative council being the consistorium principis, an assembly composed entirely of imperial favorites, who were consulted from time to time as occasion required. In the reign of Justinian, the Roman consulship ceased to exist, even in name, the only dates now employed being the years of the emperor's reign, according to the Indiction-Cycle of fifteen years. Political importance of the colors D
in the Hippodrome. The provinces were handed over to governors, who purchased their offices, and exercised almost irresponsible authority, to the great disgust of the oppressed and plundered provincials.

2. *Language and Literature.* The language of the court, 59
after its removal to Constantinople, continued for a time to be Latin, but was afterwards a corrupted Greek.

(59) Poetry was confined almost entirely to the epigram.
A Schools of the new Platonic philosophy, grammar, and rhetoric, flourished at Constantinople, at Athens, until the reign of Justinian, and at Edessa and Alexandria until the Arabian dynasty. The most renowned school of jurisprudence was at Berytus in Phœnicia. Medicinal science was most successfully cultivated at Alexandria. The writings of the Byzantine historians were either chronicles from the creation of the world to their own times (as Syncellus), or biographies of individual emperors, for the most part mere compilations without plan, judgment, or taste.

60 3. *Art.* The establishment of Christianity as the re-
B ligion of the state, and the removal of the Roman court to Byzantium, gave new life to art, especially during the brilliant reign of Justinian. The distinguishing features of ancient Christian architecture, as seen in its greatest perfection in the church of St. Sophia, built by Justinian, were the cruciform plan, and the dome resting on arches, supported by massive piles.[1] Simplicity of taste was almost lost amidst a profusion of marbles of the most varied and brilliant colors. All visible personifications of the Deity being forbidden by the Christian religion, the only works of sculpture were statues representing emperors, generals, and statesmen, in their gorgeous robes of office,
C ornaments for the altar, and sacred vessels. The interior of the churches was generally ornamented with mosaic of the most brilliant colors, composed of gold and costly marbles. The earliest specimens of Christian sculpture and painting are found in the ninth century, when images of the saints were first permitted by the Greek church. The modern Greek or Byzantine style of architecture found its way into the west as far as Britain and the Moorish settlements in Spain, as well as into Arabia. A knowledge of painting was also generally diffused by the artists who were driven from the east by the iconoclastic controversy.

61 4. *Commerce and Manufactures.* The operations of
D commerce were sorely cramped by the almost perpetual wars, barbarian invasions, the insecurity of the roads, and oppressive taxation and monopolies. A direct trade was

[[1] See Gibbon, chap. xl. § 5.]

carried on with the shores of the Mediterranean, which (61)
had been reconquered by Justinian, and were for the most A
part inhabited by rude and barbarous nations; whilst, on the other hand, the trade with India was conducted through the intervention of the Persians, and at a later period of the Arabians. The situation of Constantinople rendered it the principal emporium for western as well as eastern produce. Manufacturing industry was fostered by the luxury of a brilliant court, and was greatly promoted by the introduction of silkworms, the eggs of which were brought in hollow canes from China to Constantinople by missionaries in the reign of Justinian.

5. *Manners.*—The demoralization of this luxurious 62
court extended to the great body of the people, who gave B
themselves up to coarse and sensual enjoyment in defiance alike of ecclesiastical censures, severe laws, and the most fearful punishments.

§ 16. The Arabians.

Geography of Arabia.

The peninsula of Arabia, the superficial area of which 63
is four times greater than that of Germany or France, C
consists partly of a table-land traversed by ranges of mountains, entirely destitute of water, and forming a huge sea of shifting sands, and partly of narrow strips of flat land along the sea-coast, all equally barren, with the exception of the south-western portion, which, on account of its fertility, was called by the ancients Arabia Felix (hod. Jemen). The inhabitants are partly Bedouins, whose lives are spent in wandering, either in single families under their Scheiks, or in large clans under Emirs, in search of water and pasture, and partly inhabitants of cities (of which the most celebrated are Mecca and Medina), where they maintain themselves by agriculture, trade, and manufactures. Before the time of Mohammed, their religion was D
a worship of the stars. Their national sanctuary, the Caaba or temple at Mecca (with its black stone, formerly venerated as divine), was superintended by the family of Haschem, of the tribe of Koreisch. Circumcision and abstinence from pork, as among the Jews and Egyptians.

History of the Arabians.

64 The Arabians, who trace their origin to Ishmael, the son
A of Abraham and Hagar, have always retained their independence, with the exception of the inhabitants of Arabia Petræa, which for a short time (A.D. 106) was subject to the Romans.

1. From Mohammed to the Dynasty of the Ommaijades, 622—661.

65 Mohammed was born at Mecca in the year 571, and
B after the death of his parents (who belonged to the powerful tribe of Koreisch, and the family of Haschem), was brought up by an uncle (Abu-Taleb). By a fortunate marriage with a rich widow, he was enabled to gratify without restraint his taste for religious seclusion. One month of every year was passed in a cave in the neighborhood of Mecca, whence he sallied forth to proclaim himself the ambassador of the One God, by whom, as he declared, a commission had been granted him to restore the religion
C of Abraham. This doctrine, which at first was preached (609) only to the members of his own family, but subsequently promulgated to the world, was vehemently opposed by the Koreischites, whose persecutions at length drove him, in company with Abu-Bekr, to seek an asylum in the city of Medina, July 15, 622. From this flight the Arabians date their era Hegira (Hedschra). From Medina, where he assumed the authority of king, and married the daughter of Abu-Bekr, Mohammed propagated the doctrines of Islamism by the sword. In the year 629, he took the holy city of Mecca, converted the Caaba into the national sanctuary of the true believers (Moslem), completed the conquest of Arabia, and invited the king of Persia and the Byzantine emperor (Heraclius), to embrace
D Islamism. He died at Medina, in 632, leaving behind him only one daughter, (Fatima), the wife of Ali.

The four first caliphs, 632—661.

66 1. Abu-Bekr (632—34), the father-in-law of tne prophet, who collected the sayings of Mohammed into a book called the Koran. His general, Khaled, began a war with Persia, and the conquest of Syria.

2. Omar (634—43), another father-in-law of the pro- 67
phet. His generals took Damascus, completed the con- A
quest of Syria, and made themselves masters of Palestine,
which was visited by Omar himself (in very humble guise)
for the purpose of concluding a capitulation with the
Christians at Jerusalem, to whom he granted full toleration
on condition of receiving a yearly tribute. The conquest of
Phœnicia enabled the Arabians to take rank as a maritime
power. The war with Persia was prosecuted successfully
(victory at Cadesia in 636, and Nohavend in 642). At
the same time, Amru subdued Egypt, after a war which
lasted two years (narrative of the burning of the Alexandrian library,[1] by order of Omar, probably incorrect), and
advanced into Africa as far as Tripoli.

3. Othman (643—56). A son-in-law of the prophet. 68
The conquest of the Persian empire was completed in 651, B
together with that of the whole of northern Africa, as far
as Ceuta; Cypress was compelled to pay tribute, Rhodes
taken, and the fragments of its famous Colossus sold. The
discontent occasioned by the avarice and nepotism of
Othman, produced an insurrection in Medina, which ended
in his assassination and the accession of

4. Ali (656—661), another son-in-law of the prophet 69
(husband of Fatima), was placed on the throne by the
assassins, but not generally recognized as Caliph, many
persons believing that the murder of Othman had been
perpetrated at his instigation. In order to strengthen his C
authority, Ali confided the administration of the provinces
to friends of his own; an arrangement by no means acceptable to the governors actually in possession, most of
whom, (especially Moawijah, governor of Syria, who
caused himself to be proclaimed Caliph, and Amru, governor of Egypt), united to oppose the usurper. After several
(90) insignificant but bloody engagements, a conspiracy
was entered into by three Arabians, to restore tranquillity
by the murder of Ali, Amru, and Moawijah—all of whom
escaped the dagger of the assassin except Ali, whose son,
Hassan, succeeded him on the throne, but was compelled
to abdicate in favor of Moawijah.

[[1] Gibbon's reasoning upon this subject (ch. 51), seems conclusive. Some of his arguments had already been anticipated by the acuteness of Voltaire (Esai sur les Moeurs), and are confirmed by the learned researches of Heeren, Geschichte der Classischen Literatur im Mittehalter.]

2. The Ommaijad Caliphs 661—750.

70 *Moawijah* I., great-grandson of Ommaija, transferred
A the residence of the caliphs from Medina to Damascus, and
made the caliphate hereditary. Under the thirteen caliphs
of this dynasty, the Arabian dominions were more extensive
than at any other period of their history. a. Conquests in
the *West.* The African subjects of the Arabians, being
oppressed and compelled to pay tribute by the Byzantines
(who still retained possession of Carthage), applied for aid
to the Arabians, who stormed and sacked Carthage, expelled the Byzantines from Africa, extended their dominions to the Atlantic, and strengthened their authority by
B the conversion of the Barbary tribes to Islamism. From
this province, Musa, on the invitation of a West-Gothic
chief (Julian), despatched his lieutenant Tarek into Spain,
where he overthrew the Goths, in a battle fought at Xerez
de la Frontera (711), and had well-nigh completed the
destruction of the West-Gothic empire, when Musa himself
arrived in Spain, and threw the conqueror into a prison,
where he was treated with great cruelty. Musa was on
the eve of crossing the Pyrenees, when both generals were
recalled by an order of the Caliph (Walid). After a long and
triumphal march from Spain to Syria, the aged commander-
in-chief was exposed to the heat of the sun, scourged,
C and compelled to pay a heavy fine. Meanwhile, his son
had been murdered in Spain, and his head forwarded to the
unhappy father. The Christians in Spain were permitted,
on payment of a moderate tribute, to retain their language,
laws, and the free exercise of their religion. The attempt
of the Spanish viceroy Abderrahman to wrest Gaul from
the feeble hands of the Frankish kings, was frustrated by
his defeat at Tours and Poitiers (comp. § 13). b. In the
East, the Arabians subdued Armenia, a portion of Asia
Minor, the countries between the Black and Caspian seas,
D and Turkestan. Even in India they had acquired possessions,
of no great extent, nor occupied for any considerable length
of time, but sufficiently important to place in their hands the
whole trade of that peninsula. Two attempts on Constantinople were rendered abortive by the Greek fire (see § 15).
During the progress of these events, the reigning dynasty
was engaged in perpetual struggles with the family of
Haschem, and the adherents of Ali, as well as with the

rival caliphs, who were placed on the throne by the two (70)
contending parties. At length, on the accession (in 750) A
of Abul Abbas, a great-grandson of Abbas, uncle of the
prophet, the dynasty of the Ommaijades was swept away
in a torrent of blood (600,000 of their adherents having
been put to death in Khorassan alone), and the throne of
the Abbassides firmly established. Abderrahman alone
escaped into Spain, where he established the caliphate at
Cordova (comp. § 11).

Religion, arts, and sciences, &c.

1. The creed of the Arabians, or Islamism, was con- 71
sidered by its founder merely a restoration of the religion B
of Abraham, which, as he contended, had been also promulgated by Moses, and our Blessed Lord, but grievously
disfigured by their disciples. To Mohammed himself, as
the last and greatest of the prophets, was intrusted the task
of restoring this religion to its original purity. The Mohammedan system (Islam), is partly doctrinal (Iman), and
partly practical (Din). Its principal articles of faith are,
the unity of God, predestination, and retribution in the
world to come. The moral law enjoins control over the C
passions, war against unbelievers, prayer five times a day,
repeated purifications with water or sand, almsgiving, fasts
(during the month of Ramadan, daily, until sunset), abstinence from wine, and a pilgrimage to the Caaba. It allows
polygamy, and permits its followers to recompense evil
for evil. The sacred writings of the Mohammedans are the
Pentateuch, the Psalms, the Gospels, and the Koran, or
collection of the prophet's sayings, preserved by Abu-Bekr,
and arranged by Othman. This work was speedily followed by the Sunna, a collection of moral precepts, which
many of the Mohammedans refused to recognize. Hence D
the two sects of the Sunnites and Schiites. Conversion to
Mohammedanism was produced not so much by argu-
ment and conviction, as by the sword. All vanquished
nations were compelled either to pay tribute or conform
to the new religion; and slaves, prisoners, and malefactors
were restored to freedom on declaring their assent to the
doctrines of the Koran. These circumstances will account
for the rapidity with which the religion of the Arabian
impostor was propagated.

2. *Political Constitution.* The supreme ecclesiastical 72

(72) as well as civil authority was vested in the caliphs. At
A first they were required to render a weekly account of their administration to the people, who were consulted by them on all important occasions; but at a later period (especially since the establishment of an hereditary caliphate by Moawijah) their power was completely despotic. The mode of life of the earliest caliphs was exceedingly simple (Omar's journey to Jerusalem), but they soon learnt to imitate the luxury of the conquered nations, whose treasures supplied them with the means of enjoyment. The lieutenants of the provinces were invested with military as well as civil authority. Hence their power, and at a later period the renunciation of their allegiance to the caliphs.

73 3. *Arts and Sciences.* As early as the fifth century
B there were poetical contests at the fair of Mecca, and seven poems are still extant (the Moallakat), composed by authors whose names were inscribed in letters of gold on the walls of the Caaba. The warlike enthusiasm of the nation and the fierce eagerness with which the earlier caliphs pursued their plans of conquest, prevented the cultivation of science, properly so called, until the reign of the Abbasides, when the Arabian conquerors learnt to emulate the learning of the Greeks. The golden age of Arabian architecture began (about 700) with the erection of mosques at Jeru-
C salem and Damascus. Painting and sculpture were out of the question among a people whose religion condemned every representation of the human form.

74 4. *Trade and Manufactures* being recommended by the Koran as employments pleasing to God, were held in high estimation among the Arabians. The conquest of the Persian empire had placed in their hands the commerce of India. Westward their maritime trade extended over the whole of the Mediterranean as far as the Straits of Gibraltar; in the south, they founded the settlements along the whole eastern coast of Africa to the borders of Caffreland, and in the east they had a considerable factory at Canton in
D China. The land traffic was carried on by means of caravans, which conveyed merchandise from Egypt into the interior of Africa on the one side, and on the other into Syria, and thence into central Asia. The principal markets for the products of the extreme west and east were, Me-

dina, Mecca, Kufa, Bassora, Damascus, Bagdad, Mosul, (74)
and Madain. Notwithstanding the perpetual wars, trade A
and manufactures of every description continued to flourish, especially on the shores of Barbary and Spain.

§ 17. *The Modern Persian Empire*, 226—651.

The boundaries of the empire founded by Artaxerxes I. 75
(Ardeschir), the son of Sassan (see B. i. 2, § 49), varied at different times. Under Chosroes I. it extended from the Mediterranean to the Indus, and from the Jaxartes to Arabia and Egypt, and under Chosroes II. to Jemen. The empire was divided into four provinces, viz. Assyria,
Media, Persia, and Bactriana. The capital city was B
Ctesiphon, on the eastern bank of the Tigris, with the suburb of Seleucia on the opposite side, forming together Madain, or the "double city."

The Persians were engaged in almost perpetual warfare 76
either with the Turks or the eastern Roman empire (see § 15). The most distinguished among the (25) Sassanides, next to the founder of the dynasty, was Chosroes I., surnamed Nushirvan, or the Just, a contemporary of Justinian, who terminated a war with the Byzantines, which had been inherited by his predecessor, but subsequently recommenced hostilities in Syria at the instigation of the Ostrogoths. On the appearance, however, of Belisarius in the C
east, he retraced his steps, and devoted all his energies to the Lazic war, at the conclusion of which he renounced his claims on Colchis, on condition of receiving an annual tribute. During the forty-eight years of his reign (531—79) the prosperity of the empire was promoted not so much by foreign conquests, as by the establishment of domestic
order and tranquillity. The government of the four great D
provinces was intrusted to four viziers, whose administration was subjected to a rigid supervision; an improved system of legislation, war, and finance was introduced; agricultural enterprise encouraged by protection and by the artificial irrigation of the soil, higher and elementary schools established, learned Greeks entertained at his court, and the most celebrated Greek and Indian authors translated into Persian. Destruction of the empire by the Arabians, see § 16.

C. The North-East of Europe.

§ 18. *The Sclavonians.*

77 Until the beginning of the fifth century, the eastern
A neighbors of Germany were denominated Wendes and Sarmatians. The last of these names was exchanged for that of Slaves or Sclavonians. Under Hermanric, these tribes were incorporated into the Gothic empire, and under Attila, into that of the Huns, and after the dissolution of those kingdoms, remained possessors of the eastern portion of Germany (as far as the Elbe), which had been depopulated by the migration of the Germans. They were divided into the Baltic Wendes, who retained their independence
B the longest. 2. The Sorbes in central Germany (between the Elbe and the Saale), who were made tributary to the Franks. 3. The Slaves, in the more restricted signification of the term, southwards from the Danube to Illyria, and westwards to Bavaria. The Slaves were delivered from the dominion of the Avars by their commander Samo, a Frank who had relapsed into heathenism. This general was recognized as king by most of the Slavish tribes, from Dalmatia to the Giant Mountains (Riesengebirge). After his death, the confederacy of the Slavish tribes was again dissolved, and new empires (e. g. those of the Croatians and Servians) arose from its ruins. The southern Slaves remained under the dominion of the Lombards.

78 A certain similarity between the Slavish and Germanic
C tribes appears not only in the vigorous structure of their bodies, but also to a certain extent in their religion (worship of nature, without images), constitution (patriarchal), manner of life (avoidance of cities), and moral character, for example, in their hospitality, chastity, and fidelity to the marriage-bed. On the other hand, we find traces of physical and moral difference in the liveliness of the Slaves, their love of ornament and revelry, and the want of union among individual tribes under a common head; in their practice of attacking from an ambuscade, their rapacity after a victory, and the frequent cruelties practised towards their prisoners; the burning of widows after the death of their husbands, the alacrity with which they

adopted the customs of neighboring nations (Romans, (78)
Greeks, Germans); their commercial enterprise at an early A
period of their history, the navigation of their rivers; and,
in later times, their industrious cultivation of the soil which
had been abandoned to their occupation by the Germans.
The languages of the two nations exhibit some traces of a
common origin, but the principles on which they are constructed are totally dissimilar.

§ 19. *Other Nations in the East of Europe.*

1. The Avars, who had been compelled by the Turks 79
to evacuate their settlements in the north of Circassia, B
ascended the Danube, and after twice demanding in
vain an allotment of land in the Eastern Roman empire,
took possession of Dacia, overthrew the empire of the
Gepidæ, with the assistance of the Lombards, established
themselves in Pannonia, which had been abandoned by their
allies, and wrested Dalmatia from the Byzantines. Thus,
in the year 600, their empire extended from the Volga to
the Saale and Ems: but, in the following century, its limits
were gradually circumscribed by the secession of neighboring states,—the Bulgarians declared themselves independent, Dalmatia was wrested from them by the Croatians
and Servians, and the eastern portion of the empire fell
into the hands of the Chazares.

2. The Bulgarians.

The Bulgarians, a Tartaric tribe, who had occupied 80
from time immemorial the shores of the Volga and the Ural C
mountains, ascended the Danube, and about the end of the
fifth century made annual incursions into the Byzantine
empire, laying waste the whole of the country from the
Ionian Sea to the suburbs of Constantinople. Having
effected a breach in the wall erected by Anastasius (see
§ 15), for the defence of the Thracian Chersonese, they
crossed the Hellespont, and returned laden with the spoils
of Asia. The fortresses erected by Justinian on the Danube,
opposed a barrier equally feeble to their destructive progress. Their deliverance from the tyranny of the Avars, D
to whom they had been tributary during a period of seventy
years (562—635), was effected by one of their princes,
named Kuvrat, who founded a mighty empire, which his

(80) sons divided among themselves after his death, the third
A receiving for his portion Bulgaria Proper, or the territory
lying between the Danube and the Hæmus.

81 3. The Chazares (also a Tartaric tribe) were masters, in the seventh century, of the whole of Southern Russia, from the Volga to the Dnieper, and were engaged in almost perpetual warfare with the Persians, and the Romans of the eastern empire. The famous Caucasian wall was erected by Chosroes I., as a barrier against their invasions.

Second Period.

From the Accession of the Carlovingians and Abbasides to the first Crusade, 752—1096.

A. The West.

§ 20. *The Frankish Empire under the Carlovingians.*

(752—888.)

1. Pepin the Short (752—768)

82 governed the three united kingdoms of 1. Austrasia, which
B comprehended Alemannia or Swabia, Bavaria, Thuringia,
and a part of Friesland. 2. Neustria. 3. Burgundy with
Provence and Septimania. *War in Italy.* The Ducatus
Romanus having been threatened by the Lombards, Pope
Stephen III. (II.), after an ineffectual attempt to obtain
support from the eastern emperor, implored the aid of
Pepin, whom he a second time crowned and anointed at
St. Denys, with his two sons Charles and Carloman. The
Franks were required thenceforward to choose their kings
from the male descendants of Pepin, whom the Pope raised
to the dignity of a Roman patrician, conferring on him at
the same time the title of Protector of the Church, and
enjoining him to undertake a crusade against the Lombards, for the purpose of securing the Exarchate for the
C Holy See. In obedience to these injunctions, Pepin invaded Italy, and after two campaigns compelled the Lombard king (Aistulf), to surrender the whole line of
Adriatic coast (from Commachio to Ancona), which he
presented to the Roman Pontiff. *Wars with neighboring
nations.*—The Frieses, who had assassinated St. Boniface,

were again subdued; the Saxons (after two campaigns) com- (82)
pelled to pay tribute; the Arabians (after the surrender of A
Narbonne) expelled from Southern Gaul and Aquitania
(after the death of Duke Waifar) re-united to the Frankish
empire.

2. Charlemagne (768—814),

born in 742 (on the 2nd April?), perhaps at Aachen, or 83
Aix-la-Chapelle, during the first three years of his reign shared the throne with his brother Carloman, by whose sudden death, in 771, he became sole king of the Franks, to the exclusion of his two nephews, who fled with their mother to the Lombardic court.

The wars of Charlemagne.

a. *Conquest of Lombardy*, 774. In compliance with 84
the wishes of his mother, Charlemagne had divorced his
first wife, and married a daughter of Desiderius, king of
the Lombards, whom he soon repudiated, and formed a third
matrimonial alliance with Hildegarde, a daughter of the
Duke of Swabia. Desiderius, indignant at this treatment, B
supported the sons of Carloman in their claims to the Frankish throne, and on the refusal of the Pope (Hadrian I.) to crown them, took possession of the patrimony of St. Peter. On receiving intelligence of this outrage, Charlemagne invaded Italy, besieged Desiderius in Pavia, and entering Rome, confirmed the grant of Pepin to the Holy See, the possessions of which were now augmented by the addition of Spoleto. Desiderius was taken prisoner by Charlemagne, who caused himself to be proclaimed king of the Lombards (or of Italy), in the year 774. An attempt of the Langobardic nobles to reinstate Desiderius on the throne, was frustrated by a second invasion of Italy.

b. *Wars with the Saxons*, 772—804. The Saxon na- 85
tion was divided into Westphalia between the Rhine and C
Ems, Engern between the Ems and Weser, Eastphalia between the Weser and Elbe, and Transalbingia beyond the Elbe. From the earliest times a feeling of hostility seems to have existed between the Saxon and Frankish races, and ever since the reign of Chlotar I., the Merovingians and their Saxon neighbors had been engaged in perpetual struggles, with no more important result than the subjugation of a few gaus by the Franks. With

(85) equal obstinacy, the Saxons resisted the introduction of
A Christianity into their country, putting the missionaries
to death and demolishing the churches. At a diet held at
Worms, in 772, it was resolved to attempt the subjugation
and conversion of these obstinate unbelievers. In the first
campaign, Charlemagne stormed the Eresburg (hod. Stadt-
berg on the Diemel), and destroyed the Irminsul, a statue
to which divine honors were paid, but which does not
seem to have been dedicated exclusively to any one god.
After his first Italian campaign (and a diet at Düren, in
775), Charlemagne marched against Wittekind and Alboin,
who had invaded his kingdom at the head of a Saxon army,
stormed their fortress of Sigiburg (at the confluence of the
Ruhr and Lenne, and compelled them to give hostages.
During his second campaign in Italy, and an expedition
into Spain, the Saxons again advanced to Deutz on the
B Rhine, but were driven back by Charlemagne, who subdued their country as far as the Elbe. Charlemagne now
ventured to send detachments of Saxons with two Frankish
armies against the Sorbes, who had invaded Thuringia,
but his faithless allies turned their arms against their com-
rades, an act of treachery which was punished by the
execution of 4500 Saxons at Verden on the Aller. A
general insurrection followed, and for three years the Saxons
made head against their powerful enemy. At length, after
two indecisive engagements (at Detmold and on the Hase),
Wittekind and Alboin entered into negotiations with Char-
C lemagne, and embraced Christianity, with most of their
followers. No sooner, however, was Charlemagne occupied with the Bavarians and Avares, than the Saxons again
broke out into open rebellion. At last, after eight campaigns (793—804), Charlemagne, with the assistance of
the Obotrites (in the country now called Mecklenburg),
after transplanting many of the Saxons into other countries,
and conciliating several of their most influential nobles by
grants of land, succeeded in persuading the people to acknowledge his authority, and embrace Christianity, without
86 formally concluding a peace.[1]
D 3. *War in Spain* (778). At a diet held by Charlemagne

[[1] There was no peace concluded at Selz, as has been generally supposed.]

at Paderborn, on his return from his third campaign against (86)
the Saxons, a petition for assistance against the Emir A
Abderrahman was presented to the king by the banished governor of Saragossa. Charlemagne immediately entered Spain, and subdued the whole of the country lying between the Pyrenees and the Ebro, which was annexed, under the name of the Spanish March, to the Frankish empire, but, even during the lifetime of Charlemagne, was frequently lost and recovered. On the homeward march, his army was attacked by the mountaineers of Gascony, and well-nigh annihilated in the pass of Roncesvalles (where the renowned Roland lost his life).

4. *War with the Avars* (788—801). Duke Tassilo of 87
Bavaria, who had several times violated his oath of alle- B
giance to Charlemagne at the instigation of his wife (a daughter of Desiderius, king of Lombardy), and been overthrown after a short campaign in 787, again raised the standard of rebellion in conjunction with the Avars, but was a second time defeated, taken prisoner, and confined in a monastery. His dukedom was incorporated into the Frankish empire. Charlemagne then attacked the Avars in their own country, which he ravaged as far as the Raab; and, at a later period, his son Pepin was sent to subdue the whole of the territory from the Ems to the Raab, which was now denominated the Avaric March.

5. *A war was carried on by his son Charles against the* 88
Danes and Wilzes, who had attacked Charlemagne's C
allies, the Obotrites. After the murder of their king Gottfried, the Danes concluded a peace (810), by which the Eider was recognized as the boundary between their country and that of the Franks. The Wilzes were soon afterwards entirely subdued.

In order to secure the frontiers of his empire, which 89
now extended from the Ebro to the Raab, and from Benevento to the Eider, Charlemagne established, especially in the east, Margravates (Friuli, the Spanish, Avaric, and Danish Marches, &c.)

Restoration of the Western Roman Empire 90
(800). Pope Leo III., having been shamefully ill-treated D
by the opposite party during a solemn procession, appeared before the diet at Paderborn, and induced Charlemagne (who had already assumed the office of protector

(90) of the Church, in his character of Roman Patrician),
A to visit Rome and chastise the offenders. In return for the assistance thus afforded, Charlemagne on Christmas-day in the year 800, received from the Pope the title of Roman Emperor, and immediately required from his subjects an oath not merely of fidelity, but of unqualified submission to his commands. The new relation between the Emperor and Pope was not that of a vassal to his feudal lord, but rather the co-existence of two supreme authorities, the spiritual being exercised by
B the Pope and the temporal by the Emperor. This supremacy was mutually recognized; the Pope, as restorer of the western empire, enjoying the privilege of placing the imperial crown on the head of the Emperor, to whom he administered an oath of allegiance to the Holy See; whilst, on the other hand, no election of a Pope was valid unless approved and confirmed by the Emperor. Both parties pledged themselves to act in concert, and support one another on all occasions.

Charlemagne's administration.

91 a. *Ecclesiastical and educational establishments.* For
C the confirmation of the Saxons in their profession of Christianity, Charlemagne founded eight bishoprics in that country (Osnabrück and Münster for the Westphalians, Minden and Paderborn for the Engernians; Bremen, Verden, and Hildesheim for the Eastphalians, and Halberstadt for the Thuringians). To each of these cathedrals, as well as to the monasteries, were annexed schools for instruction in the seven liberal arts (see § 14. IV). In the establishment of these seminaries, Charlemagne was assisted by his own tutor, the Anglo-Saxon monk, Alcuin.
D At the same time measures were adopted for restoring the respectability of the clergy, by procuring for them a more liberal education, introducing among them the canonical life (a chapter of canons being attached to each cathedral), prohibiting war and the chase, exempting them from the jurisdiction of the civil courts, and appointing them to the most important offices of state. His subjects were also required to pay tithes to the Church. The affection of Charlemagne for his mother-tongue induced him to give German names to the months; to compile, with the assistance of Alcuin, a grammar of the Frankish language, and

to publish a collection of old German heroic ballads. For (91)
the improvement of church music, professors of singing A
were invited from Rome by the advice of Alcuin.

b. *Legislation.* Codes of laws in the Latin language
were given to those nations (the Frieses, Saxons, and 92
Thuringians) which possessed no written statutes; whilst,
at the same time, the ancient "leges" of the other tribes
(see § 14, 2. c.), especially the lex Salica, were enlarged
by the addition of Capitularies, which were enacted at the
diet, and thenceforth became the law, not merely of those
tribes, but of the empire in general. To facilitate the
execution of the laws, the right of asylum possessed by
churches was considerably restricted.

c. The *Constitution,* in all essential particulars, remained 93
the same as it had been under the Merovingians; the only B
changes introduced being such as were rendered necessary
by the progress of civilization. The feudal system was
more fully developed; but, in spite of the opposition of
Charlemagne, many of the fiefs became hereditary allodes.
The division of estates into gaus, under the presidence of a
count, who possessed the right of administering justice and
calling out the army, was still retained; and the officers
of the court were the same as before, with the exception
of the Majordomat, which was now merged in the royal
dignity. These officers resided at the court of Aachen C
[Aix-la-Chapelle], or at Ingelheim, and accompanied the
emperor on his yearly progress through his dominions.
The Archchaplain (Apocrisiarius) acted as the sovereign's
vicegerent in spiritual matters, and the Comes Palatii in
temporal.

Besides the "field of May," or general review of the 94
army, at which all males capable of bearing arms were
present, Charlemagne held a second diet in the autumn,
which was attended by the spiritual and temporal dignitaries of the empire. At this diet, which assembled alter- D
nately at Worms, Aachen, Düren, Paderborn, &c., questions
of inferior moment were determined summarily, the more
important being reserved for discussion at the next field of
May. For the purpose of obtaining a more accurate
knowledge of each province, Charlemagne every year sent
into certain districts (legationes or missatica, each of which
comprised several counties or dioceses) imperial commis-

(94) sioners (missi dominici), one of whom belonged to the high-
A est rank of spiritual, and the other of temporal, nobility.
The duty of these commissioners was to hold visitations
(placita), at which the assembled ecclesiastics and nobility
of the district were required to render an account of the
different branches of administration. They were also em-
powered to settle disputes, inspect the imperial demesnes,
inquire into the condition of the churches and monasteries,
and the lives of the clergy, and prepare a list of male persons capable of bearing arms. Every freeholder who
possessed three (afterwards four) mansi, or homesteads,
B was required to serve for three months in the army. Those
who possessed less than the above qualification were
allowed to club together and arm one of their number.
The militia of each province was commanded by a duke.
A fine of sixty solidi was imposed on all who neglected to
appear in arms at the place of rendezvous, and those who
were unable to pay this penalty were sent to work it out
on the imperial farms. Spiritual persons were exempt
from military service, but were required to arm their able-
bodied vassals. The punishment of death continued to be
C inflicted on deserters. It was forbidden to carry weapons
in time of peace. The *imperial revenues* were derived
from the following sources: *aa*, the (163) crown demesnes;
bb, presents from his subjects in the month of May;
cc, duties; *dd*, land and poll taxes; *ee*, tributes of dependent nations.

95 For the encouragement of commerce, which had been
severely crippled by his numerous wars, Charlemagne established depôts, opened annual markets, improved the high-
ways, and diminished the imposts.

After the conclusion of his war with the Saxons, the
emperor divided his dominions among his three sons,
Charles, Pepin, and Lewis, of whom only the youngest
D survived him. At a diet held at Aachen in 813, Lewis
was proclaimed his successor in the imperial and royal
dignities, and received the crown from the hands of his
father. Pepin's illegitimate son Bernard was permitted to
hold the kingdom of Italy as a fief from his uncle. On the
28th January in the following year Clarlemagne died at
Aachen, and was buried in the cathedral of that city, which
he himself had founded.

3. Lewis the Pious (814—840).

Lewis, whose benevolence, love of justice, and piety 96
were, in a great measure, neutralized by his weakness of A
purpose and ignorance of human nature, promulgated, at a
diet at Aachen, a number of new regulations for the government of spiritual persons, monks, and nuns. In the year
817 an imperial edict was issued, dividing the empire
among his three sons, Lothar [Lothaire], Pepin, and Lewis.
Lothar was raised to the imperial throne as the colleague of
his father; Pepin received Aquitania; and Lewis, Bavaria.
Bernard of Italy was deprived of his sight for conspiring
against his uncle, and soon afterwards died. The crown
of Italy was then placed on the head of Lothar.

Soon afterwards the emperor married a second wife 97
(Judith, daughter of Count Welf), by whom he had B
Charles the Bald. The settlement of Alemannia, Alsace,
and a part of Burgundy on this son, excited the envy of
his brothers, who entered into a conspiracy against their
father, which was followed up (after the compulsory cession of Aquitania by Pepin to Charles) by a declaration
of war. Lewis was taken prisoner in an engagement on
the plain of Colmar (called from the treachery of his
nobles the "perjurers' field"), deprived of his crown, and
compelled to do penance in a monastery at Soissons. But
the arrogance of Lothar soon disgusted his brothers, who
replaced their father on the throne. The sons of Pepin C
(who died before his father) were excluded from the succession, and the dominions of Lewis divided (by the advice
of his wife) among his surviving children; Charles the Bald
receiving the western portion as far as the Maas (Meuse),
Saone, and Rhone; Lothar the eastern; and Lewis only
Bavaria.

Pepin of Heristal † 714.

Charles Martel † 741.

Carloman (a monk) 747. Pepin the Short † 768.

Charlemagne † 814. m. Hildegarde — Carloman † 771.

Charles † 811. — Pepin † 810. — Lewis the Pious † 840. — Charles. — Pepin.

Bernard, king of Italy, † 817. — Lothar I. † 855. — Pepin † 838. — Lewis the German † 876. — Charles the Bald † 877. — Gisela.

Lewis II. † 875. — Lothar II. † 868. — Charles † 863. — Carloman † 880. — Lewis † 882. — Charles the Fat † 888. — Lewis the Stammerer † 879. — Berengar I. king of Italy, 888.

Irmengard, wife of Boso, k. of Burg. Cisjur. — Arnulf of Carinthia † 899. — Lewis III. † 882. — Carloman † 884. — Charles the Simple † 929. — Gisela, w. of Adalbert, margrave of Ivrea.

Lewis, king of Burgundy. — Lewis the Child † 911. — Lewis IV. — Berengar II. king of Italy. 950—961.

Lothar

Lewis V. † 987.

The Successors of Lewis the Pious to 887.

Immediately after the death of Lewis, a quarrel arose 98
among his sons, in consequence of an attempt on the part A
of Lothar, as emperor, to exclude his brothers from all participation in the government. A battle was fought in 841, near the village of *Fontenay* (Fontenaille), in Burgundy, in which Lothar was defeated. The war, however, continued until 843, when Lothar found himself compelled to conclude with his brothers the famous *Treaty of Verdun*, by which

Lewis (surnamed the German) received all the Frank- 99
ish territory on the right bank of the Rhine (with the exception of Friesland), together with Spiers, Worms, and Mainz.

Charles the Bald had all the western provinces as 100
far as the Scheld, Maas, Saone, and Rhone. B

Lothar had the territory eastward of those rivers to the 101
Alps and the Rhine, with the exception of three cities. The southern portion of this strip of land was called Burgundy, and the northern Lorraine (Lotharii regnum). Italy and Friesland were also settled on him.

The three new kingdoms were soon disquieted by intes- 102
tine commotions, the quarrels of their sovereigns with one another, and perpetual contests with a wild piratical race called the *Normans*, or *Northmen*, who availed themselves of the distracted condition of the empire to make
descents on the coasts, especially of western France. Sail- C
ing in their light galleys up the Loire, Garonne, and Rhone, they sacked the cities of Rouen, Paris, &c., ravaged the country, and overthrew the armies of Charles the Bald. Italy was also visited by these marauders, as well as by the Arabian pirates. In Germany, the Normans sailed up the Elbe, and burnt the city of Hamburg, but were beaten back by Lewis. During the whole period of this prince's reign, the eastern frontier of his kingdom was the scene of perpetual struggles with Sclavonic tribes, particularly with the Bohemians and Moravians.

The Emperor Lothar I. at his death, in 855, had divided 103
his kingdom among his three sons; the youngest of whom, D
Charles, died in 863, leaving his portion to be equally distributed between his surviving brothers, the Emperor

(103) Lewis II. and Lothar II. After the death of this Lothar,
A his kingdom of Lorraine was seized by his uncles, Lewis the German and Charles the Bald.

104 Lewis II. having died without male issue, in 875, Charles the Bald anticipating his elder brother, Lewis the German, hastened into Italy, where he was crowned king of that country and Roman emperor. On the death of Lewis the German, in the following year (876), his kingdom was divided among his three sons; the youngest of whom, Charles the Fat, became sole occupant of the throne
B after the decease of both his brothers. As none of the descendants of Charles the Bald survived, after the death of his son Lewis the Stammerer (877—879), and two elder grandsons, with the exception of an infant named Charles the Simple, little difficulty was experienced by Charles the Fat in reuniting the whole Frankish monarchy (885—887), with the exception of the Spanish March, the dukedom of Carinthia, and the cisjuranic kingdom of Burgundy (separated in 879), the crown of which had been conferred by the estates on Count Boso (of Vienne), brother-in-law of Charles the Bald. The power of Charles, however, was insufficient either to repress the intestine disturbances of his kingdom, or make head against the
C Normans, who burnt Cologne, Bonn, and Trèves. His pusillanimity in consenting to pay tribute, and abandoning Burgundy to the Normans, so displeased his subjects, that at a diet held at Tribur, in 887, he was set aside, and died in the beginning of the following year. The Frankish empire was then broken up into five portions, viz.:—

105 1. The western Frankish empire was assigned to Count Otho of Paris, brother-in-law of Lewis the Stammerer.

106 2. Germany to Arnulf, Duke of Carinthia, a natural
D son of Carloman, and grandson of Lewis the German.

107 3 and 4. Burgundy was divided into transjuranic and cisjuranic; the former founded by Rudolf Welf, previously Duke of the West Franks; the latter governed, since 879, by Boso, son-in-law of the Emperor Lewis II.

108 5. In Italy, the sovereignty was disputed between Guido of Spoleto, and Berengar, Margrave of Friuli.

109 Domestic History (814—887). Under the feeble successors of Charlemagne, there arose a temporal and

ecclesiastical aristocracy, whose influence increased (109)
in proportion to the decline of the imperial authority, and A
the subjugation of the common freeholders, most of whom
were compelled by violence and oppression to hold their
estates as fiefs from the nobility and clergy. These usurpations were facilitated by the practice, which daily became
more general, of making fiefs hereditary, and by the right
which the nobles had gradually acquired of electing their
own sovereign on the extinction of a dynasty, as well as
by the suppression of the royal commissioners. Instead of B
offering any effectual opposition to these encroachments,
the kings were only too happy, amidst partitions of the
empire, intestine disputes, and foreign wars, to conciliate
the favor of the nobles by the most unlimited concessions.
Among other instances of weakness, it may be mentioned,
that Charles the Bald granted to the West Frankish nobility
the right of resisting with the strong hand the introduction
of any measure which they might consider unjust. The
dukedoms which had been suppressed by Charlemagne
were now restored, especially in those provinces which
were threatened with foreign invasion, where the authority
of the king was inadequate to the maintenance of peace: in
Thuringia, for instance, against the Sorbes, and in Saxony
against the Normans, in the reign of Lewis the German.
The influence of the clergy over all classes became daily C
more confirmed, as the institutions of the Church developed
themselves; and men discovered that the ecclesiastical body
enjoyed exclusive possession of the learning of those days.
The so-called decretals of St. Isidore did not, it is true,
establish a power which existed in its fullest extent before
their publication, but they served, by authoritatively proclaiming the actual supremacy of the Church, to consolidate
and uphold her claims to universal dominion.[1]

[[1] About the year 867, a German deacon, named Benedictus Levita, published a collection of ecclesiastical statutes, or "decretals," in which the supremacy of the Pope over general councils, and his right of appointing bishops and settling all ecclesiastical controversies, were distinctly asserted. As it was important to assign to these decretals a date antecedent to the empire, Benedict pretended that they were the production of St. Isidore, a Spaniard who flourished in the seventh century. Their genuineness was asserted by Pope Nicholas I., who made them the groundwork of the papal claims to

§ 21. *The East Frankish Empire under the two last Carlovingians* (887—911).

110 1. Arnulf (887—899) compelled Guido and the two
A kings of Burgundy to acknowledge him as their feudal lord, and thus re-united Italy and Burgundy, as fiefs, to the German empire. The utter defeat of the Normans (891) served to raise the military reputation of Arnulf, but not to scare them from their acts of piracy, in which they were encouraged by the knowledge that the Moravians (who, since the fall of the Avaric monarchy, had advanced as far as Hungary) were now, under their leader Zwentibold, menacing the eastern frontier of Germany.
B By the aid of the Magyars, or Hungarians (who had proceeded up the Danube after their expulsion from their settlements on the Ural mountains by the Petschenegers), the Moravians were compelled to evacuate their country (from the Gran to the Morawa), which was soon afterwards occupied by the Magyars. Arnulf was crowned emperor, but was unable to settle the disputes of the different candidates for the crown of Italy.

111 2. Lewis the Child (900—911). During the regency
C of Archbishop Hatto of Mainz, and Duke Otho of Saxony (guardians of Lewis), the nobles had many opportunities of consolidating their power. In Bavaria and Alemannia national dukedoms were established for the protection of those countries against the marauding incursions of the Hungarians, who, since the overthrow of the Moravian empire, had almost every year invaded Carinthia and Bavaria, and, after the defeat of Lewis's army, had ravaged Alemannia, Thuringia, and Saxona. The ducal dignity was also re-established about this time in Lorraine and Franconia; so that, at the termination of the Carlovingian dynasty, there were no less than six national dukes in Germany.

§ *Empire of the East Franks under Conrad I. of Franconia* (911—918).

112 After the extinction of the Carlovingian race, an attempt

universal supremacy.—*Wolfgang Menzels Geschichte der Deutschen; Capitel* 137.]

was made by the nations in the south of Germany (the (112)
Alemanni and Bavarians) to establish independent king- A
doms. On the other hand, the Eastern Franks and Saxons proceeded to the election of an emperor, and chose Otho the Illustrious, duke of Saxony; but that prince having refused the crown on account of his advanced age, a second election took place, and the East Frankish Duke Conrad was chosen on his recommendation, the Alemanni and Bavarians acquiescing in the choice. Lorraine, on the other hand, became a province of the West Frankish empire. During the whole of his reign, Conrad was occupied B
in fruitless attempts to render the vassals, especially the dukes, subject to his authority; the provinces being left in the mean time to defend themselves, as best they might, against repeated invasions of the Normans. Lorraine continued to be a dependency of the West Frankish empire. The Duke of Bavaria, after sustaining a defeat, went over to the Hungarians, hoping with their assistance to maintain his independence. Henry, son of Otho the Illustrious, not only held possession of all his father's fiefs, but even established his right to the independent duchies of Saxony
and Thuringia. On his deathbed Conrad recommended C
Henry as his successor. There were now four German dukedoms, viz., Eastern Franconia, Saxony, Swabia, and Bavaria.

§ 23. *The German Empire under kings of the house of Saxony* (919—1024).

1. Henry I., surnamed the Fowler (919—936), 113
quickly carried into effect the plans of his predecessor, subduing the Duke of Alemannia, who had availed himself of the change of sovereigns to declare his country independent, as well as the Duke of Bavaria (who had returned from Hungary), and re-uniting Lorraine to the
empire. An armistice for nine years was granted by the D
Hungarians in return for the restoration to liberty of one of their princes, who had been taken prisoner in Hungary, the Germans engaging to pay an annual tribute during the whole of that period. This breathing time was employed by Henry in placing the army on a more efficient footing, building strongholds (Merseburg, Meissen, Quedlinburg, Nordhausen, Goslar—hence his surname of

(113) the "City-builder"), establishing an order of knighthood,
A and restoring the military games (the origin of tournaments). At the same time the army was exercised in warfare: 1. Against the Sclavonians from the Elbe to the Baltic. The conquest of these tribes enabled him to extend the boundaries of the empire from the Elbe to the Middle Oder. 2. Against the Normans, who were compelled to evacuate their territory from the Eider to Schleswig. Three Margravates were established for the defence of the frontiers, viz.: *a.* North Saxony, against the Wilzes; *b.* Meissen, against the Sclavonians; *c.* Schleswig, against
B the Normans. Having completed his preparations, Henry refused the further payment of tribute, and when the Hungarians invaded Thuringia, overthrew them at Merseburg, in the year 933. He was succeeded by his second son,

2. Otho I. (surnamed the Great),

114 the first king elected by the common suffrages of the five principal nations. From this time the ceremony of coronation was always performed at Aachen [Aix-la-Chapelle]. The first years of his reign were passed in disputes with the Dukes of Bohemia, Bavaria, Franconia, and Lorraine, who had formed a confederacy with Otho's discontented brothers Tankmar and Henry, and even with Lewis IV., king of
C France. After the termination of this contest, an attempt was made by Otho to diminish the influence of the dukes by the establishment in each province of a Count Palatine, or imperial lieutenant; his own authority being at the same time strengthened by the elevation of four of his relations to the dukedom. His friend Herman Billing was invested with Otho's own dukedom of Saxony, in return for his services in putting an end to the Bohemian war. The
D feudal supremacy of the emperor over the united (since 933) kingdoms of Burgundy, which had been in abeyance since the death of Arnulph, was re-established; and in the year 933 Lorraine was divided into two dukedoms, viz., Upper Lorraine on the Moselle, and Lower Lorraine on the Maas [Meuse] and the sea-coast. The same care was bestowed by Otho on ecclesiastical affairs and the establishment of schools, as on the improvement of the constitution; laws were enacted against simony, the privileges of the

Church augmented, and bishoprics established, especially (114)
in the Sclavonic countries, Brandenburg and Havelberg.
Foreign Wars. 1. The *Danes*, who had invaded and laid 115
waste the Margravate of Schleswig (founded by Henry I.), A
were compelled (after a single campaign, in which Otho
advanced into Jutland as far as Ottesund) to recognize the
feudal supremacy of Germany, and embrace Christianity.
2. The Duke of Bohemia (Boleslav), who had a second
time thrown off his allegiance, submitted to Otho, became
a Christian, and founded the bishopric of Prague. 3. *First
Italian campaign.* Italy had been severed from Germany
since the days of Arnulf. Lothar, king of that country,
having been assassinated by Berengar II., (Margrave of
Ivrea), an appeal was made by Adelaide, widow of the murdered man, to Otho, who entered Italy, and having liberated
and married the queen, was crowned king of the Lombards at
Pavia, and soon afterwards (at Augsburg) invested Berengar
with the sovereignty of Italy as a fief of Germany. 4. The B
Hungarians, who had entered Bavaria with an army of
100,000 men, were totally defeated on the plain of the
Lech, and never again appeared in Germany. The Christian religion was soon afterwards generally received among
them. 5. A victory over the Wendish Sclavonians was
followed by the recognition, on the part of the Duke of
Poland, of the feudal supremacy of the German empire, as
well as by the subjugation and conversion of all the Sclavonian tribes as far as the Vistula. 6. *Second Italian
campaign.* The complaints of Berengar's tyranny, which
reached Otho from all quarters, induced him to send his
son Ludolf into Italy, and after his death to visit that
country in person. Having deposed Berengar, and assumed C
the iron crown at Milan, Otho proceeded to Rome, where
he revived the title of Emperor of the West,
which, from that time (962), until the period of its extinction
in 1806, was always borne by the German kings. After
quelling repeated disturbances, and obtaining from the
Romans a promise that no Pope should be chosen without
his consent, Otho returned to Germany, where he endeavored to improve the condition of his cities by encou-
raging trade and manufactures, and especially by the
establishment of markets. 7. *In a third Italian campaign*
he wrested from the Greeks their possessions in Lower

(115) Italy, with the exception of Benevento and Capua, which
A were ceded to him by treaty; the hand of the Greek princess Theophania being at the same time bestowed on his son Otho, who had already been crowned king and emperor.

3. Otho II. (973—983).

116 A war with France (during which King Lothar surprised Otho II. in Aachen, but was driven back as far as Paris) was terminated by Lothar's consenting to hold Lorraine as a fief of the empire. The refusal of the Greeks to give up certain lands in Apulia and Calabria, which he claimed as the dowry of his wife, furnished Otho with an excuse for entering Lower Italy, where he was defeated near Basantello, by the forces of the Greeks, assisted by the Arabians, whom they had summoned from Sicily for that purpose.
B He died at Rome, in the midst of his preparations for a fresh campaign, and was succeeded by his son

4. Otho III. (983—1002),

117 a child of three years old, under the guardianship of his mother Theophania, and, after her death, of his grandmother Adelaide and his aunt the Abbess Matilda. Carinthia was separated from Bavaria, and erected into a seventh duchy. An attempt having been made by a party at Rome, headed by the Consul Crescentius, to emancipate themselves from the German yoke, Otho three times visited that city, and, after restoring tranquillity, assumed the imperial crown, and raised a nominee of his own to the papal chair, but, happily for Germany, was unable to carry out his favorite plan of making Rome the capital of the German empire.
C A separate election of each province placed on the throne as his successor a great-grandson of Henry I.,

5. Henry II. (surnamed the Saint) (1002—1024),

118 the first king who was required, as the condition of his election, to guarantee to each nation all the privileges which had been at any time enjoyed by the people. During the absence of Henry in Germany, where he was detained by the intrigues of his enemies, an attempt was made by some of the provinces to throw off the German yoke. Harduin, Margrave of Ivrea, caused himself to be proclaimed king of Italy, whilst at the same time Duke Boleslav, of Poland,

overran Bohemia and Moravia, and formed an alliance with (118)
the discontented German princes. After defeating Har- A
duin, and assuming the crown of Italy (at Pavia), Henry compelled Boleslav to evacuate Bohemia, and recognize him as his liege lord (probably only with reference to the provinces of Lusatia and Silesia). During a second visit to Italy, occasioned by a fresh attempt on the part of Harduin to obtain possession of that country, Henry was solemnly crowned emperor; and soon afterwards the death of Harduin terminated for ever the contests between the native and German princes for the possession of the Italian
crown. A third Italian campaign was signalized by the B
defeat of the Greeks, and the establishment in Apulia of the Norman allies, to whose co-operation Henry was in some measure indebted for his victory.

§ 24. *The German Empire under the Franconian Emperors* (1024—1125).

1. Conrad II. (1024—1039)

was chosen at Mainz by the unanimous suffrages of the 119
eight German dukes, and crowned at Aachen, Milan, and Rome. The first act of his reign was to confirm the Normans in their settlements in Lower Italy. After the decease of Rudolph III., king of Burgundy, who died without issue, that country was added, as a lapsed fief, to the German empire, and at the same time the supremacy of Germany
over Poland and Bohemia was re-established. On the C
other hand, the March of Schleswig, which was no longer of any value as a barrier against the Normans, was ceded by Conrad to Canute, the king of Denmark, Norway, and England: and thus the Eider became again the northern boundary of the German empire. During his second visit to Italy, Conrad passed a law by which the smaller fiefs were made hereditary both in Germany and Italy. His family influence was extended by the nomination of four members of the royal house to the vacant dukedoms of Bavaria, Swabia, Franconia, and Carinthia.

2. Henry III. (1039—1056).

The first act of Henry's administration was to consoli- 120
date the family influence of which his father had laid D
the foundation. By retaining the dukedoms of Bavaria and Swabia, which he had held before his elevation to the

(120) throne, and allowing those of Carinthia and Franconia to
A remain vacant, he established the imperial authority, without the intervention of any secondary power, over the whole
of Southern Germany, as well as Italy and Burgundy. At
the same time Bretislav, duke of Bohemia, who had invaded Poland, was reduced to submission, and the feudal
sovereignty over Hungary insured for a season (1045—
1063) by the restoration of Peter, the exiled sovereign of
that country. At this period the German empire comprised three kingdoms (Italy, Burgundy, and Hungary);
six German dukedoms (Alemannia, Bavaria, Franconia,
Saxony, Upper and Lower Lorraine); and three Sclavo-
B nian (Bohemia with Moravia, Poland, and Carinthia). For
the better maintenance of peace in Alemannia, Bavaria, and
Carinthia, dukes were re-established in those countries, but
the dignity was never conferred on a native, and its possessor was entirely dependent on the imperial crown.
Franconia was already considered the hereditary property
of the royal house. Introduction into Germany of the
"Truce of God" (treuga Dei), by which all quarrels were
suspended from Wednesday evening to Monday morning,
as well as during the seasons of Lent and Advent.

121 Henry's next project was the *reformation of the*
Church, especially in Germany, with reference especially
to its two most glaring abuses,—simony, or the sale of
benefices, and the immoral lives of the clergy. As it was
desirable that these reforms should emanate from the pope
himself, Henry endeavored to re-establish unity in the
Church, by setting aside three rival pontiffs, and raising a
C German (Clement II.) to the papal throne. In return for
these services the new pope placed the imperial crown on the
head of Henry, and entered into a solemn engagement that
thenceforth no election of a pope should be considered
valid unless confirmed by the emperor. Stringent laws
against the luxury of the clergy, and against simony, were
enacted by Henry and four popes, who were successively
elevated by him to the throne of St. Peter; whilst, on the
other hand, all his plans for subjecting the Church to the
temporal power were cautiously but effectually resisted by
D the papal chancellor, Hildebrand. The Normans were
confirmed by Henry in the possession of their conquests
in Apulia and Calabria, which they were afterwards content to hold as vassals of the see of Rome.

3. Henry IV. (1056—1106),

a child of six years old, succeeded his father, under the guardianship of his mother the empress Agnes. The administration of the kingdom, which had been usurped by Hanno, archbishop of Cologne, who had secured the person of the young king, was wrested from his grasp by Adalbert, archbishop of Bremen, whose insolence at last so irritated the nobles of Germany, that, at a diet held at Tribur, they offered Henry the choice either of renouncing his favorite or resigning the crown. Adalbert was banished in consequence of these threats, but at the end of three years he reappeared at the imperial court, and endeavored to annihilate the party of his opponents. Otho, duke of Bavaria, was falsely accused of high treason and deprived of his dukedom (which was conferred on his son-in-law Welf [Guelph], founder of the junior Welfic [Guelphic] line; and his ally Magnus, son of the Duke of Saxony, was thrown into prison. After the death of Adalbert in 1072, Hanno again resumed the reins, which the infirmities of old age compelled him to resign at the end of a year. Being now left to himself and his own evil passions, Henry committed the most capricious excesses, conferring dukedoms and bishoprics on his unworthy favorites, and endeavoring to render Saxony immediately subject to the imperial crown. With this view fortresses were built, and garrisons distributed over the whole country; and Magnus, who had been elected duke on the death of his father, was still detained a prisoner. 122 A B C

War with the Saxons (1073—1075).

The oppressive administration of the king, the insolence with which he treated the assembled nobles of Saxony, and the lawless proceedings of the royal garrisons, so irritated the Saxons, that an insurrection at length broke out, and 60,000 men appeared before Goslar, where Henry was at that time residing. In the extremity of his terror Henry fled to Harzburg, and thence to Worms, where he was received with every mark of respect by the citizens, notwithstanding the opposition of their bishop. A peace was concluded at Gerstungen, the chief condition of which was, that all Henry's fortresses in Saxony should be levelled with the ground. This peace the princes of Upper Germany and the Rhineland refused to ratify; and Henry in consequence again took the field, and overthrew the Saxons at Hohenburg on the Unstrut. 123 D

Contest between Gregory VII. and the princes of Germany (1073—1085).

124 As archdeacon and chancellor of five successive popes,
A Hildebrand had been gradually preparing the way for the development of his mighty project *of rendering the Church independent of the State, and using the authority thus acquired for the improvement and reformation of the Church itself.*[1]
B With this view he had, as early as the year 1059, persuaded a council held in the church of St. John Lateran, to pass a resolution that thenceforth the pope should be elected by a college of cardinals, and accepted by the rest of the clergy and the Roman people; the emperor's right of confirming their choice being conferred on him, after each election, by the pope himself. As the most effectual mode of carrying this decree into effect, the pope conferred the title of Duke on the Norman prince Robert Guiscard, together with the fiefs of Apulia and Calabria, and invested him, by anticipation, with the sove-
C reignty of the still unconquered island of Sicily. In return for these benefits, Guiscard solemnly pledged himself to secure freedom of election to the college of cardinals. In the year 1073 Hildebrand himself became pope, and by way of protest against the illegal removal of Gregory VI. by the Emperor Henry III. assumed the title of Gregory VII. In order fully to establish the independence of the clergy, Gregory renewed the laws against the marriage of spiritual persons and against simony, forbidding bishops and abbots to receive investiture (i. e. the ring and staff, which were in most instances purchased simoniacally) from the hands of
D temporal sovereigns. Henry, who still continued this practice in defiance of the pope's prohibition, was summoned to plead before a synod at Rome; but, instead of obeying the mandate, he immediately assembled (at Worms, in 1076) a council of German and Lombard bishops, who deposed Gregory from the popedom. On receiving intelligence of this bold proceeding, Gregory pronounced sentence of excommunication against the emperor, and absolved all his subjects from their

[1] ["The object of Gregory VII. in attempting to redress those more flagrant abuses which for two centuries had deformed the face of the Latin Church, is not incapable, perhaps, of vindication, though no sufficient apology can be offered for the means he employed. But the disinterested love of reformation, to which candor might ascribe the condition against investitures, is belied by the general tenor of his conduct, exhibiting an arrogance without parallel, and an ambition that grasped at universal and unlimited monarchy."—*Hallam*, vol. ii. p. 270.]

oath of allegiance. An attempt was now made by Henry (124)
to place Pope Gregory under the ban of the empire ; but a A
meeting of German princes at Tribur, for the purpose of
electing a new emperor, so alarmed him, that he crossed
the Alps in the winter of 1077, and after three days of
humiliation in the castle of Canossa, obtained from Gregory
the reversal of the sentence of excommunication ; he, on his
part, engaging to exercise none of the functions of royalty,
until a diet of the empire should decide whether he might
continue to wear the crown of Germany or not. During B
Henry's absence the nobles had chosen in his room Duke
Rudolph of Swabia, who pledged himself not to inter-
fere in the election of bishops, and agreed that thenceforward
the king's son should succeed to the throne only in virtue
of his election, and not by hereditary right. After two indecisive engagements (at Melrichstadt near Fulda, and
Flarcheim near Mühlhausen) between Rudolph and Henry,
the latter was again excommunicated by the pope, and in
return deposed Gregory, and placed the Archbishop of
Ravenna (Clement III.) on the papal throne. In a third
battle (on the Elster), Rudolph was mortally wounded by
Duke Godfrey of Bouillon. Henry now left the prosecu- C
tion of the war in Germany to Frederic of Hohenstaufen
(on whom he had conferred the dukedom of Swabia, void
by the elevation of Rudolph to the throne), and marching
into Italy, took Rome after a siege of three years, and received the imperial crown from the hands of Clement III.
Gregory, who had taken refuge in the castle of St. Angelo,
was released by Robert Guiscard, and immediately fled to
Monte Cassino, and subsequently to Salerno, where he died
in 1085, after again pronouncing sentence of excommunication against Henry. During Henry's absence the Saxons D
and Swabians had elected Count Herman of Luxemburg (1081—1088), who obtained one victory over Henry
(at Bleichfield near Würtzburg in 1086), and soon afterwards resigned his crown.

Rebellion of the sons of Henry IV. against their father (1093—1105).

Henry's eldest son Conrad, who had already been 125
crowned as his successor in Germany, raised the standard
of rebellion against his father, and assumed the crown of

(125) Italy at the instigation of the adversaries of Clement III.,
A who had elevated Urban II. to the papal throne. For this act of treason Conrad was deprived of the succession by sentence of a diet assembled at Cologne, and the crown secured to his brother Henry, who was required to promise that he would not claim the sovereign authority during the lifetime of his father. Henry, however, soon violated his engagement, and headed an insurrection under the auspices of Pope Pascal II., who had renewed the bull of excommunication against Henry IV. on learning that the emperor was making preparations for the election of an
B anti-pope. Although his personal liberty had been three times guaranteed by his son, Henry was seized and compelled to sign his abdication at Ingelheim. Thence he fled to Liege, where he died in the year **1106**. His body was afterwards disinterred, and removed to Spiers, where it was buried on the removal of the ban of excommunication in **1111**.

4. Henry V. (1106—1125)

126 had a twofold object in view: 1. The restoration of the royal authority, which had fallen into contempt; 2. The termination of the disputes with the pope respecting investiture, which had been revived by a
C fresh decree of Pascal II. The first of these objects was promoted by the re-assertion of the almost obsolete claims of the German king to feudal supremacy over Bohemia and Poland, both of which countries were again compelled to pay tribute. A proposal of the pope, that the king should renounce the right of investiture, on condition of the bishops restoring to the empire all the fiefs which had belonged to it since the days of Charlemagne, having been generally resisted by the German clergy, Henry seized the person of the pope, and compelled him to renounce his own claim to the right of investiture, and place the imperial
D crown on the head of his adversary. No sooner, however, had he quitted Italy, than the pope annulled the decree, on the ground of its having been obtained by intimidation, and pronounced the ban of excommunication against Henry, which was renewed by the two succeeding popes. At length the contest, which had lasted fifty years, was terminated by the conclusion, in the year **1122**, of the Con-

cordat of Worms, in which Henry, whose kingdom was (126)
disquieted by the insurrections of his nobles, agreed to A
renounce the right of investiture with the ring and staff, retaining only the sceptre; the pope, on his part, consenting that the election of bishops and abbots should take place in the imperial presence, and that, in the event of a disputed election, the question should be decided by the emperor, the archbishop and provincial bishops acting as his assessors.

Changes in the constitution during the Saxon and Franconian period.

The Monarchy. With the extinction of the Carlovingian 127
line disappeared also the practice of dividing the kingdom B
among sons; but the hereditary right of succession was in some sort retained; inasmuch as the heir was invariably chosen by the electors as long as any member of the family survived. The election (from the same dynasty), and at a later period the coronation of the successor to the throne, took place during the lifetime of the reigning monarch. Whilst the officers appointed by the king were acquiring the right of hereditary succession, the monarchy itself was gradually becoming elective; and the legality of this mode of proceeding was at length formally asserted at the election
of Rudolph of Swabia. The limits of the royal authority C
were not defined by statute, its greater or less extent depending principally on the family or personal influence of the sovereign.

The *Dukes*, who had been restricted by Charlemagne 128
to the duty of leading the people in time of war, for which they were originally appointed, extended their sphere of action, after his death, by assuming the functions of the suppressed royal missi or commissioners, especially as regarded the presidency in courts of justice and provincial assemblies. Thus they acquired no inconsiderable D
influence in the election of kings; whilst, on the other hand, their authority was crippled by the rising power of the cities, and the establishment of principalities under Margraves, Landgraves, &c. They were nominated by the king, but could only be removed for scandalous offences, and with the consent of the diet. Under Henry IV. most of the dukedoms became hereditary.

129 The *Margraves*, the number of whom was increased in
A the reign of Henry I. by conquests in the east, remained almost entirely independent of the dukes, whose military power they possessed in conjunction with the judicial authority of the counts.

130 The *Counts Palatine* were appointed partly for the superintendence of single palaces or fortresses with their districts, and partly for the government of entire provinces, in which, as the king's lieutenants, they watched over the administration of the law. The most important among them was the Count Palatine of the Rhine.

131 The *Counties* were all hereditary under the Franconian
B princes. The most important duty of the count was the administration of justice.

§ 25. *Italy* (888—1125).

A. The kingdom of Italy,

132 comprising upper and central Italy, was governed 1) *by kings of its own* until the year 961. After the death of Arnulf, whose claims to the Italian crown could only be supported as long as he remained in Italy, fresh disputes arose between Friuli and Spoleto; and until the reign of Otho I., who re-united Italy to Germany in 961 (see § 78), each king had to contest the possession of the crown with
C a rival claimant. At the same time the country was ravaged by the Hungarians, whose assistance was invoked sometimes by one party, and sometimes by the other.

133 2) *by German kings*, who remained in undisturbed possession of the Italian throne, with the exception of a fruitless attempt on the part of the Margrave Harduin of Ivrea (see § 80) to depose Henry II. From the time of Otho I., Italy seems to have been split into a number of fiefs, some of them spiritual (in which episcopal vicecomites exercised the functions of counts), and some temporal
D (under counts and margraves). Under the Othos, all the privileges which had before belonged to the kings (the right of imposing duties, of coining money, establishing markets, &c., were gradually conferred on Italian subjects, principally on the priesthood; but in order to prevent the great feudal lords from becoming too powerful,

the inferior fiefs were made hereditary by a constitution of (133)
the Emperor Conrad, promulgated on the plains of Ron- A
caglia in 1038; and a law was at the same time passed,
securing to every man the right of being tried by his peers.
During the decline of the imperial authority, consequent on
the disputes of Henry IV. and V. with the Church, the
Lombard cities repudiated the government of the emperor's
lieutenants, and formed themselves into republics, under
consuls and magistrates of their own, the German king still
retaining his title of King of Italy.

B. Venice.

The Venetian islands, which had been peopled by the 134
emigration consequent on Attila's invasion of Italy, were, B
in the first instance, governed by tribunes, and subject to
the Roman empire, then to the Ostrogothic, and at a later
period again to the Roman. In the year 697 the whole
group was placed under the administration of an officer
named Dux or Doge; but their political relations with the
eastern empire continued until the separation of Venice
and the other Italian states from the Byzantine government,
occasioned by the edicts of the iconoclastic emperors.
About the year 800, the seat of government was established on the Rialto, an island which had successfully
resisted the attacks of King Pepin (son of Charlemagne).
Being joined by bridges to the other islands, it became the C
centre of a maritime city, which enlarged its dominions by
conquests in Dalmatia, about the year 1000; and by means
of an extensive commerce, for which its position between
two of the most powerful states of Europe afforded extraordinary facilities, soon became one of the most important
cities of Italy, and eventually of the world.

C. Papal Italy, or the States of the Church.

The foundation of the pope's temporal power was laid 135
by Pepin (see § 59), who settled on the popedom the pro- D
vinces of Romagna and Urbino, an endowment which
Charlemagne not only confirmed, but augmented by grants
of land in Tuscany; and perhaps of those estates on the
other side of the Tiber, which had been ceded to the
empire by the Duke of Benevento. To this patrimony of
St. Peter, as it was called, Henry III. added the city of

(135) Benevento, in return for the renunciation by the pope
A (Leo IX.) of the revenues and patronage of certain
Frankish churches; and a still more important accession of
territory was obtained through the liberality of the Margravine Matilda of Tuscany, who bequeathed (in 1077, not
in 1102) all her allodes to the see of Rome. Lastly, the
Normans consented to hold Apulia and Calabria as fiefs;
but, during this period, no temporal authority was exercised
by the pope over Rome itself, or the dukedom in which it
was situated.

D. Lower Italy.

136 On the ruins of the Lombard empire arose the Lom-
B bardic dukedom of Benevento, which comprehended
the greater part of the present kingdom of Naples, and was
at first independent, but subsequently became a Frankish
fief. At a later period Salerno and Capua separated
from Benevento, and formed a second and third Lombardic
principality. The Greeks retained only Calabria, and a
narrow strip of territory along the western coast (with the
cities of Terracina, Naples, Gaeta, and Amalfi), which
were exposed to perpetual attacks from the Arabians, who
had been settled in Sicily since the year 827, and in a
short time established themselves also in Bari.

137 In the fourteenth century the whole of lower Italy
C became a prey to the Normans, who had first visited Italy
as adventurers in the year 1017, and, in return for certain
military services, had obtained from the Greek duke a strip
of land, on which they built the city of Aversa. From this
stronghold the twelve sons of Count Tancred, of Hauteville, sallied forth to subdue Calabria and Apulia; and
one of them, Robert Guiscard (surnamed the Cunning), was
invested by Pope Nicholas II. with the dignity of duke,
and the fiefs of Apulia, Calabria, and Sicily, the last of which
had been conquered by his brother Roger after a thirty
D years' war. Under pretence of replacing on the throne
the deposed Emperor Michael VIII. (father-in-law of his
daughter), Robert Guiscard raised an army, and after
obtaining a victory at Durazzo, and placing a garrison in
that key of the eastern empire, advanced towards Constantinople; but the exhaustion of his army, an insurrection of the Apulian cities, and the expedition of Henry IV.

against Pope Gregory VII., compelled him to retrace his (137)
steps. After liberating the pope, Robert undertook a A
second expedition against Greece, and died during the campaign (at Cephalonia, in 1085). After the decease of his grandson (who died without issue), Apulia and Calabria were united with Sicily, by Roger II., son of his youngest brother, who was crowned King of the Two Sicilies in 1130.

E. The Islands.

1. Sicily was taken from the Byzantines (in 827) by 138
the Arabians, who were compelled to surrender it to the B
Normans in 1060.

2. Sardinia was wrested from the Byzantines (850) by 139
the Arabians, and from the Arabians by Pisa (1022).

3. Corsica at first was subject to the Arabians, and 140
then became the object of a struggle, which lasted 200 years, between Genoa and Pisa.

§ 26. *France under the last Carlovingians.*

As Charles, third son of Lewis the Stammerer, was still 141
a child, when the Frankish empire was divided for the third time, the nobles, who were hard-pressed by the invading Normans, elected

1. Otho, Count of Paris (888—898), who was unable 142
either to restrain the insolence of the Normans, or obtain C
a general recognition of his title to the throne.

2. Charles III., surnamed the Simple (898—929), 143
who was elected in opposition to Otho (in 893), and after his death recognized as sole king, conferred on Rollo (or Rolf, a Norman prince, who had embraced Christianity, and been baptized by the name of Robert), the dukedom of Normandy with the feudal sovereignty of Bretagne, an arrangement which put an end to the Norman invasions.
After the extinction of the Carlovingian race in Germany, D
Charles took possession of Lorraine. Several nobles of the kingdom, being discontented with Hagano, the minister of Charles, conspired against the king, and elected (922)

3. Robert, duke of Francia, brother of Count Otho, 144
who was slain (after reigning one year) in a battle against Charles at Soissons. He was succeeded by his son-in-law,

145 4. Rudolph, duke of Burgundy (923—936). Charles
A died in prison in 929. Lorraine re-united with Germany by Henry I. Repeated invasions of the Hungarians. On the death of Rudolph, without male issue,

146 5. Lewis IV. (surnamed the Stranger), the son of Charles the Simple, returned from England, and ascended the throne (936—954). Unsuccessful attempt to recover Normandy. His son and successor

147 6. Lothar (954—986) carried on a war with Otho II.
B for the re-conquest of Lorraine, with no success, beyond obtaining for his brother Charles a grant of Lower Lorraine, to be held as a fief of Germany. On the death of his son

148 7. Lewis V. (Fainéant) without male issue, after a reign of fourteen months, his uncle Charles, duke of Lower Lorraine, was excluded from the succession, as being a German vassal, and Hugo [Hugh], surnamed Capet (from the robe, *cappa,* which he wore as a lay abbot ?), duke of Francia, was proclaimed king by his vassals in 987.

149 France about this time was split into a multitude of
C greater and smaller fiefs, which became at length so numerous, as to leave no territory subject to the immediate control of the last Carlovingians except Soissons, Laon, and a few insignificant provinces. The immediate fiefs of the crown, the possessors of which might be said to share the sovereignty of the country with the king, rather than to be dependent on him, were the four dukedoms of Francia (between the Seine and Loire), Normandy with Bretagne, Aquitania or Guienne (to which the dukedom of Gascony was united at a later period), and Burgundy, and the three counties of Toulouse, Flanders, and Vermandois (of which St.
D Quentin was the capital). At the same time a distinction was established between northern and southern France, founded on the difference of *language* (the langue d'oil, or d'oui, also langue Française, being spoken north of the Loire, and southwards of that river the langue d'oc, which at a later period was termed the Provençal tongue), *manners* (the northern French character being more daring, warlike, and fond of display; the southern more quick-witted and cunning, but at the same time more industrious and

contented), and *legal codes* (in the north the Territorial; in (149)
the south the Roman). A

§ 27. *France under the four first Capets* (987—1108).

1. Hugh Capet (987—996), Duke of Francia and 150
Count of Orleans, annexed the dukedom of Francia to the crown, and having gained over the clergy by granting them benefices, and the lay nobles by confirming them in the hereditary possession of their fiefs, was universally recognized as king, after the death of Duke Charles of Lower Lorraine, the last scion of the Carlovingian house. He was, however, merely the first of more than forty nobles. His son B

2. Robert (996—1031) added the dukedom of Bur- 151
gundy to the possessions of the crown, and bestowed it as a fief on his third son Robert (founder of the younger Burgundian line, and ancestor of the kings of Portugal).

3. Henry (1031—1060). Establishment of the Treuga 152
Dei by the decrees of several councils.

4. Philip I. (1060—1108). At the beginning of his 153
reign, under the guardianship of Count Baldwin of Flan- C
ders, Duke William of Normandy conquers England, which is separated from Normandy after his death, his son William (Rufus) inheriting the former, and his eldest son Robert the latter.

§ 28. *England under the West Saxon kings* (827—1016).

The Seven Anglo-Saxon kingdoms, or Saxon Heptarchy, 154
after a series of struggles, were united under one crown by Egbert, king of Wessex, the first who gave the name of
England (in 800) to the island of Britain. The Danes or D
Normans, who for half a century (since 787) had harassed the separate Anglo-Saxon kingdoms by repeated invasions, renewed their attacks towards the end of Egbert's reign, and continued to ravage the country until the time of his youngest grandson

Alfred the Great (871—901),

who had been anointed by the pope while yet a child. On 155
his accession, Alfred found the whole of England, as far as Wessex, and subsequently as far as Somerset, in the hands of the Danes; and as most of the native inhabitants had

(155) either abandoned the island, or submitted to the invader,
A he was compelled to pass one winter as a fugitive in the
forests of Somersetshire. In the disguise of a minstrel,
Alfred visited the Danish camp, and, availing himself of
the information thus acquired, he took the field at the head of
the loyal inhabitants of three Gaus, and defeated the Danes
at Heddington. Gothrun, the Danish leader, was persuaded
to embrace Christianity, and surrender East Anglia,
Northumbria, and a few cities of Mercia to the conqueror.

156 Having thus secured peace, at least for a season, Alfred
B employed the time in restoring the cities (London among
the rest) and fortresses which had been demolished by the
Danes, building a fleet, fortifying the coasts against foreign
invaders, and facilitating the administration of justice by
the publication of a code of laws, and the division of the
country into counties, hundreds, and tithings. Schools were
also established in all parts of the country, learned men
invited to visit England, and Latin authors translated into
the vernacular language of England by Alfred himself.
From these peaceful occupations, Alfred was summoned to
defend his kingdom against the Normans, who had landed
on the coast of Britain after their defeat at Louvain by
C Arnulph. At the same time his hereditary dominions were
assailed by two fleets manned by rebellious East Anglians
and Northumbrians, who were soon compelled to return to
their allegiance; but it required a war of three years, and
a succession of decisive battles, to drive the Normans out
of England. The reigns of Alfred's successors were disquieted
by repeated insurrections of the Anglo-Danes,
reinforced by bands of their continental brethren. Ethelred
three times purchased peace at the expense of an
annual tribute, termed the Danegeld; but these concessions
D only incited the Danes to fresh acts of plunder. The discovery
of a conspiracy against the king's life induced
Ethelred to command the massacre of all the Danes in his
dominions on the same day (Nov. 13, 1002), an act of
cruelty which Sweyn and his son and successor Canute
avenged by conquering the whole of England.

§ 29. *Supremacy of the Danes in England* (1016—1042).

157 Canute (1016—1035), who at first shared the throne
with Edmund Ironsides, the son of Ethelred, became, by

the death of his colleague, monarch of all England, which (157)
he divided into four provinces, viz., Wessex, Mercia, A
East Anglia, and Northumbria, secured their rights of property to the Anglo-Saxons as well as to the Danes, by legislative enactments, forbad heathenish rites, increased the number of churches and convents, and enriched them with liberal gifts. By a convention with the Emperor Conrad II., Canute became master of the March of Schleswig. In the year 1028 he also conquered Norway and the north British kingdoms of Scotland and
Cumberland. His pilgrimage to Rome. After his death, B
his mighty empire was divided between his son Hardicanute, who received Denmark as his portion, and his two (probably) supposititious sons, Sweyn and Harold, the former of whom was crowned King of Norway, and the latter of England. After Harold's death, Hardicanute became also king of England, and, dying suddenly without issue, was succeeded by an Anglo-Saxon prince, Edward the Confessor, youngest and only surviving son of Ethelred.

§ 30. *Restoration and extinction of the Anglo-Saxon dynasty* (1042—1066).

Edward III. (The Confessor (1042—1066) was 158
entirely under the influence of Norman favorites and of C
Earl Godwin, whose daughter was married to the king, and who with his sons possessed the larger and richer half of England. The introduction of the Norman language, manners and customs into England excited universal discontent among the Saxon inhabitants. After his death the throne
was occupied by his brother-in-law, Harold II., who D
made head against his rebellious brother and his ally the King of Norway, but was overthrown and lost his life in a battle fought near Hastings (Oct. 14, 1066), where William of Normandy had landed with 60,000 picked soldiers. By this victory William gained the English crown, and the surname of "The Conqueror."

§ 31. *Scotland.*

The earliest inhabitants of Scotland were the Picts and 159
Scots, the one a Celtic, the other an Irish race, both governed by kings of their own until the year 842, when

(159) Kenneth II., King of the Scots, having conquered the
A Picts, united the two kingdoms under the name of Scotland. The Norman piratical hordes from Denmark and England were successfully withstood by the Scots, who formed an alliance with the Anglo-Saxons. The kingdom of Cumberland was conferred as a fief on Malcolm I. by Edmund Ironsides, grandson of Alfred ; the Scotch monarch pledging himself to render military service whenever called on. Scotland and Cumberland were conquered by Canute, but permitted to retain their own kings as feudatories of England.

§ 32. *Ireland.*

160 Ireland, at its conquest by the English in 1172, seems to
B have been divided into five states—Connaught, Ulster, Leinster, Munster, and Meath, each governed by its own king, but on some occasions subject also to one of the number, who exercised a sort of feudal authority over the others. As early as the fifth century the Irish were converted to Christianity (by St. Patrick ?), convents and schools were established, and holy men visited the continent for the purpose of converting the heathen German
C tribes (Comp. § 14, 1, a). A code of Irish laws (Brehon laws, *i. e.* decisions of the judges) is still extant. The progress of civilization was retarded for three centuries (from 795) by the piratical invasions of the Normans, who conquered portions, but were never able to establish their authority over the whole island.

§ 33. *Spain.*

161 1. The Arabian portion of the Peninsula, which
D (until the year 1087) was separated from Christian Spain by the river Duero [Douro], enjoyed a period of uninterrupted prosperity under the Ommaijad Caliphs of Cordova (756—1028), especially during the fifty years administration of Abderrahman III., (who subjugated the whole of Mauritania), and the reigns of his learned son Hakim II. and the great leader Almanzor. The country south of the Duero [Douro] had a population of twenty-five to thirty millions, with eighty cities of the first class. Cordova, the capital, contained more than a million of inhabitants, 600 mosques, eighty public schools, and a university with a library of

600,000 volumes. The descriptions given by contem- (161)
porary writers of the splendor of the court and the mag- A
nificence of the royal palaces (Azzehra with its 4300 marble columns), border on the fabulous. Agriculture, horticulture, mining operations, and commerce (principally with Constantinople) employed a large portion of the population, whilst at the same time architecture, poetry, and the sciences, especially mathematics, astronomy, with astrology, chemistry, and medicine, were cultivated with great zeal and success.

After the death of the last Ommaijad, the lieutenants of 162
the different cities established a number of petty king- B
doms, all of which, with the exception of Saragossa, were overthrown by Jussof, king of Morocco (of the dynasty of the Morabethes), who annexed Arabian Spain to his own dominions.

2. Christian Kingdoms. *a.* The kingdom of Asturia, 163
founded by the Visigoths (who had been driven by the Arabians into the mountains of the North), was also called the kingdom of *Leon*, after the removal of the seat of government from Oviedo to that city.

b. The Spanish March, which had been conquered 164
by Charlemagne, was divided by his feeble successors into C
two counties—*Barcelona* and *Navarre*. As the Counts of Navarre assumed the title of king, there were at this period two Christian kingdoms in Spain. After the death of King Sancho III., (Mayor), Navarre was subdivided into four, and soon afterwards into three provinces—*Castille*, *Arragon* and *Navarre*, which were subsequently re-
united. At the conclusion of this period Christian Spain D
comprised—

a. The county of Barcelona (independent of France since the year 997).

b. The kingdom of Castile and Leon, of which Portugal formed a portion, until the year 1095, when it was granted as a county by King Alfonso VI. to his son-in-law, Henry of Burgundy.

c. The kingdom of Arragon and Navarre.

B. The East.

§ 34. *The Byzantine empire under the Macedonian emperors* (867—1056).

165 At the commencement of this period the empire com-
A prehended Thrace, Macedonia, Greece, and the islands of the Ægean Sea, a portion of Lower Italy and Asia Minor. The code of Justinian was republished under the title of "Basilikai," by Basilius, who also reformed the financial administration of the empire. His successors, the philosophical Leo VI. and Constantine V. (Porphyrogenētus), devoted themselves entirely to literary and scientific pursuits, whilst the Arabians, Bulgarians, and Russians ravaged their domi-
B nions without encountering any opposition. On the other hand, Armenia, the countries between the Black and Caspian Seas, with the islands of Crete and Cyprus, Northern Syria and Sicily, were wrested from the Arabians by the Emperors Nicephŏrus, Phocas, and John Tzimisces. Basilius II. conquered Bulgaria, and put out the eyes of 15,000 Bulgarians. After the extinction of the Macedonian male line, five individuals were raised to the throne by the daughters of the last emperor (Zoë and Theodora). The last of these rulers was deposed by Isaac Comnenus, who was proclaimed emperor by the army.

166 Notwithstanding its gradual decline, the Eastern empire
C was still the most considerable among the kingdoms of the Christian world, its population the most numerous and industrious, and its capital city the largest. Until the period of its dissolution the people continued to reject with scorn the appellation of "Greeks," bestowed on them by the Franks, and to speak of themselves as the "Roman"
D people. Luxury, profuse expenditure, and unmeaning etiquette still reigned at the imperial court. The legislative and executive authorities were united in the person of the monarch; and even the shadow of power retained by the senate was at last annihilated by a decree of Leo the Philosopher.

§ 35. *The Arabians under the Abbasides* (750—1258).

167 Soon after the accession of the Abbasides, the seat of government was transferred to Bagdad, a city on the

western bank of the Tigris, which had been built on (167)
a magnificent scale by Al Mansur, and soon became the A
capital of the commercial enterprise and civilization of the
world. For the separation of Spain from the Caliphate,
and establishment of a Caliphate at Cordova, see § **11.**
In the fifth Caliph, Harun al Raschid, the contemporary
and friend of Charlemagne, and still more in his son,
Mamun (the seventh Abbaside), the arts and sciences, as
well as commercial and manufacturing industry, found
enlightened and liberal protectors; and throughout the
empire, at that period the largest in the world, the munificent example of the sovereign was followed by the provincial governors. Notwithstanding these appearances of B
prosperity, the work of dissolution had already commenced—**1.** In the secession, at first of the more remote,
and subsequently of the nearer provinces, which were
erected into independent sovereignties by their rulers.
Thus, for example, in Spain, the empire of the Ommaijades was established at Cordova as early as the year 756;
in Africa those of the Aglabides, Edrisides, Fatimides,
and Morabethes; and in Asia a multitude of dynasties,
almost all of which gradually became subject to the Seldschuks, by whom towards the end of the eleventh century
most of the Asiatic possessions of the caliphs were united
under one crown. Scarcely, however, had the empire of C
the Seldschuks been established on this extensive basis,
when it was again split (after the death of the third sultan
in 1092) into several small sovereignties (in Iran, Kerman,
Aleppo, Damascus, and Iconium, or Rum), nothing remaining to the caliphs but the city of Bagdad, with its
immediate neighborhood. **2.** In the admission into Bagdad of a *Turkish body-guard* of 50,000 men, who soon
exercised uncontrolled influence, deposing and appointing
caliphs at their pleasure. **3.** *In constant political and* D
religious dissensions (formidable sects of the Carmathians
and Assassins). **4.** In a succession of *feeble*, and at the
same time cruel and oppressive rulers, who since the year
955 had intrusted the affairs of government to a Turk,
under the title of Emir al Omrah, reserving to themselves only the high priesthood.

C. The North-east of Europe.

§ 36. *Scandinavia.*

168 1. Norway and Iceland. The provinces of Norway
A existed as independent sovereignties, each governed by its own petty monarch until the end of the ninth century, when they were united under Harald Harfagr, who founded a Norwegian kingdom, to which he soon afterwards added, by conquest, the Hebrides, Feröe, and Shetland islands, and the Isle of Man. The chieftains who refused to submit to his authority, either emigrated to Western Europe or Sweden, or colonized the recently (in 861) discovered island of Iceland, where they established a fourth Scandinavian state, which was soon raised into importance by the commercial and manufacturing activity of its founders, and their extensive voyages of discovery (to Greenland,
B North America, &c.). About the year 1000 Christianity was introduced by Olaf I. and Olaf the Saint. At the same time Norway was conquered and divided by the Danes and Swedes. Olaf the Saint, who had made head for a long period against the invaders, was at length conquered and slain in a battle with Canute the Great; but the independence of Norway was re-established by his son Magnus.

169 2. Sweden was inhabited by two principal races, the
C Fins and Germans; the latter being also subdivided into Goths and Swedes, who, (about the time when Harald formed the petty principalities of Norway into *one* kingdom) were placed by Erich, the son of Edmund, under *one* sovereign, who resided at Upsala, the city of the gods. The Christian religion, although known in Sweden as early as 800, was not generally received until the year 1000, when the repeated attempts of missionaries from Hamburg and Bremen, to convert the people, were at length crowned with success.

170 3. Denmark. The Danish islands and Jutland had
D each their own king, until the time of Gorm the Elder, king of Zealand (of the race of the Skioldings, who trace their descent from Odin), who overthrew the other chieftains, and compelled the whole nation to recognize him as their sovereign, in the year 900. His male descendants occupied the throne until the middle of the eleventh cen-

tury. For the conquest of Schleswig, by Henry I., and (170)
the expedition of Otho the Great to Jutland, see § 23. A
Sweyn conquered England, to avenge the murder of the
Danes, and also Norway (in conjunction with the Swedes).
He was succeeded in England by Canute the Great
(1014), who also ascended the Danish throne after the
death of his elder brother Harold (in † 1016). Under
this sovereign Schleswig was annexed to the kingdom of
Denmark, by a convention with the Emperor Conrad II.;
and Norway, which had re-asserted its independence under
Olaf the Saint, was again reduced to submission. For the B
confirmation of the Christian religion, which had been
established by his father, Canute founded churches, convents, and bishoprics. After his death and that of his son,
Denmark was for a short time subject to Magnus, king of
Norway, until its emancipation by Sweyn Estritson, who
founded the dynasty of the Estritides (1047—1375).

§ 37. *Russia.*

Russia, the southern portion of which was inhabited by 171
the Chazares, and the north and centre by Tschudish and C
Sclavonian tribes, was visited in the year 862, on the
invitation of the Sclavonians, by the Varogian chieftain
Ruric (a prince of the Swedish tribe of Russ), who
founded the grand-dukedom of Russia, with its capital
Novgorod, from which the government was soon afterwards
transferred to Kiev, where the family of Ruric continued
to reign until the end of the sixteenth century (1598).
Under his immediate successors, the Normans, in conjunc- D
tion with the Sclavonians, following the course of the
Dnieper, made several predatory descents on the coasts of
the Byzantine empire; but being unable to withstand the
destructive Greek fire, they concluded a truce, the result
of which was a peaceful commercial intercourse with their
former enemies, and the introduction of Christianity into
Russia. Vladimir the Great (988) embraced Christianity
on his marriage with a Byzantine princess (Anna), and
endeavored to spread the knowledge of the true faith by
building churches and convents. The district known as
"Red Russia" was conquered by this sovereign, who
endeavored to introduce Byzantine civilization among his

A subjects. Kiev, with its 400 churches, was popularly
spoken of as a second Constantinople.

§ 38. *Poland.*

172 The Slaves on the middle Vistula (whose capital was
Gnesen) were called Poles. In the year 840 they chose
for their Duke a peasant named Piast, whose family
continued to reign for more than five centuries (until
1370). In the year 965, one of their dukes named
Miecislav, embraced Christianity, founded a bishopric at
Posen, and recognized the Emperor of Germany as his
B feudal sovereign. His son Boleslav, with the assistance
of St. Adalbert, exterminated the remnants of heathenism,
and founded bishoprics at Breslau, Colberg, and Cracow,
and an archbishopric at Gnesen. This prince carried on
several wars successfully against the Russians, united under
his rule the Lechites, Poles, Masovians, Cracowians, and
Silesians, compelled the Pomeranians to pay tribute, and
a short time before his death caused himself (in 1024) to
be crowned King of Poland, by his bishops. Bolislav
II. having abandoned his dominions, in consequence of
a sentence of excommunication pronounced against him by
Pope Gregory VII. for the murder of St. Stanislaus, bishop
of Cracow, Poland again became a dukedom (from 1079
to 1295).

§ 39. *Hungary.*

173 Towards the end of the ninth century (889) the Hunga-
C rians (called also Magyars from the name of their principal
tribe) advanced from the centre of Asia into the country of
the Avares, under the command of a leader named Arpad,
whose family continued to reign until the end of the thirteenth
century. After assisting King Arnulf against the
Moravians, and taking possession of their country, squadrons
of Hungarian cavalry overran Southern Germany,
Burgundy, and Italy, until they were driven back by Henry
D I. and Otho I. Christianity was introduced among them
towards the end of the tenth century, and several bishoprics
(nine or ten, including the archbishopric of Gran) were
founded by Duke Stephen the Saint, who was crowned
king by Pope Sylvester II. in the year 1000. Peter, the
son and successor of this Stephen, having irritated the

people beyond endurance by his excesses, was deprived of (173)
the throne, which he recovered by the aid of Henry III., A
to whom he took the oath of fealty as a vassal of the empire. He was deprived of his sight by a savage faction (who desired the re-establishment of paganism), and died in prison. After thirty years of intestine confusion, tranquillity was at length restored by Ladislav the Saint.

§ 40. *Religion, arts, sciences, &c., during the second period.*

The *Church.* The increasing influence of the clergy 174
was viewed by the temporal power with a jealousy, which B
was the natural result of the vague and ill-defined position occupied by the two parties with reference to each other. To the pope belonged the privilege of crowning the emperors, the supreme legislative authority in ecclesiastical matters, and judicial power, not only over spiritual persons, but in questions affecting the interests of the Church, over laymen also (the interdict and excommunication). He also enjoyed the right of appointment to the highest ecclesiastical offices (gift of the pallium to the bishops), and the possession of the territories conferred on the Church by Pepin.
The number of converts was greatly increased, especially C
in Germany, between the ninth and eleventh centuries. The monks, most of whom (since the tenth century) were priests, employed themselves, according to the rule of St. Benedict, in agriculture, various handicrafts, the instruction of youth, transcribing of ancient writers, the compilation of chronicles, &c.; but the general profligacy and coarseness of the times, the introduction of lay brethren, and, more than all, the increasing wealth of these establishments, produced, in many instances, a laxity of discipline utterly subversive of morality. A partial reformation was effected D
by the establishment of a convent at Clugny in Burgundy, after the rule of St. Benedict, whose improvements were adopted in seventeen other convents. At the same time strenuous efforts were made by the Abbot Dunstan for the introduction of the same rule into the convents of England. Some additions to the rule of St. Benedict in the eleventh century occasioned the establishment of the Cistercian order (so named from their first convent at Citeaux near Dijon), out of which arose the Bernardine (founded by St.

(174) Bernard of Clairvaux) and the Carthusian (by St. Bruno of
A Cologne in 1086). Cathedral chapters, the members of which, from the regularity of their lives, were termed canonici or canons,[1] were founded in 760, by Chrodogang, bishop of Metz, and generally established by a diet held by Lewis the Pious at Aachen (Aix-la-Chapelle) in 816; but as early as the eleventh century, many of them had relaxed the strictness of their original discipline.

175 For the propagation of Christianity, and the development of the *various political constitutions*, see the history of the different countries.

176 *Arts and Sciences*. During the whole of this period
B the arts and sciences flourished not only among the Asiatic, but in a still higher degree among the Spanish Arabians (see § 33). The Caliphs (especially Mamun) spared no expense for the purpose of procuring Greek, Persian, Coptic, and Chaldaic manuscripts, which were translated into Arabic by societies of learned men. In all the Arabian provinces, particularly in Bagdad, Alexandria, Ispahan, Samarcand, Damascus, Kufa, Bassora, and, above all, in Cordova, there existed schools and universities, in which not only Mussulmans, but Christians and Jews, and even some of the Caliphs themselves, received instruction in philosophy, medicine, mathematics, and physical science.
C The poetry of this period, although fostered by poetical contests at the courts of the Caliphs, was deficient in comprehensiveness, variety, and arrangement. The literature of the Arabians is rich in legendary tales and romances of chivalry, the latter of which were invented by the writers of that country; but their best works have all the
D dryness of ancient chronicles. Geographical science was also greatly advanced by their conquests, voyages, and pilgrimages; but their most successful efforts were in the department of natural science, including every branch of medicine except anatomy, the practice of which was forbidden by the Koran. This defect was, however, in some measure supplied by a diligent study of botany, and by the discoveries for which chemistry was indebted to the persevering but fruitless attempts of the alchemists to produce the philosophers' stone. In philosophy and physics they

[1] [From the Greek word, *κανών*, a rule.]

never advanced beyond the principles of Aristotle, which (176)
were often misunderstood. Algebra, trigonometry, and A
astronomy were simplified, and enriched with new discoveries: astrology was also highly esteemed. The Arabian school of architecture, the characteristics of which were lightness and profuse ornament, produced several magnificent works, especially in Spain. In *Persia* also poetry flourished under the Ghasnavides and Seldschuks. The most renowned of the Persian epic poets, Firdûsi, who celebrated in his verses the heroic deeds of the Persian
kings, lived at the court of Ghasna about A.D. 1000. In B
the *Byzantine empire*, Greek literature, which had been neglected during the iconoclastic controversy, began again to be cultivated in the ninth century, but with little result beyond the publication of extracts (by Photius and Constantinus Porphyrogenetus) from the ancient writers. Historical writing was almost entirely limited to the compilation of dry chronicles. Suidas in his grammatical and historical Lexicon, and the author of the Etymologicum Magnum, exhibit an intimate acqaintance with the works of classical writers. In sculpture and painting, simplicity and good taste were rapidly disappearing before a love of the elaborate and minute. In the *West*, learning was exclusively C
in the hands of the clergy, who studied in the renowned convents and capitular schools of St. Gall, Corvey, Fulda, Paderborn, and Hildesheim, as well as at Paris and in Normandy. Several historical works, all in the Latin language, were published by the German clergy; Wittehind (history of the Saxons), Dithmar (History of the Saxon Emperors, 876 to 1018), Wippo (Life of Conrad II.), Hermannus Contractus (Chronicles), Lambert of Aschaffenburg (Annals). The scholastic philosophy taught in the D
church schools, especially at Paris, consisted in the adaptation of the dialectics of Aristotle to the discussion of theological theses. The most distinguished professors of this philosophy and of the mysticism of the Middle Ages were Joh. Scotus Erigena (at the court of Charles the Bald), and two archbishops of Canterbury, Lanfranc and Anselm. The most renowned school of jurisprudence was at Bologna, and of medicine at Salerno. The study of mathematical science was promoted in France by Gerbert, archbishop of Rheims (afterwards Pope Sylvester II.), who had received his education in Moorish Spain. Natural

(176) philosophy was rather speculative than experimental;
A hence the study of astrology, magic and alchemy. Latin
ceased to be a living tongue in the ninth century, the
Roman and German languages having now assumed a
settled form. The earliest specimens of German literature
are the Ludwigslied (Lay of Lewis), Otfried's Christ (a
harmony of the Gospels in rhyme), and Notker's translation of the Psalms.—Among the arts, architecture produced
the most considerable works in a mixed Lombardo-Byzantine style, e. g. in the noble Minsters at Bamberg, Worms,
B Mainz, Spiers, &c. Baronial castles were first built in
the eleventh century (the Wartburg in 1067).—Sculpture
and painting seem to have been at the lowest ebb in this
century, with the exception of painting on glass, which had
become very general. Music made considerable progress,
in consequence of the invention of a new system of notes,
by Guido of Arezzo; and of time, by Franco of Cologne.

177 Trade and manufacturing industry flourished
C principally in the Arabian countries, especially in Spain
(compare § 33), where they found in the Abbasides patrons
no less zealous than the Ommaijades had been at an
earlier period. The commerce of Byzantium was gradually
transferred to the Italian sea-ports of Venice, Pisa, Genoa,
and Amalfi, which had already established themselves as
emporia, whilst the trade of the other western ports was
still limited to the mere supply of the daily wants of the
inhabitants. Indian and Levantine wares were brought
D into Germany up the Danube from Constantinople. Regensburg [Ratisbon], at that period the most populous and
important city of Germany, was the emporium of the
commerce not only between the East and West, but also
between the North and South, that is to say, between
Poland, Prussia, and Russia on the one side, and Italy on
the other. The cities of the South of France, especially
Marseilles, traded for the most part to the Levant; and
those of the North (as well as of Friesland and the North of
Germany) to England. Commercial relations also existed
between the Sclavonians on the Elbe and Baltic, and the
neighboring countries. Manufacturing industry was promoted by the rapid increase in the number of cities, the
establishment of fairs, and the discovery of gold and silver
mines in the Hartz mountains, in the reign of Otho the
Great.

Third Period.

AGE OF THE CRUSADES (1096—1273).

§ 41. *The Crusades* (1096—1273).

The First Crusade (1696—1100).

For many years it had been the practice of Christians 178
from all parts of the Roman empire, to perform pilgrim- A
ages to the Holy Sepulchre, where a magnificent church
had been erected by Constantine the Great. The number
of those who visited Jerusalem had gone on steadily increasing, even after the occupation of the city by the
Arabians (636); but under the Fatimides and Seldschuks
a system of persecution was carried on against the Christians, who were compelled by the Turks to pay a heavy
tax for the privilege of visiting the Holy City. Instead, B
however, of diminishing the number of pilgrims, the effect
of this intolerant measure was to excite throughout Chris-
tendom a general desire to make *Palestine again a
Christian kingdom*. The complaints of the Eastern
Christians were seconded by *Peter of Amiens*, or Peter
the Hermit, as he is generally called, who had recently
returned from the Holy Land, and was now traversing
Italy, France, and Germany, and every where describing
the atrocities of which he had himself been an eye-witness.
Councils of the Church were also held at Piacenza and C
Clermont, at which Pope Urban II. exhorted the people to
assist in the good work of delivering Jerusalem out of the
hands of the unbelievers. In the Spring of 1096, the
crusade was commenced by detached bands of adventurers
from France, Italy, and Lorraine, who penetrated as far as
Hungary and Bulgaria, where most of them were cut to
pieces by the inhabitants. The remainder, under Peter
the Hermit and Walter of Pexeijo, a needy adventurer,
surnamed in derision the Lord of Lackland (Habenichts),

(178) advanced as far as Nicæa, where their army was well nigh
A annihilated. On the 15th of August, 1096, an expedition
on a larger scale, and under more favorable auspices, was
undertaken by Godfrey de Bouillon, duke of Lower
Lorraine, his brother Baldwin, Count Robert of Normandy
(brother of the King of England), Robert, count of Flanders, Raymond, count of Toulouse, Boëmund, prince of
Tarento, and his nephew Tancred. The grand army, the
several divisions of which reached Asia Minor by different
routes, numbered, we are told, more than half a million of
B men. The city of Nicæa was first attacked and carried
by storm. Then the crusaders took Edessa, and conferred
the sovereignty of that district on Baldwin of Lorraine.
Antiochia, which had surrendered after a siege of nine
months, was on the eve of falling again into the hands of
the Turks, when the besieged, re-assured, it is said, by the
discovery of the sacred lance,[1] made a sally from the gates,
dispersed the Turkish army, and established a Christian
C principality under Boëmund of Tarento. The army of the
crusaders, reduced to 20,000 infantry and 1500 cavalry, at
last reached Jerusalem, which, a few years before (in 1095)
had been re-conquered by the Fatimides. After closely
investing the city for thirty-nine days, the assailants scaled
the walls on the 15th of July, 1099, and put the infidels to
death without mercy. Godfrey de Bouillon, as the
best and bravest of their leaders, was proclaimed King of
Jerusalem, but refused to accept any higher title than that
of duke.

179 A Christian state was also founded at Tripolis, by Ray-
D mond of Toulouse. An army of 140,000 men was collected
for the re-conquest of Palestine, by the Caliph of Egypt,
who was drawn into an ambuscade near Ascalon, and
defeated by Godfrey de Bouillon, with only 20,000 men.
In the year 1100 Godfrey died, in consequence of the
fatigues which he had undergone during the siege, and was
succeeded by his brother Baldwin I., prince of Edessa,
who accepted the title of king, and being supported by the
free states of Italy, Genoa, Pisa, and Venice, added the
maritime cities of Cæsarea, Tripolis, Berytus, and Sidon
to the kingdom of Jerusalem, which at its first establish-

[[1] The spear, according to tradition, with which the side of our Blessed Saviour was pierced.]

ment consisted merely of the capital with the city of (179)
Joppa, and about twenty hamlets. Division of the king- A
dom into—1. the crown-lands; 2. the county of Tripolis; 3. the principality of Antiochia; 4. the county of
Edessa.

The Second Crusade (1147—1149).

After repeated attempts on the part of the Egyptian 180
caliphs to regain possession of the Holy Land, Edessa was B
taken by storm, during the minority of Baldwin III., and
its inhabitants put to the sword, or sold as slaves. On
receiving intelligence of this disaster, Bernard, abbot of
Clairvaux, persuaded the emperor, Conrad III., and
Louis VII., king of France, to undertake a second crusade. The two armies marched through Hungary with
little loss, and entered the Byzantine dominions; but soon
afterwards the German division was abandoned by its
Greek guides near Iconium, and, after suffering severely
from want of provisions, was attacked by the forces of the
Sultan of Iconium so fiercely, that scarcely a tenth part
survived the engagement. After sustaining considerable C
loss, some joined Conrad at Jerusalem, and the two sovereigns proceeded to lay siege to Damascus; but, failing in
their attempt, they abandoned the Holy Land, and returned to their own dominions.

The Third Crusade (1189—1193).

The dynasty of the Fatimides in Egypt was sustained 181
(1163) by the generals of Nureddin, sultan of Damascus, D
who was soon succeeded by his nephew Saladin. This
monarch revived the claims of Egypt to Syria and Palestine, defeated the Christians near Damascus, took their
king, Guy de Lusignan, prisoner, and entering Jerusalem
in triumph, put an end to the kingdom which had lasted
eighty-eight years.

The loss of the Holy City occasioned the third crusade, 182
which was undertaken by the emperor, Frederic I. (Barbarossa), now in his seventieth year, Philip Augustus, king
of France, and Richard Cœur de Lion of England, with the

(182) flower of their chivalry. Barbarossa, whose army was the
A first in the field, entered Asia Minor, and, having defeated
the Sultan of Iconium, stormed that city, but soon afterwards was drowned in the river Calycadnos.

183 The remains of his army, the ranks of which were daily thinned by pestilence and desertion, at last reached Accon, Acra, or Ptolemais (St. Jean d'Acre), where their commander, Duke Frederick of Swabia, son of the late emperor, instituted the order of Teutonic Knights, and soon afterwards died of the plague, during the siege of the city,
B in the year **1191**. Soon after his death the place was surrendered to the kings of France and England. It was on this occasion that Richard Cœur de Lion insulted Leopold, duke of Austria, by trampling on his banner. Philip and Richard having disagreed respecting the partition of their conquests, and the mode of carrying on the war, the former returned to France; and Richard, after raising the siege of Joppa, concluded an armistice with Saladin, by the terms of which the whole line of coast from Joppa to Accon remained in the hands of the Christians, free access to the holy places being also secured to them.
C The island of Cyprus, which had been conquered by Richard, was sold by him to Guy, the last king of Jerusalem: hence the kingdom of Cyprus (to the year **1480**). On his return from Palestine, Richard was seized by Leopold VI. of Austria, and delivered up to the emperor, Henry VI., by whom he was released after two years' imprisonment, on payment of a ransom of **150,000** marks.

The (so-named) Fourth Crusade (1202—1204).

184 Fresh bands of crusaders were sent out by the emperor,
D Henry VI., and, having reached Syria by the route of Constantinople, regained possession of Sidon, Tyre, and Berytus. Meanwhile the emperor himself died in Sicily. The (so-called) fourth crusade was undertaken by the Franks and Venetians, whose forces, instead of advancing into Palestine, remained at Byzantium, for the purpose of restoring the emperor, Isaac Angelus, who had been deposed and blinded by his brother Alexius. Finding, however that the promises made on behalf of his father by

Alexius the younger (son of the Emperor Isaac), were not (184)
likely to be fulfilled (Isaac having died of grief and terror A
during an insurrection of the Greeks), the French and Venetians a second time took possession of Constantinople, chose Baldwin, count of Flanders and Hennegau, for their emperor, and thus founded the Latin Empire (1204—1261). Baldwin received only a fourth part of the empire, with the title and authority of feudal sovereign over the rest, which was divided among the Venetians, who obtained possession of the shores of the Adriatic, Ægean, and Black Seas, together with most of the Greek islands; and the French and Lombard nobles, one of whom, the Marquis of Montferrat, received for his share the whole of Macedonia and a portion of Greece, which were named the kingdom of Thessalonica. A Greek empire was soon after- B
wards established at Nicæa by Theodore Lascaris (one of the family of the Comneni), whilst at the same time another Byzantine prince reigned independently, with the title of emperor, at Trebizond. In the year 1261, the Emperor of Nicæa, Michael Palæolŏgus (with the assistance of the Genoese, who were jealous of the Venetians), took Constantinople, and put an end to the Latin empire.

The Crusade of Frederic II. (1228).

The attempts of Pope Innocent III. to regain Palestine, 185
by means of a general crusade, were utterly unsuccessful. C
The children's crusade in 1213, and the expedition to Syria of Andrew II., king of Hungary, terminated in disappointment and disgrace, whilst the advantage obtained by the titular King of Jerusalem (John of Brienne), through the capture of Damietta, was again lost by the surrender of that fortress to the infidels in the year 1221. On D
receiving intelligence of this calamity, Pope Honorius III. vehemently urged on the emperor, Frederic II., the necessity of fulfilling the promise which he had made at his accession, and again at his coronation; but so many difficulties intervened, that the commencement of the crusade was deferred until the year 1227. Scarcely had the emperor assembled his forces, when sickness compelled him again to defer the expedition; and the pope (Gregory IX.), who believed this to be a mere pretext, at once published

(185) the sentence of excommunication against him. In the year
A 1228, Frederic visited Palestine, and placed on his own
head the crown of Jerusalem, which had been ceded to
him, together with the surrounding territory as far as Tyre,
by Camel, sultan of Egypt.

The Sixth Crusade (1248).

186 A violation of the armistice by some pilgrims, under the
B command of the King of Navarre, again occasioned the
loss of Jerusalem in 1239; and five years later (1244) the
city was taken from the Turks by the Carizmians, who had
been driven out of Khorassan by the Monguls. About
this time Louis IX., king of France, commonly called
St. Louis, undertook his crusade in fulfilment of a vow which
he had made during a severe illness, and landing in Egypt,
the possession of which seemed an indispensable prelude
to an attempt on the Holy Land, took Damietta, and
C defeated the Turks. Advancing towards Cairo, he was
taken prisoner, with his whole army; and after a long negotiation
was at length released, on condition of evacuating
Damietta, and paying a ransom of 800,000 pieces of gold.
After his liberation, Louis still lingered in Accon until the
year 1254, and fortified the sea-ports of Palestine.

The Seventh Crusade (1270).

187 The possessions of the Christians in the East having
D fallen one by one into the hands of the Mamelukes, who
had overthrown the dynasty of Saladin, and raised themselves
to the rank of sultans of Egypt (1254—1517),
Louis undertook another crusade, and at the instance of
his brother, Charles of Anjou, king of Sicily, landed at
Tunis, where a pestilence carried off himself and the
greater part of his army. In the year 1291, Accon, the
last of the Christian possessions in Palestine, fell into the
hands of the Mamelukes.

Results of the Crusades.

A. Political Consquences.

188 1. *To the Hierarchy.* *a.* The exaltation of the papal
power was the natural consequence of a system in which

the pope appeared as the originator of plans, which the (188)
temporal sovereigns of Europe were called on to execute. A
b. The authority of the pope over the clergy was also augmented by the opportunities which the crusades afforded him of appointing legates, who exercised, as representatives of the Holy See, considerable influence over the archbishops and bishops, and of placing episcopal vicars in the dioceses during the absence of the bishops. *c.* The wealth of the clergy was greatly increased by the opportunities afforded to churches and convents of purchasing, at a cheap rate, the estates of those who were anxious to join the crusades.

2. *To the Sovereigns of Europe.* Increase in the num- 189
ber of estates belonging immediately to the crown, occa- B
sioned by the falling in of several fiefs, especially in France under Philip II.—Another result of the wars against the infidels, was the extension in European countries of the dominions of Christian sovereigns (e. g. in Spain), and the establishment (e.g. in Prussia) of new Christian states.

3. *To the Nobility,* the consequences of the crusades 190
were most important. *a.* The *spirit* of aristocracy de- C
veloped itself in the formation of the knightly character, which was a compound of religious enthusiasm, reckless courage, and love of adventure in the service of religion or of beauty. *b.* The distinctive *forms* of nobility were created by the adoption of family names and coats of arms, and the institution of degrees of chivalry (pages, esquires,
knights). *c.* Origin of the religious orders of knight- D
hood. *aa.* The *Knights Hospitallers,* or *Knights of St. John.* Some merchants from Amalfi had founded at Jerusalem a convent and hospital for sick pilgrims. The monks of this institution, which was dedicated to St. John, were afterwards sworn to do battle against the infidels, and were divided into three classes, viz. chaplains, who conducted the public worship; knights, who bore arms; and lay-brethren, on whom devolved the care of the sick and poor. This order spread over the whole of Europe, and was divided into eight "tongues," according to the languages of the different states in which it was established. The president had at first the title of "Master," and afterwards of "Grand Master." After the loss of Palestine, the Knights Hospitallers established themselves at Cyprus,

(190) and in the year 1309 took possession of Rhodes (hence
A their title of *Knights of Rhodes*), which they held against the
Turks until 1522, when they were driven from it by
Soliman. In 1530, they were presented by the emperor,
Charles V., with Malta, Gozzo, and Comino (hence their
title of *Knights of Malta*), on condition of their waging
perpetual war against infidels and pirates. Malta was
B taken from them by Napoleon, in the year 1798. *bb.* The
Knights Templars. The nucleus of this order existed as
early as the year 1118, in an association of nine French
knights, for the protection of pilgrims on the high roads.
Their name was derived from their residence near the site
of Solomon's temple, in a building granted to them by
Baldwin II. After the loss of the Holy Land, most of the
Templars sought an asylum in France, where they were
cruelly put to death by Philip IV. (1312), after a mock
trial on charges substantiated by no better evidence than
C confessions extorted from them by the rack. *cc. The
Teutonic Order* was founded during the siege of Accon (in
1190) by a number of German knights and pilgrims, who
formed an association for the relief of persons attacked by
a pestilential disease, which at that time raged in the German camp. The knights were exclusively Germans. Their
president had the title of Teutonic Master, or Grand
Master. Their residence was removed from Jerusalem to
Venice by their fourth grand master, the renowned Herman of Salza, who undertook the conversion of the heathen
Prussians. After a struggle, which lasted fifty-three years,
Herman obtained possession of Prussia, and transferred his
D residence from Venice to Marienburg in 1309. The establishment of these orders contributed essentially to the
formation and consolidation of an aristocracy, and prepared
the way for the institution of similar orders of knighthood
in Europe. In Palestine they supplied the place of a standing army, and in the struggles between the ecclesiastical
and temporal powers, rendered essential service to the party which had the good fortune to secure their adherence.

191 4. *To the Burgher Order.* Guilds, or fraternities of
Burghers, were established, which obtained various privileges, generally by purchase, when their lords were in want
of money. The growth and prosperity of their cities were
promoted by the absence of the nobles, as well as by the
increasing activity displayed in commercial pursuits.

5. *To the peasant order.* The necessity which existed of (191)
employing freemen in the cultivation of those farms from A
which the serfs had been withdrawn, to supply the ranks of
the crusaders, occasioned a diminution in the number of
vassals, and the gradual establishment of a free peasantry.

B. Consequences to Trade and Manufactures.

1. *To maritime enterprise.* Important commercial privi- 192
leges were acquired by the Venetians, and to a certain B
extent by the Genoese and Pisans, in all the principal cities
of the Byzantine empire, as well as of Syria and Palestine.
During the fourth crusade, the Venetians obtained possession
of most of the seaports and islands of the empire, where
they established colonies; the command of the Black Sea
securing to their merchants a monopoly of the northern
trade, and a considerable share in that of Asia. On the C
re-establishment of the Byzantine government at Constantinople, the Venetians were expelled from the capital, their
place being occupied by the Genoese; but this disaster was
comparatively of little importance, as they were at the same
time enabled to conclude commercial treaties with the
Saracens, by which the Ægypto-Indian trade, and a share
in the commerce carried on by caravans in the interior of
Africa, were secured to them, together with permission
to establish settlements on the northern coast of that peninsula.

2. *To the overland trade.* The commerce of the inte- 193
rior, which in former days had been for the most part D
confined to the beaten route from Constantinople to Germany, along the banks of the Danube by Vienna and Ratisbon, was diverted into various other channels during the
period of the crusades: *a.* from the seaports of Italy into
Germany: *b.* from the ports of the South of France into
the interior of that country, as well as into Brabant and
Flanders. It was not, however, until the following period,
that this commercial intercourse was fully developed.

3. *To manufacturing industry.* Extension to Europe 194
(to the South in the first instance) of the manufacture of
silk and cotton stuffs, and the production of sugar, together
with a more active exportation of European produce to

(194) Greece and the East. Increase of luxury in the cities, a
A consequence of their manufacturing prosperity.

C. To the Sciences.

195 The mass of geographical information was considerably
augmented by the knowledge of eastern lands, acquired
through the crusaders, as well as by the accounts of missionaries (since the thirteenth century), and the travels of
Marco Polo, a Venetian merchant; but the defective state
of mathematical science occasioned grievous mistakes re-
B specting the position of different countries. Historical
works, for which there was abundant material, began now
to be written (after the example of the Orientals) in the
vernacular tongue. Natural history and medicine were
more generally studied.

A. The West.

§ 42. *The German empire under Lothar the Saxon.*

(1125—1137.)

196 Henry V. had nominated as his successors the two sons
C of his sister Agnes, Frederick and Conrad of Hohenstaufen;
but, under the influence of the Archbishop of Mainz, the
choice of the electors fell on Lothar [Lothaire] duke of
Saxony, who agreed, as the condition of his election, that
the Church should enjoy the undisputed right of appointing
her own officers, and that the investiture of bishops by the
emperor should not take place until after their consecra-
tion. The vacant dukedom of Saxony, and the hand of
his daughter, were conferred by Lothar on Henry the Proud,
duke of Bavaria (of the house of Welf [Guelph]), by whose
aid he defeated Frederick and Conrad of Hohenstaufen,
and compelled the latter to renounce the title of King of
D Germany. Lothar made two journeys to Rome. On the
first occasion he restored Pope Innocent II., who had been
expelled from Rome by his rival, Anaclete II., and received the imperial crown from his hands, together with a
grant of the lands of Matilda, margravine of Tuscany, to
be held as a fief of the Holy See. On the second, he
expelled Roger II. from Apulia and Calabria; but no
sooner had he quitted Italy, than the exiled king returned
to his dominions.

197

The Welfs (Guelphs).

Welf IV.,
duke of Bavaria.

Henry the Black,
duke of Bavaria, † 1126.

5 Henry the Proud, duke of Bavaria and Saxony, † 1139. mar. Gertrude, daughter of Lothar the Saxon. — Welf † 1191. — Judith married Frederick, duke of Swabia, † 1147.

Henry the Lion,
duke of Saxony (1142), of Bavaria (1156, † 1195.

Otho IV. † 1218. — William.

Otho the Child,
first duke of Brunswick and Lünenburg.

The Hohenstaufen.

Frederick, duke of Swabia, † 1105,
mar. Agnes, daughter of the Emperor Henry IV.

Frederick, duke of Swabia, † 1147. — Conrad III. † 1152.

Frederick I. (Barbarossa) † 1190. — Henry, † 1150. — Frederick, † 1167.

Henry VI. † 1197, mar. Constantia. — Frederick, duke of Swabia. — Philip, † 1208.

Frederick II. †1250.

Henry, — Conrad IV., † 1254. — Enzio, — Manfred.

Conradin, † 1268. — Constantia, mar. Peter III. of Arragon.

§ 43. *The German empire under the Hohenstaufen.*

(1138—1254.)

1. Conrad III. (1138—1152.)

198 After Lothar's death, the claims of his unpopular son-in-
A law, Henry the Proud, who had already possessed himself of the crown jewels, were set aside by the electors, whose choice fell on a Hohenstaufen, Conrad, duke of Franconia. Henry, on being required to resign one of his two dukedoms, renounced his allegiance, and was placed under the ban of the empire; his dukedom of Bavaria being conferred on Leopold, margrave of Austria (half-brother of Conrad III.); and Saxony on Albert the Bear (grandson of Duke Magnus of Saxony). After Henry's death, the war was carried on by his brother Guelph (his son, Henry the
B Lion, being still a mere child). The city of Weinsburg, in which Guelph had shut himself up, was taken after a long siege (in **1140**), and the lives of the garrison saved through the fidelity of their wives: hence the name of "Weibertreue" (woman's fidelity), which the hill still retains. A treaty was concluded, by which Saxony was restored to Henry the Lion. Conrad was the first king, since Otho the Great, on whose head the imperial crown was not placed by the pope.—For his crusade, see page 89.

2. Frederick I., Barbarossa (Red-beard).

(1152—1190.)

199 Conrad was succeeded by his nephew, his son being still
C a child. Frederick, who was a Hohenstaufen, or Ghibelline, on the side of his father, and a Guelph on that of his mother, endeavored to reconcile the two houses; and with that view restored Bavaria to Henry the Lion (who had accompanied him in his first Italian campaign); the Margrave of Austria being indemnified by the elevation of his marquisate to the rank of an independent dukedom, hereditary in the female as well as the male line. His great object was to re-establish the imperial authority, which, in Italy especially, had sunk into insignificance during the reigns of his predecessors. For this purpose he visited Italy six times.

First Italian campaign (1154). The city of Milan 200
having declared itself independent, Henry addressed a A
letter of remonstrance to the magistrates, which was torn
in pieces, and thrown into the face of his messenger. On
entering Italy for the first time, Frederick, although un-
prepared to attack Milan, was able to reduce three other
rebellious towns (Asti, Chieri, and Tortona). After their
surrender, he assumed the iron crown of Italy in the city
of Pavia, and marched at once to Rome, whither he had
been summoned by Pope Adrian IV., whose subjects had
been persuaded by Arnold of Brescia to throw off the
papal yoke, and establish a senate with sovereign authority,
as in days of yore. Arnold was taken prisoner by Frede- B
rick, delivered up to the prefect of the city, and hung.
His body was burnt, and the ashes thrown into the Tiber
(1155). Frederick now received the imperial crown from
the hands of the pope, whose stirrup he held previously to
the ceremony. A terrible disease, which soon afterwards
broke out among his troops, compelled Frederick to return
to Germany, where he re-united the Burgundian and German kingdoms by a marriage with Beatrice, heiress of
Burgundy, compelled the Poles again to pay tribute, and
elevated the Duke of Bohemia to the rank of king.

In his second Italian campaign (1158—1162), Frederick 201
placed Milan (which had been perseveringly enlarging its C
territories) under the ban of the empire, and laid siege to
the city. After sustaining great hardships, the Milanese
signed a capitulation, one of the principal conditions of
which was, that the election of their magistrates should
thenceforward be subject to the emperor's approval. At
a diet held on the Roncalian plain near Piacenza, the relations of Italy to the emperor were settled on terms exceedingly advantageous to the latter. Even the Milanese were D
willing to accept of the new constitution, although it deprived
them of the right secured to them by the capitulation of
electing their own magistrates, who were thenceforth to
be nominated by the emperor himself. An attempt on the
part of the citizens of Milan to re-assert this right, occasioned a fresh war. After a siege of two years, Milan
surrendered unconditionally; the fortifications of the city
were dismantled, and the inhabitants, after sustaining fresh
humiliations, were compelled to establish themselves in

(201) four separate townships. A double election having been
A made by the college of cardinals, Victor IV., and after his death Paschal III., were recognized by Frederick and the bishops immediately under his influence, in opposition to Alexander III., who was supported by a large majority of the priesthood.

202 *In his third visit to Italy* (1163) without an army, Frederick, who had been excommunicated by Pope Alexander III., endeavored to allay the discontent occasioned by the severity of his functionaries.

203 *In his fourth Italian campaign* (1166—1163) he com-
B pelled the Romans to receive Paschal III. in the place of Alexander III., who had fled from the city. Frederick and his consort were crowned by the new pope; but soon afterwards a frightful pestilence well-nigh annihilated his army, and compelled him to re-cross the Alps in disguise, and almost alone. The Lombard cities, being unable to obtain redress for the cruelties perpetrated by the imperial governors, entered into a confederacy, re-established the exiled Milanese in Milan, and built a fortress, to which, in defiance of the emperor, they gave the name of Alexandria.

204 *In his fifth campaign* (1174—1178) he was abandoned
C by Henry the Lion during the siege of Alexandria, and in consequence of this defection was compelled, after sustaining a defeat at Legnano on the Ticino (1176) to conclude (at Venice) a peace with Alexander III., and an armistice with the Lombards for six years; at the expiration of which a formal peace was concluded at Constance. By this new treaty the right was confirmed to the emperor of appointing magistrates and levying taxes; the cities being permitted to retain their own laws and institutions, and to continue members of the confederacy which they had formed a few years previously.

205 On his return to Germany, Frederick published the ban
D of the empire against Henry the Lion, (who had neglected to appear after being five times cited), gave Bavaria to the Count Palatine Otho of Wittelsbach, and West Saxony to the Archbishop of Cologne, conferred the dignity of Duke of Saxony on Count Bernard of Anhalt, and having subdued Henry after a war of two years, released him from the ban, and restored his family estates of Brunswick and

Lüneburg, on condition of his absenting himself from (205)
Germany for three years. Henry acceded to these terms, A
and sought an asylum at the court of his father-in-law,
Henry II. king of England.

After holding a brilliant diet at Mainz (1184), at which 206
his two eldest sons, Henry and Frederick, were admitted to
the degree of knighthood, Frederick appeared *for the sixth
time in Italy*, where he was received with enthusiasm, and
celebrated in the city of Milan, which had been lately
rebuilt, the marriage of his eldest son, the Roman King
Henry, with Constance, daughter of Roger II., and heiress
of the kingdom of Apulia and Sicily,—For an account of
his crusade and death, see pages 89, 90.

3. Henry VI. (1190—1197).

Henry, who had governed the empire as regent, during 207
the absence of his father in the Holy Land, hastened into B
Italy on receiving intelligence of the death of William II.
of Sicily, for the purpose of securing the birthright of his
consort; but the Sicilians, who hated the Germans, had
already placed on the throne Count Tancred, an illegitimate scion of the Norman royal house. Henry, after
receiving the imperial crown at Rome, advanced by forced
marches to Naples, but was soon compelled by the sick-
liness of his troops, and the intelligence which reached him
of his brother's death, to return to Germany. The ransom C
of Richard Cœur de Lion (see page 90), afforded him the
means of undertaking a second campaign to Italy, where
all opposition had ceased since the death of Tancred. At
Palermo, the crown of Sicily was added to the four which
he already possessed. The discovery of an unsuccessful
conspiracy furnished the emperor with a pretext for in-
flicting the most terrible punishments on his enemies.
Tancred's widow and daughters were thrown into prison, D
his son William deprived of his eyes, and archbishops,
bishops, counts, and nobles, put to death by tortures too
horrible to relate. These acts of cruelty, together with
his treatment of Richard Cœur de Lion, provoked the
pope (Cælestine III.) to pronounce sentence of excommunication on Henry. A plan which he had long cherished,
of making the imperial dignity hereditary in his family,
was rendered abortive by the opposition of the nobility,

(207) especially of the higher orders of the clergy. The following
A year, during his preparations for the conquest of the Byzantine empire, Henry suddenly expired at Messina, to the great delight of all the Italians.

208 Henry the Lion had returned from England to Germany, where he found many adherents; but all his attempts to recover his former possessions ended in disappointment. He died at Brunswick, in the year 1195.

4. Philip of Swabia (1198—1208).

Otho IV. (1198—1215.)

209 After Henry's death, the German nobles were divided into
B two parties: that of the Hohenstaufen, which supported Henry's youngest brother, Philip of Swabia (Henry's son Frederick being scarcely three years old when his father died); and the Guelphic, which chose Otho, second son of Henry the Lion. Innocent III. (1198—1216), to whose arbitration the disputed election was referred, decided in favor of Otho. Philip, who had conferred the hereditary sovereignty of Bohemia on Ottocar (1198), and had already obtained some advantages over Otho, and entered into negotiations with the pope, was murdered at Bamberg, in the year 1208, by the Count Palatine Otho of Wittelsbach, to whom he had promised one of his daughters in marriage, and neglected to fulfil the engagement.

110 The first act of Otho's reign, after the death of his rival,
C was to place Otho of Wittelsbach under the ban of the empire, and command his assassination. After effecting a reconciliation with the house of Hohenstaufen by means of a marriage with Beatrice, the youngest daughter of Philip of Swabia, Otho visited Rome, and received the Italian and imperial crowns; but soon afterwards having involved himself in a dispute with Pope Innocent III., through an attempt to re-establish the imperial authority in Italy, he
D conquered Apulia, and attacked the King of Sicily, who happened to be the pope's ward. Innocent immediately excommunicated him, and invited the German nobles to confirm their former election of Frederick, the only surviving prince of the house of Hohenstaufen, who was crowned at Aix-la-Chapelle in 1215. Otho, who previously to this event had been defeated by the French king,

Philip Augustus, at Bovines, in Flanders (where he was (210)
assisted by his ally, King John of England), was compelled A
to retire to his hereditary estate of Brunswick, where he
died (at Harzburg) in 1218.

5. Frederick II. (1215—1250).

On his accession, Frederick had promised the pope, 211
(1) that thenceforward the German and Sicilian crowns
should be disunited; and (2) that he would undertake a
crusade. Both these engagements were violated; the first
by his nominating his son Henry (to whom he had resigned
the kingdom of Sicily) to be his successor on the German
throne, and causing him to be crowned Roman king in 1222;
and the second (which he had renewed at his coronation),
by his deferring the crusade until the year 1227, the inter-
vening time being occupied in arranging the affairs of his
hereditary estates. On his return from Palestine, Frede- B
rick found Apulia in the occupation of the papal troops;
and having re-conquered that province, effected a reconciliation with the pope, through the intervention of Herman of Salza, grand master of the Teutonic order, and
thoroughly reformed the legal code of his hereditary dominions, he re-visited Germany, where his son Henry had
raised the standard of rebellion during his absence. Henry
was taken, solemnly disinherited at Mainz, and thrown into
prison, where he remained until his death in 1242. At C
the same diet, Frederick conferred on Otho [the Child] the
allodes of his father, to be held thenceforward as the hereditary duchy of Brunswick Lüneburg, with succession in
the female as well as the male line. After proclaiming a
general peace throughout Germany, the emperor revisited
Italy, for the purpose of chastising those Lombard cities
which had taken part with his eldest son, leaving the
second, Conrad, to administer the affairs of the kingdom
during his absence. Having reduced all the cities to sub- D
mission with the exception of four, and obtained a decisive
victory at *Cortenuova* (1237) by the aid of his general,
Ezzelino Romano, Frederick summoned the Milanese to
surrender at discretion, but was prevented from attaining
his object, by a misunderstanding with Pope Gregory IX.,
in consequence of the elevation of the emperor's natural

(211) son, Enzio, to the throne of Sardinia, of which the sove-
A reignty was claimed by the holy see, as a part of St.
Peter's patrimony.

212 Sentence of excommunication was passed on Frederick; but the endeavors of the pope to place a rival on the imperial throne were unsuccessful. About the same time, Russia and Poland were overrun by the Mongols, who penetrated as far as Silesia, and defeated the army of Henry the Pious, duke of Lower Silesia, at a place called from this engagement Wahlstatt, or the battle-field. Then they marched through Morovia and Hungary, and after sustaining a defeat somewhere in Austria, retired to the steppes, whence they had originally sallied forth.

213 In the same year, Gregory IX. died, at the age of one
B hundred years. In the year 1243, Pope Innocent IV. fled
to Lyons, where he called together a general council, and
solemnly deposed the emperor and his son Conrad. The
bishops then elected the Landgrave Henry Raspe of
Thuringia (1246), whose elevation to the throne by the
votes of the clergy, without the consent of the temporal
electors, procured him the nick-name of the "Parson's
King" (der Pfaffenkönig). The usurper obtained some
advantages near Frankfort; but died in the following year
at the Wartburg, in consequence of wounds received in an
C engagement in the neighborhood of Ulm. The choice of
the three Rhenish archbishops then fell on Count William
of Holland, who was also supported by one of the temporal electors, the King of Bohemia. Leaving his son
Conrad to oppose the usurper in Germany, Frederick, in
conjunction with his natural son Enzio (who was taken
prisoner in a bloody engagement near Fossalta), and his
general, Ezzelino Romano, resumed the war in Lombardy,
which continued with various success until his death (at
Firenzuelo, near Luceria), in 1250.

6. Conrad IV. (1250—1254). William (1256).

214 After sustaining a defeat at Oppenheim, Conrad quitted
D Germany, where the mendicant friars were preaching a
crusade against him, and sought an asylum in Apulia,
which was occupied by the forces of his illegitimate brother Manfred. He died in 1254, leaving behind him one

son, named Conradin, an infant of two years old. Almost (214)
the only public act of William of Holland was the giving A
his sanction to a confederacy which had been formed by a
number of towns on the Rhine about the time of his own
election. He was slain in a frozen morass, by the inhabitants of Friesland, from whom he had attempted to extort tribute.

§ 44. *The interregnum in Germany* (1257—1273).

So distracted was the empire at this period of our history, 215
that no native prince would suffer himself to be put in B
nomination as William's successor: the choice, therefore, of the electors fell on two foreigners, Richard of Cornwall (who obtained the majority of votes), and Alfonso of Castille. The former, who was crowned at Aix-la-Chapelle, visited Germany four times. After his death, in 1272, Alfonso, who had never quitted Spain since his election, was set aside by the electors, and Count Rudolph, of Habsburg, raised to the imperial throne, in 1273, chiefly through the influence of the Archbishop of Mainz.

§ 45. *The kingdom of the two Sicilies* (1130—1282).

a. *Under the Normans* (1130—1194). The immediate 216
successors of Roger II., founder of the kingdom of the Two C
Sicilies (see § 25, D), and conqueror of the northern coast of Africa, from Tunis to Tripoli, were William I., surnamed the Bad, who lost the possessions of the Sicilian crown in Africa; and William (II.) the Good. The legitimate successors of the latter were Constance, daughter of Roger II., and her consort, the emperor Henry VI.; but the throne was usurped during a period of five years, by Tancred, a natural son of Roger II., and his son William III.

b. *Under the Hohenstaufen* (1194—1266). Henry I. 217
(VI.) was succeeded by his son Frederick I. (II.) a child D
of three years old, who was placed under the guardianship of the pope. This sovereign transferred the royal residence from Palermo to Naples (where he founded a university), and gave the nation a new code of laws, most of which were borrowed from the ancient Norman constitutions. All peculiar jurisdictions were abolished, and thus a check

(217) was given to the progress of immorality and luxury. His A son Conrad IV. left behind him one son, named Conradin, a minor, whose guardian, Manfred, assumed the crown without the sanction of his feudal sovereign the pope. On receiving intelligence of this proceeding, Urban conferred the kingdom on Charles of Anjou, brother of St. Louis of France. In the year 1266, a battle was fought near Benevento, in which Manfred lost his life.

218 c. *Under the house of Anjou* (1266—1282). The ad- B herents of Manfred fled to Germany, and joined the army of Conradin, who entered Italy accompanied by his friend Frederick of Austria, and after sustaining a defeat at Tagliacozzo, or Scurcola, in the neighborhood of Alba (August 23), was taken prisoner and executed (with his companion) in the market-place of Naples (1268). On the scaffold he bequeathed his claims to Peter III. of Arragon, Manfred's son-in-law. The flames of discontent, kindled by the insolence and tyranny of Charles of Anjou, burst forth on Easter-Monday, 1282, during the Vesper service at Palermo (the Sicilian vespers), when all the Frenchmen in the island were massacred, and the crown of Sicily placed on the head of Peter of Arragon, Charles still retaining the kingdom of Naples.

§ 46. *France* (1108—1270).

219 5. Louis (VI.) the Fat (1108—1137). The gradual C abolition of serfdom and the formation of free guilds, or companies (communes) in the cities, contributed in no small degree to the consolidation of the sovereign authority, and the depression of the powerful vassals of the crown. Normandy was still held by the King of England as a French fief, in spite of three attempts made by Louis VI. to restore Robert, duke of that country, who had been deposed and imprisoned by his brother, Henry I.

220 6. Louis VII. (1137—1180) was persuaded by the D Abbot Bernard of Clairvaux to take part in the second crusade (see page 89), during which the affairs of his kingdom were well administered by the Abbot Suger. On his return, Louis divorced his wife Eleonora, heiress of Poitou, Guienne, and Gascony, who immediately married

Henry, duke of Normandy and count of Anjou. Two (220)
years later, on the accession of this prince to the English A
throne, the whole western half of France was annexed to
England.

7. Philip II. (1180—1223), surnamed Augustus (on 221
account of his conquests), quarrelled with Richard Cœur
de Lion during the third crusade, and made an unsuccessful attempt on the English possessions in France. On the
other hand, Richard's successor, John (surnamed Lackland), whom Philip had in vain cited to appear before the
chamber of peers at Paris, and clear himself from the
charge of having murdered his nephew, Arthur of Brittany,
was compelled to relinquish all his French fiefs except
Guienne. By the consolidation of these fiefs, the crown of
France obtained an influence infinitely greater than that
possessed by its vassals individually. King John having B
quarrelled with the pope respecting the election of an
Archbishop of Canterbury, Innocent III. excommunicated
him, and invited Philip II. to take possession of England.
An arrangement was subsequently effected, by which John
consented to hold his territories as a fief of the see of
Rome; but, notwithstanding this change in the aspect of
affairs, Philip, who had obtained a victory at Bovines over
John and his allies (the Emperor Otho IV. and the Count
of Flanders), sent his son Louis into England, whence he
was expelled at the end of a year. During the progress of C
these events a fierce civil war was raging in the south of
France, where the Albigenses (a designation common to
several sects which had arisen in that quarter of the kingdom, especially in the province of Albigeois, towards the
close of the twelfth century) had refused to recognize
either the spiritual or secular authority of the pope, and
placing themselves under the protection of Count Raimond VI. of Thoulouse, had destroyed several churches
and ill-treated the clergy. Sentence of excommunication D
having been passed on the count by Pope Innocent III.,
and preachers sent forth to proclaim a crusade against the
heretics, the cities of Beziers and Carcassonne were laid in
ashes (1209), the inhabitants butchered without distinction
of age or sex, and the greater part of Languedoc overrun
by the crusaders. Origin of the "pairs de France" (six
temporal, viz. the dukes of Normandy, Guienne, and Bur-

(221) gundy, the counts of Thoulouse, Champagne, and Flanders;
A and six spiritual, viz. the Archbishop of Rheims and five bishops); and of appeals from the baronial courts to the king.

222 8. Louis VIII. (1213—1226) undertook a fresh crusade against the Albigenses and Raimond VII., and died before its termination.

223 9. Louis IX. (St. Louis, 1226—1270), the most pious prince of the middle ages, commenced his reign under the guardianship of his mother, Blanche of Castille, and terminated the Albigensian war in 1229, by concluding a peace with Raimond VII., who was compelled to cede a portion of his dominions to the crown, and bequeath the remainder
B to his son-in-law, a brother of the king. The Albigenses were exterminated partly through the vigilance of the recently-established inquisition, and the exertions of the Dominican preachers, and partly by actual violence.—For his first crusade, see page 92. A permanent peace with England was established by the restoration of four provinces south of the Charente to Henry III., who, on his part, consented to abandon his claims to all other portions of the French territory formerly possessed by England, and to take the oath of feudal allegiance to Louis; after which he was enrolled among the peers of France, as duke
C of Guienne. For the preservation of peace at home, all private feuds were strictly forbidden, wager of battle abolished on the estates belonging to the crown, the rights of the Church secured by a pragmatic sanction, and the baronial jurisdiction gradually subjected to the royal courts, which were duly supplied with advocates.—For his second crusade and death, see page 92.

§ 47. *England* (1066—1272).

a. Under Norman kings (1066—1154).

William I. † 1087. 224

Robert, Duke of Normandy.	William II. † 1100.	Henry I. † 1135.	Adelaide, mar. Stephen, Count of Blois. A
		Matilda, mar. 1. The Emperor Henry V. 2. Geoffrey Plantagenet, Count of Anjou.	Stephen, King, † 1154.
		Henry II. † 1189.	

1. William (I.) the Conqueror (1066—1087), in- 225
troduced the feudal system into England, and divided the B
conquered territory into 60,215 portions, of which 14,000 were retained by the crown, and 20,215 conferred on the clergy, who were bound, no less than the temporal barons, to render military service for their fiefs. As the best security for the stability of his usurped throne, William filled all the great offices of state with Normans, introduced the French language into the courts of law and schools, and published an exact register of the lands of England, which still exists, under the title of Domesday Book.

2. William (II.) Rufus (1087—1100), succeeded 226
his father on the English throne, to the exclusion of his C
elder brother Robert, who inherited the dukedom of Normandy, and joined the crusaders.

3. Henry I. (1100—1135) seized on the crown during 227
the absence of his elder brother in Palestine, and on his return robbed him also of Normandy, which was united to England in 1106. Robert was deprived of his eyes, and
died in prison. A charter by which the severity of the D
feudal constitution was in some degree qualified, was granted by Henry to the nobility and the city of London. The recognition by the nobility of Henry's daughter Matilda, and her second husband Geoffrey Plantagenet, introduced the principle of female succession into England; but Henry having died in Normandy, a rival candidate for the throne appeared in the person of

4. Stephen of Blois, who was defeated by the forces 228

(228) of Matilda near Lincoln, thrown into prison, and only per-
A mitted to retain the crown during his life, on condition of
nominating Matilda's son Henry as his successor.

b. Under the four first kings of the house of Anjou or Plantagenet (1154—1272).

229 1. Henry II. (1154—1189) inherited Normandy from
his mother, and Anjou, Maine, and Touraine, from his
father; and held Guienne and Poitou (see § 45) in right
of his wife. The attempts of Henry to subject (by the
constitutions of Clarendon) ecclesiastics to the jurisdiction of the temporal courts in matters purely secular, and
to restrain the practice of appealing to Rome, were defeated by the pertinacity of Thomas à Becket, archbishop
of Canterbury, who was murdered in his own cathedral by
B four noblemen. To satisfy the people, Henry did penance
at the archbishop's tomb. Ireland, which was distracted
by intestine feuds, was conquered in 1172, and the King of
Scotland compelled to take the oath of vassalage to the
crown of England. Henry died of grief, occasioned by
repeated acts of rebellion, committed at the instigation of
his consort, by his two sons, who were abetted in their
treason by the King of France.

230 2. Richard Cœur de Lion (1189—1199) sold his
C feudal supremacy over Scotland, passed three years in
Palestine, and two in a German prison, and lost his life
before a fortress during a war which he had undertaken
against France, in consequence of the support afforded by
that power to his rebellious brother John.

281 3. John (surnamed Lackland) (1199—1216 was
deprived of all his French fiefs, except Guienne, as a
punishment for the murder of his nephew, Arthur of Brittany, whose claims to the English crown were supported by
D Philip Augustus. About the same time, John was excommunicated by Pope Innocent III. (in consequence of a dispute
respecting the nomination of an archbishop of Canterbury),
and the sovereignty of England offered to the King of
France (compare § 46). Having effected a reconciliation
with the pope, by consenting to hold his kingdom as a
fief of the Holy See, John made an unsuccessful attempt to
abrogate the charter of English liberty (Magna Charta

libertatum), which his insurgent barons had forced him (231)
to sign in 1215, and soon afterwards died of fever, occa- A
sioned by the fatigue of a precipitate flight.

4. Henry III. (1216—1272) was only ten years of age 232
when he ascended the throne. Prince Louis of France,
who had assumed the title of King of England, in consequence of the pope's invitation (compare page 107), was
defeated by the Earl of Pembroke (Henry's guardian) near
Lincoln, and also in a naval engagement, and compelled
to renounce his claims. Scarcely, however, was Henry
securely seated on the throne, when his incapacity manifested itself in the injudicious selection of his generals and
ministers, and the favor shown to foreign adventurers,
as well as in the oppression of his own subjects, notwithstanding his assurances (renewed during a period of thirty
years, on the occasion of every fresh subsidy) that their
privileges should be respected. The discontent excited by B
his weakness and treachery burst forth at last in an insurrection of the barons (1258, headed by Henry's brother-
in-law, Simon de Montfort, earl of Leicester). Henry was
compelled to assemble a parliament at Oxford, and commit
the administration of his kingdom to a council composed of
twenty-four barons. An attempt on the part of the king C
to resume the reins of government, occasioned the battle of
Lewes (1264), in which Henry (with his brother, Richard
of Cornwall, king of Germany) was taken prisoner, and
forced to purchase his freedom by consenting to re-establish
the council of barons. The haughty demeanor of Leicester offended the barons; but, on the other hand, the favor
of the people was conciliated by his calling to the parliament two knights from each county, and two burgesses as
representatives of each town, thus laying the foundation of
a House of Commons. Meanwhile Edward, the heir- D
apparent to the throne, had assembled the adherents of the
king, and marched to Evesham, where a battle was fought
in 1265, in which Leicester was slain, and the baronial
aristocracy completely crushed. The result of this victory
was the re-establishment of peace between the king and
his people.—For an account of the termination of the disputes with France, by a peace with Louis IX., see page 108.

§ 48. *Spain.*

233 1. The kingdom established by the Arabians in Spain
A remained until the end of this period (1269) in close connection with the empire of Morocco; but the Moorish power, both in Africa and in the peninsula, had been gradually declining since the defeat of their forces at Tolosa (1212), by the united armies of the kings of Arragon, Castille, and Navarre. In Spain especially, Christianity had gradually obtained a preponderance over Islamism, through the acquisition of provinces, which had either been re-conquered from the unbelievers, or conferred by them as fiefs on the native princes.

234 2. Christian Spain. *a.* The kingdom of *Leon* and
B *Castille* (compare § 33, 2) was divided by Alfonso VII. into two sovereignties (1157), which were re-united by Ferdinand the Saint (1230), and augmented by the addition of several Moorish provinces (Cordova, Estremadura, Murcia, Jaen, and Seville), the conquest of which was principally achieved by the knights of the three Castilian orders (Alcantara, Calatrava, and St. Jago de Compostella), established towards the middle of the twelfth century. His son Alfonso X. (surnamed the Wise) was elected
C King of Germany (compare § 44). *b. Navarre* was again separated from Arragon, and continued to be an independent kingdom until 1284, when it was annexed to France. *c.* On the other hand, Barcelona, the Balearic isles, and the kingdom of Valencia, were added to the kingdom of *Arragon*, the first through the marriage of Count Raimond of Barcelona with the heiress of Arragon, and the others by the sword of James I., surnamed the Conqueror.
D Pedro III., son of this monarch, whom Conradin immediately before his execution had nominated heir of his claims to the Neapolitan throne, became King of Sicily after the Sicilian vespers.

§ 49. *Portugal.*

235 About the time of the first crusade (1096), Alfonso VI., of Castille, granted to his brave son-in-law, Henry, duke of Burgundy (great-grandson of Hugh Capet), the whole of the territory between the Minho and Douro, which derived

its name of Portugal from the city of Porto.[1] The capital (235)
was Coimbra. Alfonso I., who had been enabled to extend A
the boundaries of his infant kingdom by a victory over the
Arabians at Ourique (1139), assumed the title of king (for
the recognition of which he engaged to pay a yearly tribute
to the pope), obtained a constitution for his new kingdom
from the Cortes of Lamego, and with the assistance of
some English and North-German crusaders, wrested Lisbon
from the infidels. Alfonso III. further enlarged the
kingdom by the conquest of Algarves in 1253.

B. The East.

§ 50. *The Byzantine empire.*

1. Under the Comneni and Dukas (1157—1185]. 236
The soldiers, weary of their dependence on the two prin- B
cesses (compare § 34), had placed their comrade Isaac
Comnenus on the imperial throne; but the newly-elected
emperor was soon compelled by bodily infirmity to resign
his crown and retire into a monastery. A friend of his
house, named Constantine Dukas, was then invested with
the purple, which he bequeathed to his wife (Eudocia), to be
held in trust for his three sons, subject to the condition that
the empress should remain unmarried. Scarcely, however, C
had seven months expired, when Eudocia, disregarding
her lord's injunctions, bestowed her hand on her general,
Romanus Diogenes, who was defeated and taken prisoner
in a war with the Seldschuks. After a short captivity,
Diogenes was generously set at liberty by his conquerors,
and returning home, found his wife imprisoned in a convent, and the throne in possession of Michael VII. (eldest
son of Constantine Dukas), who defeated him and put out
his eyes. The greater part of Asia Minor had been D
already wrested from the empire by the Seldschuks (hence
the Sultanate of Iconium, or Rum), and the whole of
Lower Italy by the Normans, when the Comneni again
ascended the throne. Three emperors of that house, each
distinguished for his bravery, viz. Alexius Comnenus,
his son Kalo-Johannes, and grandson Manuel (whose
united reigns occupied 100 years, 1081—1180), resisted
manfully the encroachments of the Seldschuks in the east,

[[1] Called by us "O Porto, *the* port."]

(236) the Normans in Lower Italy, and the Petschenegens and
A Cumanes in the north, notwithstanding the feebleness to which the empire had been reduced by the corruption of the court and the struggles of party. Manuel's son, Alexius II. (a minor) was murdered after a short reign by his guardian, Andronicus, whose cruel reign of three years was terminated by an insurrection of Isaac Angelus, a collateral relation of the Comneni, who had been condemned to suffer an ignominious death.

237 2. Under the house of Angelus (1185—1204). The weak Isaac Angelus, who had been unable to prevent the revolt of the Bulgarians, and the loss of Cyprus, was set aside by his brother Alexius III., who
B put out his eyes and threw him into prison. The fourth crusade, as it was called, was undertaken by the Venetians and French, for the purpose of replacing him on the throne, from which he was a second time deposed (see page 90).

238 3. The Latin empire (1204—1261). For an account of this empire, as well as those of Nicæa and Trebizond, see page 91.

§ 51. *The Arabians.*

239 The Caliphate of the Abbasides was extin-
C guished in the year 1258 by the Mongols, who stormed Bagdad (the only city still possessed by the caliphs), and for seven days deluged its streets with blood. Motazem, the fifty-sixth and last caliph, was sewn up in a cow's hide, and dragged by the conquerors through the streets of his capital. The descendants of Prince Hakim, who escaped the general destruction, continued to exercise a spiritual supremacy in Egypt (without any admixture of secular authority) until the conquest of that country by the Turks
D in 1517. Of the African dynasties, the Aglabides and Edrisides had become extinct during the preceding period; the Fatimides in Egypt were overthrown by Nureddin; and the Morabethes, who had founded the empire of Morocco and conquered the south of Spain, were expelled by the Almohades (whose supremacy terminated in 1269). The whole, therefore, of Arabian Africa was now shared by three recent dynasties (the Abuhassians, Merinides, and Zianides),

who had already from time to time obtained possession of (239)
particular portions.

§ 52. *The Seldschuks.*

About fifty years before the commencement of the cru- 240
sades, a nomadic Turkish tribe, named the Seldschuks, A
under the command of their Sultan Togrul Beg, a grandson of the Turkish Emir Seldschuk, conquered all the
countries between the Oxus and Euphrates, and having
established their head-quarters at Bagdad (where their
leader enjoyed the dignity of emir al Omrah), made themselves also masters of Syria and Asia Minor. After the B
death of their third Sultan (Malek) in 1092, the mighty
empire, which in its palmy days extended from the frontier
of China to the Mediterranean, and from Samarcand to the
southern coast of Arabia, after a succession of civil wars,
was split into five small governments, which during the
crusades fell into the hands of other Turkish hordes. The
kingdom of Iconium alone continued to exist, although in
a state of dependence on the Mongols, until the thirteenth
century.

§ 53. *The Mongols.*

The Mongols, a nomadic tribe closely connected with 241
the Huns, who inhabited the trackless plains stretching C
southwards from Siberia to the greater Bucharia and the
Desert of Kobi, in the year 1206 conferred the title of
Dschingis-Khan (i. e. Khan of Khans), on Temud
Schin, the son of a khan. Under the command of this
chieftain, they conquered a portion of northern China,
expelled Mohammed, sultan of the Chowaresmians,
(whose dominions extended from India to the Caspian Sea), invaded Russia, and overthrew the Prince of
Kiev (on the Kalka). Under the four sons of Dschingis- D
Khan (among whom the empire of Kiev was divided),
the whole of Northern China fell into the hands of the
Mongols, who then overran Russia, Poland, Silesia (where
they were victorious in the bloody battle of Wahlstadt,
compare page 104), Moravia, and Hungary, and entering
Austria, sustained a defeat, which compelled them to retrace their march through Asia Minor,—a measure which
was rendered still more necessary by the death of their

(241) great khan. In the year 1258 they took Bagdad, and put
A an end to the dynasty of the Abbasides. Towards the end
of the thirteenth century, the empire of the Mongols, which
now included Thibet and southern China, had reached its
widest limits, extending from the wall of China to the
frontier of Poland, and from India to Siberia. The residence
of the great khan was at Pekin. The administration
of the provinces was committed to inferior khans, of
the race of Dschingis-Khan; the most powerful of whom
were the khans of Kaptschak on the Wolga, and Dschagatai
in Turkestan.

C. The North-East of Europe.

§ 54. *Scandinavia.*

242 1. Iceland remained independent until nearly the end
B of this period (1261?), when it became a province of
Norway. In no country were the ancient Scandinavian
manners, language, and literature so little affected by
the influence of western Europe, of which scarcely any
traces are discernible, except in the ecclesiastical constitution
of the island.

243 2. In Norway, the dynasty of the legitimate descendants
of Harald Harfagr expired in 1103, with Magnus III.,
whose natural children threw the whole kingdom into
confusion by their contests for the crown. Iceland and
Greenland were annexed to Norway, and the Hebrides
sold to Scotland.

244 3. Sweden, like Norway, was distracted during this
C period by factions and civil wars, occasioned not so much
by disputed successions, as by the antagonism which subsisted
between the Gothic and Swedish races, as well as
between the Christians and heathens. The frequent result
of these disputes was the division of Norway into two
kingdoms, at first into Christian and heathen, and subsequently
into a Gothic and Swedish.

245 4. In Denmark, which comprehended also southern
D Sweden, or Schonen, the reigning family was that of the
Estrides, who conquered the island of Rügen, as well as
the whole line of coast from Esthonia to Holstein, together
with the towns of Lübeck and Hamburg. The whole of
this conquered territory, with the exception of northern

Esthonia, was afterwards surrendered by Waldemar II. to (245)
the Count of Schwerin, as the price of his liberation from A
prison. Since the abandonment of voyages to England, the
intercourse between the two countries had given place to
an intimate connection with Germany (especially after the
conquest of the south-eastern shores of the Baltic), which
produced an imitation of German institutions, especially as
regarded the creation of orders of chivalry, and the establishment of regulations for the government of their cities.

§ 55. *Russia.*

Besides the two grand principalities of Kiev and Vladi- 246
mir, there existed no less than fifty of inferior note. In B
the year 1238, the whole of Russia was occupied (after the
victories on the banks of the Kalka and at Sita) by the
Mongols, who burnt the cities of Vladimir, Moscow, and
Kiev. Novgorod alone (which had been a distinct principality since 1137) retained its independence, and became
in 1267 one of the commercial stations of the Hanseatic
league. The grand principalities were permitted to remain, their rulers engaging to pay tribute to the Mongols.
During this period of dependence, the grand prince of C
Vladimir (Jaroslav) conquered Finland, and his son Alexander, prince of Novgorod, and afterwards of Vladimir,
obtained a brilliant victory over the Swedes on the banks
of the Neva. Hence his surname of Nevskoi.

§ 56. *Poland under the Piasts.*

During this period Poland, which had again become a 247
dukedom, and now comprehended Silesia and eastern Pomerania, with its capital Dantzic, improved rapidly under
the influence of German civilization, notwithstanding the
wars in which she was engaged with the wild tribes on her
northern and eastern frontiers, and the civil commotions
occasioned by the partition of the dukedom among the
four sons of Boleslav III. The new sovereignties were— D
1. Cracow and Silesia; 2. Great Poland; 3. Masovia
and Cujavia; 4. Sendomir and Lublin. In addition to his
dukedom of Cracow and Silesia, the eldest exercised a sort
of feudal supremacy over the others. Conrad, duke of
Masovia, being too feeble to withstand the attacks of the
Prussians, called in the knights of the Teutonic order, who
were rewarded for their services with a grant of the territory of Culm. The invasion of Poland and Silesia by the

A Mongols, although of short duration, occasioned fearful
havoc, but no actual loss of territory.

§ 57. *Prussia.*

248 The Prussians, a half-civilized horde, inhabiting the line
of coast from the Vistula to the Niemen, not only resisted
successfully the attempts of the Poles to reduce them to
submission, under pretence of converting them to Christianity, but becoming themselves the aggressors, compelled
Conrad, duke of Masovia, to apply for assistance to the
"Brethren of the Sword" (an order originally established
in Livonia), and subsequently to the knights of the Teutonic
B order. After an obstinate struggle, in which they were
supported during a period of fifty-three years (1230—
1283) by crowds of adventurers from Pomerania, Austria,
and Brandenburg, the Teutonic knights became masters of
Prussia, where they founded the cities of Thorn, Marienwerder, Elbing, &c., and introduced German civilization.
The government of the conquered territory was administered by a provincial master, until the establishment of the
order itself at Marienberg, in the year 1309.

§ 58. *Hungary under the Arpads.*

249 Ladislav the Saint (see § 39) was succeeded by fifteen
C kings of the Arpadic family, which became extinct in 1301.
During the whole of this period the Hungarians were engaged in wars with German kings and dukes, with Venice,
the revolted maritime cities of Croatia and Dalmatia, with
the Byzantine emperors, the Bohemians, Poles, and Russians, and in domestic feuds occasioned partly by disputed
successions, and partly by insurrections of the nobles, who
compelled King Andrew II. (after his return from Syria)
D to grant them a charter, called "the Golden Book." But
the heaviest calamity of all was the terrible invasion of
the Mongols, in 1241. Bela IV., who then occupied the
throne, was compelled to seek an asylum in Dalmatia;
but on his return he exerted himself manfully to restore
the prosperity of his kingdom, which had been well-nigh
depopulated by the war.

§ 59. *Religion, Arts, Manufactures, &c., during the Third Period.*

250 1. The Church. The attempts of Gregory VII. *to
exalt the spiritual above the temporal power* were followed
up by his successors, particularly by Urban II., Paschal II.,

Innocent III. and IV., and towards the end of this period (250)
produced not only the complete emancipation of the Church A
from secular control, but the elevation of the pope to the
rank of supreme judge over all temporal princes, whose
crowns were placed at his absolute disposal. At the same B
time, the *ecclesiastical authority* of the popes was strengthened—I. By assemblies of the Church, in which term are
comprehended, (1) œcumenical councils, convoked and pre-
sided over by the pope himself; (2) synods held annually
at Rome; and (3) provincial synods summoned by the
pope's legates. II. By sending legates with unlimited
powers to all the countries of Europe. III. By the establishment of an appeal to Rome from the sentences of
metropolitans and bishops. IV. By an unscrupulous exercise of the right of suspending refractory sovereigns, or
placing their kingdoms under an interdict. The *monastic* C
system was also greatly enlarged: 1. By the establishment of the three religious orders of chivalry in Palestine, of three similar orders in Spain, and of the order
of Knights of the Sword in Livonia (1199). 2. By
the creation, from time to time, of fresh orders, with
more stringent rules of discipline. a. The Præmonstra-
tenses (founded by S. Norbert of Xanten, at Premontré,
near Laon). b. The Trinitarians. c. The Carmelites (on
Mount Carmel). d. The Dominicans, or Preachers (founded
by S. Dominic, a Spaniard), especially for the conversion
of heretics in the south of France. c. The Franciscans
(founded by S. Francis of Assisi). The rules of the three
last enjoined poverty, in the strictest sense of the term.
All attempts to re-unite the Greek and Latin churches D
were fruitless; but, on the other hand, the Maronites, and,
to a certain extent, the Armenians, were reconciled to the
Church of Rome. The teaching of Peter Abelard, his disciple Arnold of Brescia, and other schoolmen of the twelfth
century, produced a variety of *sects*—the Cathari in Germany and Italy; the Waldenses, or Vaudois (founded by
Peter Waldes, a rich merchant of Lyons); and the Albigenses, in the south of France, which united towards the
end of the 12th century, and were supported by many of
the temporal nobles in their resistance to their bishops. For
the suppression of these *heresies*[1] crusades were preached,

[1 "It is beyond a doubt that many of these sectaries [the Cathari, Picards, Paterins, and Albigenses] owed their origin to the Paulicians."——"Those who

A and the court of inquisition established, subject at first to the authority of the bishops, but at a later period almost exclusively under the control of the Dominicans.

251 2. Political Constitution. The distinguishing characteristic of this and the following period is the spirit of political communism which pervades every relation of life, and manifests itself in the establishment of orders of chivalry, Hanseatic leagues among merchants, guilds and companies of handicraftsmen, universities and their nations, bands of mercenary soldiers, unions of architects and
B painters, &c. Two of the most important results of this spirit are—1. *Chivalry*, the germ of which may be found in the practice of the ancient Franks (among whom the horse-soldier was highly esteemed), but for its development it is indebted to the military exercises, at the courts of the German kings, and the combats of the Christians
C with the Moors in Spain. Since the establishment of the feudal system, it had been the custom for proprietors of the larger estates to serve on horseback; and this union of persons, pledged to the performance of the same duties, soon assumed the form of a distinct order of chivalry, which spread, by means of the crusades, over the east as well as the west; its character being of course modified by the various circumstances of the countries in which it was
D established. The degrees of chivalry were—(*a*) The page (from seven years old to fourteen), who was raised to the rank of (*b*) Esquire, and declared capable of bearing arms, by the delivery of a sword. The esquire was dubbed (*c*) a Knight (generally in his twenty-first year) by the blow of a sword on his shoulder. The chief duties of knighthood were protection of the Church, widows, and orphans; maintenance of personal honor, even at the cost of life; and a courteous and modest demeanor towards ladies (galanterie). For the faithful performance of these duties, the knight was rewarded with the approbation of mankind and the panegyrical strains of minstrels. The most splendid exhibition of chivalry was the tournament,—a develop-

are absolutely free from any taint of Manichæism are properly called Waldenses; a name perpetually confounded in later times with that of Albigenses, but distinguishing a sect probably of separate origin, and at least of different tenets." ——"These pious and innocent sectaries [the Waldenses], of whom the very monkish historians speak well, appear to have nearly resembled the modern Moravians." "The Waldenses were always considered as much less erroneous in their tenets than the Albigenses or Manichæans."—*Hallam*, vol. iii. p. 45.

ment of the ancient military exercises, which assumed a (251)
more systematic character towards the end of the twelfth A
century, and soon became popular in every country of
Europe. For the union of chivalry and monasticism, see
p. 119.—2. *The establishment and development of a free* 221
and privileged Burgher order throughout the whole of what
was once the Carlovingian empire, (*a*) especially in Upper
and Central Italy, where, during the disputes respecting the
right of investiture, all affairs of police, finance, and executive government in the cities, had been administered by
civic magistrates, with the consules communis at their head.
At a diet held on the Roncalian plain during the second B
campaign of Frederick I. in Italy, the supremacy of the
emperor was established, and imperial lieutenants (podestà)
appointed to execute his decrees; but the misconduct of
these officers soon occasioned their removal, and the appointment of civic podestà. At a later period, even the
handicraftsmen claimed a share in the government, which
until that time had been entirely in the hands of the patricians, and compelled the authorities to sanction the appointment of a capitano del popolo, who became thenceforward
the opponent of the podestà. Whenever it was requisite C
that the contending parties should act in concert, the
supreme political authority (signoria) was placed for a
definite period in the hands of some neighboring prince,
or renowned leader (condottiere). All these free cities
adopted the Roman code, and a system of indirect taxation.
(*b*) In Germany, especially in the times of Frederick II. and
the interregnum, the cities, partly by purchase and partly
by the strong hand, became possessed of similar though
less extensive immunities, such as immediate dependence
on the empire, self-government, the right of coining money,
imposing taxes, and holding markets, with various commercial privileges, and free trade to a certain extent. The D
conservation of these privileges was intrusted to a burgo-
master, assisted by a college of counsellors, until the fourteenth century, when the guilds, or trades-unions, seem to
have taken forcible possession if not of all, at least of the
most important civic offices. (*c*) In France, political
privileges were granted to the cities by the nobility and
clergy, either for a pecuniary consideration, or because
they had sagacity enough to perceive that their own pros-

(251) perity was closely interwoven with that of their vassals.
A (*d*) In Arragon, the executive authority was shared by royal
and civic functionaries. In the north and east of Europe,
towards the middle of the thirteenth century, cities were
founded after the model of those in the west, or civic
privileges granted to existing communities. It was only,
however, in the maritime cities of Upper Italy that the
attempt to emancipate themselves from the authority of
their feudal sovereign was entirely successful. In Germany, especially, the imperial cities remained subject to the
B emperor, and the others to the great nobles. Delegates
from the cities appeared at diets first at Barcelona, then in
Italy, and at a later period in England.

252 3. Legislation and legal practice. The written
codes of this period were either abstracts of existing laws compiled by command of princes, or the works of private individuals, which in process of time were recognized as public
documents; such, for example, as the Lombardic feudal
code and the Saxon and Swabian mirrors (Sachsenspiegel
and Schwabenspiegel), the former for Northern, and the lat-
C ter for Southern Germany: or they were charters granted by
kings to their subjects, *e. g.* the Charta Magna Libertatum
of King John, and the Charter of Andrew II. of Hungary.
The compilation of civil codes was also common during
this period. Towards its conclusion the judicial combat
and the ordeal fell into disuse, but the practice of torturing
suspected persons became more frequent, and the punishments inflicted on criminals more cruel and sanguinary.

253 4. During this period the sciences, the study of which
had hitherto been confined to the cloister, began to be
cultivated by laity as well as clergy, under the auspices of
the spiritual and temporal princes, whose object was greatly
promoted by the increased number of schools and the
D *establishment of universities.* The most ancient of these
foundations owe their origin to the assemblages of young
persons, who flocked to the theological and philosophical
schools of Paris, where Abelard lectured, and to the
schools of jurisprudence at Bologna, in which the principles
of the Roman law were expounded by Irnevius. The
pupils and teachers formed a privileged corporation, or
universitas, with peculiar jurisdiction. After the model
of these two universities (at which the other sciences began

gradually to be taught), establishments were formed during (253)
this period at Padua, Naples, Thoulouse, Salamanca, Fer- A
rara, Oxford, and Cambridge. The scholastic mode of
treating theological subjects, which had been introduced by
Lanfranc and Anselm († 1143), was pursued by Abelard
(whose dogmas were condemned as heretical by St. Bernard)
and by his disciple Peter Lombard, whose manual of
theology was used as a text book for more than 300 years.
In the thirteenth century, the discovery of the metaphysical,
physical, and ethical works of Aristotle (his Logic having
been the only one of his treatises hitherto studied) laid the
foundation of *philosophical* scholastics, in which Albertus
(count of Bollstadt) Magnus († 1280), his disciple, Thomas
Aquinas († 1274), and Duns Scotus († 1308) especially distinguished themselves. Next to theology and philosophy the B
canon and Roman *laws* were most zealously studied. *History*, in central and western Europe, was written in Latin,
until the time of Geoffroy and Joinville, two Frenchmen,
who published the first historical work in the vernacular
tongue. *Mathematical* science was learnt from the Arabian writers or from Arabic translations of Greek treatises.
The most celebrated student in this department, and in
chemistry, was Roger Bacon († 1294). Mechanics were C
brought to great perfection during the erection of the noble
buildings of this period. The use of the mariner's compass was also discovered. *Byzantine literature* was confined to historical works (Anna Comnena, Joh. Zonăras),
critical expositions of the ancient Greek writers (Homer,
by Eustathius), and treatises on jurisprudence and theology. Among the *Arabians*, Averroes was distinguished as
a philosophical writer, Abulfaradsh as a historian, and
Geber as a mathematician.

5. Art. 254

(*a*) The *poetry* of this period was deeply imbued with D
the romantic spirit of the crusades and of chivalry. In
Germany epic and lyric poetry attained their highest degree
of excellence under the patronage of the Hohenstaufen.
The productions of the former were of three sorts: 1.
Original German compositions (the Nibelungen Noth, and
other poems); 2. Imitations of northern French works
(legends of Charlemagne, Arthur, and the Knights of the
Round Table) or of Provençal romances; 3. Poetical ver-

(254) sions of ancient myths. The most distinguished professors
A of lyric poetry were the Minne-singers; Henry von Valdeck, Hartmann von der Aue, Wolfram von Eschenbach, Walter von der Vogelweide, &c. "The war on the Wartburg" is a curious specimen of the poetical contests of those days. In the *south* of *France*, Provençal minstrelsy was cultivated successfully during an entire century by the Troubadours, who recited their compositions at the courts of the counts of Thoulouse, Provence, &c., whilst in the *north*, epic (principally the chivalrous romance, the contes and fabliaux), and at a later period didactic, allegoric, and lyric poetry flourished in the hands of the Trouvères. The minstrelsy of the Troubadours travelled from Provence
B to the east of Spain and Lombardy. In Castille the exploits of the Cid furnished a fruitful subject for romance. In the north, *Scandinavian* poetry was cultivated with considerable success, especially in Iceland, where the mythic songs of the ancient Scalds and innumerable Sagas were brought together in the older and more recent Edda.

255 (*b*) The German or new Gothic style of *architecture*, with its characteristic features, the pointed arch, slender column, and elegant tracery, was imported from England by brotherhoods or unions of architects (freemasons' lodges), and attained its highest perfection in the thirteenth
C century. The most magnificent specimens of this style of architecture, such as the minsters of Strasburg (begun in 1018) and Friburg, the church of St. Stephen at Vienna (1140), the domes of Magdeburg and Cologne (1248); in France, the cathedrals of Rouen, Rheims, and Amiens; in England, St. Peter's at York, and Westminster Abbey in London; and in Spain, the cathedrals of Burgos and Toledo, were at least commenced in this century. Secular buildings of every description, such as bridges, palaces, council-houses, monasteries, &c., were also erected at an enormous cost of labor and money.

256 (*c*) Of the other arts, those were especially cultivated
D which contributed to the embellishment of churches, *casting in bronze*, for instance, and *painting on glass*, which was invented in the eleventh century, and had now attained great perfection. Sculpture and painting were not elevated to the rank of independent arts until the thirteenth century (the former by Nicolo Pisano, † 1270, and the latter by

Cimabue, 1249—1300). Companies or unions of painters A
were also formed in the thirteenth century.

6. Commerce.—(*a*) *Maritime trade*, (*aa*) in the Mediter- 257
ranean, was carried on, for the most part, by Genoa, Venice,
and Pisa, and also by Marseilles and Barcelona, with the
sea-ports of the Holy Land and Syria, the northern coast of
Africa, Egypt, Cyprus, Asia Minor, and the Byzantine
empire. For the trade of the Venetians and Genoese out
of Constantinople, see page 95. (*bb*) The commerce of
the north of Europe flourished principally in (*α*) northern
Germany, including Lübeck, Bremen, and Hamburg; (*β*)
in the Netherlands, especially in the cities of Ypres, B
Bruges, and Ghent, where Germans, Frenchmen, and
Italians, were accustomed to meet for the purposes of trade;
(*γ*) in the island of Gothland, with its capital Wisby, the
general emporium of the commerce carried on by German,
Norman, and Sclavonian adventurers in the Baltic, and
thence overland by Novgorod into the interior of Russia.
(*b*) The chief stations of the *inland trade* were Ratisbon,
Vienna, Troyes, Lyons, Beaucaire, Augsburg, Nürnberg,
Frankfort on the Main, and Cologne. The natural result
of a commercial league between the cities of Southern
Germany (Ratisbon, Zürich, Augsburg, and Strasburg), and
the Italian towns of Genoa and Venice, was an active in-
terchange of merchandise through the passes of the Alps.
Even among merchants, especially those of Germany, the C
spirit of the age manifested itself in the formation—1. Of
several Hansas, or unions of commercial men, in one or
more cities, for the promotion and protection of their trade
with foreign countries, in which they obtained various privileges, and were permitted to erect warehouses and halls
for the transaction of their business (*e. g.* the merchants of
Cologne and other cities in the Netherlands enjoyed a
monopoly of the trade with England, and had a Guildhall in
London). 2. Provincial unions, especially of cities in the D
south of France and north of Germany, for the conservation
of peace within the district over which their commerce extended. Out of these two elements was formed in the following century the great German Hansa. During this period
the enactments respecting maritime enterprise and commerce consisted, for the most part, of letters-patent granting
privileges to particular unions or places. The Church

(257) raised her voice in vain against commercial intercourse
A with the Mahometans, but was more successful in her efforts to suppress the slave-trade.

258 7. Manufactures, &c. Agriculture flourished during this period under the protection of the Treuga Dei, and derived considerable advantage from the establishment of a free peasant order during the crusades, and the settlement of Netherlanders in north-eastern Germany. The cultivation of the vine was eminently successful in the south of France and Christian Spain, and mining operations in
B Bohemia and Moorish Spain. The importance of manual crafts was greatly augmented by the establishment of guilds, or companies, the freemen of which dwelt in the same street or quarter of the city, and exposed their wares for sale on rows of benches or in halls. The manufacture of cloth flourished chiefly in Flanders, Upper Italy, Germany, and the south of France; that of silk, in Italy; of leather, in Moorish Spain; of paper, in Italy and Spain. The best articles of hardware, especially swords, were produced in the Netherlands, Upper Italy,
C and Moorish Spain. The trade in glass was almost monopolized by Venice. Commercial prosperity was greatly promoted by the establishment of annual fairs, the erection of warehouses and depôts, and the invention by the Lombards of bills of exchange.

Fourth Period.

From the termination of the Crusades to the discovery of America, 1273—1492.

A. The West.

§ 60. *Germany and Switzerland.*

Geographical view of Germany between the years 1300 and 1500.

259 1. The seven *electorates*. *a*. Three archbishoprics:—
D viz. Mainz, Trèves, and Cologne. *b*. Four temporal principalities: viz. 1, the Palatinate (cap. Heidelberg); 2, Saxony (Wittenberg); 3, Bohemia (Prague), with Moravia and Silesia; 4, Brandenburg (Brandenburg).

2. The *Duchies*. *a*. In the west:—1. Lorraine (cap. (259)
Nancy); 2, Lützelburg or Luxemburg (Luxemburg), A
with the county of Saarbrücken; 3, Limburg (Limburg), Brabant (Brussels); 4, Cleves (Cleves), with the counties of Mark, Juliers, and Berg (Düsseldorf); 5, Guelderland. *b*. In the south:—1, Würtemberg (Stuttgart); 2, Bavaria (Munich); 3, Austria (Vienna), with Styria and Carniola; 4, Carinthia. *c*. In the north:—1, Brunswick-Lüneburg; 2, Holstein; 3, Lauenburg; 4, Mecklenburg (Schwerin and Stargard); 5, Pomerania.

3. The *Principalities*—Nassau and Anhalt. B

4. The *Margravate* of Baden.

5. The *Landgravates*—Alsace, Hesse, and Thüringia.

6. The *Burgravate* of Nürnberg.

7. Several *Counties* (Holland, Hennegan, Flanders, Namur, &c.)

8. The *Archbishoprics* (exclusive of the three spiritual electorates), Salzburg, Magdeburg, and Bremen.

9. Several (21) *Bishoprics*.

10. The (95) *free imperial cities*. Of these the most C
considerable were:—*a*. In Franconia—Spires, Worms, Mainz, Frankfort, Wetzlar, Erfurt. *b*. In Bavaria, Nürnberg and Ratisbon. *c*. In Swabia—Ulm and Augsburg. *d*. In Alsace—Strasburg. *e*. In Lorraine—Metz, Trèves, Cologne, Aachen or Aix-la-Chapelle, Düren. *f*. In Saxony—Dortmund, Magdeburg, Bremen, Hamburg, Lübeck.

The kingdom of Burgundy, after its dismemberment, was divided between France and the Dukes of Burgundy.

A. Kings of different houses, 1273—1347.

1. Rudolf of Habsburg (1273—1291). As early as 260
the beginning of the thirteenth century, the right of election D
to the throne of Germany had been transferred from the ancient dukes, or popular leaders, to the great officers of the imperial household: viz. 1, the Archbishop of Mainz, as Arch-Chancellor of the German empire; 2, the Archbishop of Trèves, as Arch-Chancellor of the kingdom of Arles; 3, the Archbishop of Cologne, as Arch-Chancellor of the kingdom of Lombardy; 4, the Count Palatine of the Rhine, as Grand-Sewer; 5, the Duke of Saxony, as Grand

(260) Marshal; 6, the King of Bohemia, as Grand Butler; 7, the
A Margrave of Brandenburg, as Grand Chamberlain. After
the death of Richard of Cornwall, the electors, on the
motion of the Archbishop of Mainz, chose Rudolf of
Habsburg, a nobleman of very moderate political influence.
The ambassador of Bohemia having been
excluded from the hall of election, his master Ottocar
refused to recognize Rudolf; and being placed under the
ban of the empire, was compelled to relinquish his claims
to the sovereignty of Austria, Styria, Carinthia, and Carniola;
and in a second war was defeated and slain on the
B Marchfield (1278). Rudolf granted Carinthia to Count
Mainhard of the Tyrol, and the three remaining principalities
to his sons Albert and Rudolf. Ottocar's son,
Wenceslaus, was allowed to retain Bohemia and Moravia.
From this period the grand object of the German kings
seems to have been to establish hereditary power in their
families.

261 2. Adolphus of Nassau (1291—1298), a cousin
C of the Archbishop of Mainz, was placed on the throne
through the influence of his kinsman, and in order to
strengthen the interests of his family, purchased Thuringia
and Meissen from the Landgrave, Albert the Degenerate,
whose sons, Frederick with the Bitten Cheek, and Diezman,
refused to recognize the compact. In the war which
ensued, such fearful barbarities were perpetrated by
Adolphus, that three of the electors, who were already
disgusted at his breach of faith, declared the throne void,
and chose Albert of Austria, a son of Rudolf I. Adolphus
was killed in the battle of Gelheim, near Worms.

262 3. The choice of the electors, which had fallen on
D Albert I. of Austria (1298—1308), during the lifetime
of Adolphus, was now confirmed by a second election. His
plans for the aggrandizement of his house, and for rendering
the imperial dignity hereditary in the family of Habsburg,
were unsuccessful; nor was he more fortunate in
the revival of his claims to the sovereignty of Thuringia.
The extinction of the ancient royal family in Bohemia
afforded him an opportunity of placing his son Albert on
the throne of that country; but this connection was soon
dissolved by the death of the new sovereign, and the election
of the Duke of Carinthia by the Bohemian people.

The three forest cantons of Switzerland, Schwyz, Uri, (262)
and Unterwalden (which had voluntarily placed them- A
selves under the protection of the empire), having resisted
an attempt of Albert to render them hereditary possessions
of his own family, were grievously oppressed by the imperial governors Herman Gessler of Bruneck and Berin-
ger of Landenberg (?) The conspiracy of Werner
Stauffacher of Schwyz, Walter Fürst (of Attinghausen
in Uri), and Arnold Melchthal of Unterwalden, with
thirty confederates, including the renowned William Tell,
laid the foundation of the Swiss Confederacy (1307).
Gessler was shot dead by an arrow from the bow of Tell, B
and Landenberg defeated by a stratagem, and expelled the
country. In the midst of his preparations for a Swiss campaign, Albert was assassinated in Aargau by his nephew
Duke John (Parricida), from whom he had unjustly withheld his portion of the Habsburg estates.

4. Henry VII., of Luxemburg (1308—1313), a 263
brave and experienced warrior, was chosen by the electors
on the motion of the Archbishop of Mainz. The attempts
of Henry to extend the influence of his family were more
successful than those of his predecessors, Bohemia having
been made a fief of his house by the marriage of his son
John with the heiress of that kingdom. A succession of C
victories enabled him to enter Rome in triumph, and place
on his head the imperial crown, thus restoring the empire,
which had been in a state of abeyance for sixty-two years.
He was on the point of attacking the King of Naples, the
head of the Guelphic party, when death put an end to his
ambitious projects.

5. Louis IV., the Bavarian (1313—1347), and Fre- 264
derick of Austria (1313—1330), the former chosen by D
the Luxemburg, the latter by the Habsburg party. The
house of Habsburg engaged in hostilities with the Swiss,
who defeated Frederick's brother, Duke Leopold of Austria,
at Morgarten (1315), and with the rival king at Mühldorf (1322), where Frederick was defeated and taken
prisoner (by Schweppermann). A reconciliation was afterwards effected (at Trausnitz) between the two kings, who
shared the throne until the death of Frederick, in 1330.
After the battle of Mühldorf, Louis had sent an army into
Italy to assist the Ghibellines against the Guelphs, the

(264) devoted adherents of the pope, and was in consequence
A excommunicated by John XXII. (at Avignon), his kingdom placed under an interdict, and the German crown offered to France. In defiance of this sentence, Louis marched to Milan, where he was crowned King of Lombardy, and then proceeding to Rome, received the imperial crown from the hands of the capitano del popolo, and placed a rival pope, Nicholas V., on the papal throne.
B Finding himself, however, too feeble to maintain his authority in Italy, he returned, after the death of Frederick, to Germany, where the electors, after endeavoring without success to effect a reconciliation between the pope and emperor, assembled the first electoral diet at Rense (from which the King of Bohemia alone was absent), and declared *the empire independent of the popedom*, swearing at the same time to maintain the privileges of the emperor and their own rights. Louis increased the possessions of his family by—1, granting the March of Brandenburg as a fief to his son Lewis, after the extinction of the Ascanian family; 2, annexing the Tyrol to his hereditary dominions, by the marriage of his son Lewis with the Countess Margaret
C Maultasch. In this instance he usurped the authority of the pope, by himself divorcing Margaret from her husband (John Henry of Bohemia), and granting a dispensation for marriage within the third degree of consanguinity; 3, by seizing on the counties of Holland, Zealand, Friesland, and Hennegau, as lapsed fiefs of the empire, and conferring them on his wife (a sister of the Count of Holland, who had died without issue). The unconstitutional annexation of the Tyrol so disgusted the nobles of Germany, that the pope found little difficulty in persuading five of the electors to declare the throne vacant, and elect (in 1346) Charles, son
D of John, king of Bohemia. The Bohemian party, on the death of Louis in the following year, elected Count Günther of Schwartzburg, who contested the possession of the crown until his decease in 1349, when Charles was universally recognized as King of Germany.

B. Kings of the house of Luxemburg.

265 1. Charles IV. (1347—1378). After receiving the

imperial crown, through his ambassador, from the hands of (265)
the pope, Charles devoted his chief attention to the re- A
moval of the evils necessarily attendant on the ill-defined
form of election to the imperial throne which had hitherto
been adopted. For the promotion of this object, he published (at the diets of Nürnberg and Metz, in 1356) a
document termed the *golden bull*, in which the mode
of election, the rights of the electors, and the terms on
which peace was thenceforth to be maintained in Germany,
were definitively settled. By this constitution it was pro- B
vided, that within three months of the death of an emperor,
the Archbishop of Mainz, as arch-chancellor, should sum-
mon the seven electors to hold a new election, the result of
which should be decided by a plurality of votes: that the
coronation of the sovereign should take place at Aachen;
the electors should hold the first rank among the dignitaries of the empire, and their territories be indivisible. All
the other efforts of Charles were directed to the aggrandizement of his hereditary kingdom of Bohemia, to which,
under various pretences, he contrived to annex the March
of Brandenburg, Silesia, the two Lusaces, and a portion of
the Upper Palatinate. In pursuance of his plan, he also C
founded the first German university at Prague (1348),
which soon numbered from 5000 to 7000 students, increased the number of convents and churches, promoted
commerce, agriculture, and mining, effected an improvement in the framing and administration of the laws, and demolished the robber-castles. The funds necessary for these
improvements were obtained by granting extensive privileges to the imperial cities, in return for large sums of
money, or equivalent advantages. The most important of
these privileges were, the right of self-taxation, forming
alliances, and making war and peace; exemption from all
external jurisdiction and inviolability. During his reign, D
the influence of the *aristocratic order* was augmented by
the addition of five new dukedoms, viz. Mecklenburg,
Luxemburg, Bar, Liège or Lüttich, and Berg; and the
number of *confederacies of towns* increased to five, viz. the
German Hansa, now at the summit of its power, the confederacy of the seven Frieslandic maritime districts, the
Rhenish, Swiss, and Swabian confederacies; besides
those of the nobility (the order of St. George, in Swabia;

A the associations of the Lion and Falcon, &c.) Charles
was succeeded by his eldest son, the Roman king.

266 2. *Wenzel*, or *Wenceslaus* (1378—1400), who retained Bohemia and Silesia, to which the dukedom of Luxemburg was added after the death (without issue) of his uncle
Wenzel. His brother Sigismund received Brandenburg as
his portion. The cities and knights having renewed and
strengthened their confederacies, and a union of the three
estates, princes, knights, and cities, having been formed in
Swabia, under the auspices of Count Eberhard of Würtemberg, Wenceslaus, in order to maintain his influence, established a general union in southern Germany, and placed
B himself at its head. A plan was already in progress for
establishing a confederacy of the entire empire, when the disputes between the nobles and cities occasioned a war, which
terminated in the defeat of the cities (near Döffingen and
Worms in 1388). Wenzel now took part with the victorious
nobles, dissolved the confederacies of the cities, and proclaimed a general peace. About the same time the Swiss
confederation (which had been recently strengthened by the
accession of Lucerne, Zürich, Glarus, Zug, and Bern)
defeated their oppressor Leopold of Austria, near *Sempach* (1386), chiefly through the patriotic self-sacrifice of
C *Arnold of Winkelried*. A second victory, obtained
in 1388 over the duke's sons at Näfels, secured to the
Swiss the undisturbed possession of their conquests. The
capricious tyranny exercised by Wenceslaus in Bohemia,
where he constantly resided, and his utter indifference to
the interests of the empire, rendered him an object of
universal contempt. He was at length imprisoned by his
brother Sigismund, and set aside by the three spiritual
electors, who chose the Count Palatine Rupert as his
successor (1400); but the recognition of this prince was
by no means universal.

267 3. *Wenzel* and *Rupert* (1400—1410). An attempt
D to force his way through Italy to Rome ended in defeat,
and lost Rupert the confidence of the nation. On his
return to Germany he endeavored to restore order by
measures of extreme severity, which were vehemently
opposed by a confederacy of nobles and cities. After his
death a double return was made by the electors, one party
choosing Wenzel's brother Sigismund, Margrave of Bran-

denburg, and by marriage King of Hungary; the other (267)
giving their votes to his cousin Jobst (Jodacus), Margrave A
of Moravia. Germany had now three kings; but Jodacus
dying a few months after his election, Sigismund remained
undisputed occupant of the throne.

4. Sigismund, universally recognized from 1410 to 268
1437. The great object of his reign was the extermination of schism. For nearly forty of the seventy years
during which the popes had been resident at Avignon, it
had been the practice of the Roman and French colleges of
cardinals to elect each its own pope. A council held at B
Pisa in 1409, instead of suppressing, increased this irregu-
larity, by deposing both Gregory XII. and Benedict XIII.,
and recognizing Alexander V., and after his death
John XXIII. as sovereign pontiff; but the previously
elected popes refusing to resign, there were now three rival
claimants to the papal throne. For the removal of these C
irregularities, a general council was summoned by the
emperor (and pope ?) to meet at Constance in 1414. The
council was divided, for the convenience of voting, into
four nations—the Italian, French, German, and English, to
which were afterwards added five votes of the Spaniards.
Its three principal objects were (1) *The entire suppression
of schism.* This was attained by the removal of the three
rival popes. Benedict XIII. and John XXIII., who had
fled from Constance, were deposed; Gregory XII. abdi-
cated voluntarily. A new pope, Martin V., was then
elected. 2. *The extirpation of heresy.* The writings of D
the Oxford theologian, John Wickliffe, who had attacked
not only the system of monachism and the supremacy of
the pope, but the doctrine of transubstantiation and other
dogmas of the Church, had been brought to Prague by a
Bohemian nobleman, Hieronymus, or Jerome, Faulfisch
(commonly called Jerome of Prague), who had studied at
Oxford. The Bohemian theologians, who were for the
most part realists, in opposition to the German nominalists,[1]
eagerly embraced doctrines which accorded so well with

[[1] The realists maintained that universal or general ideas of things were *objective, i. e.* independent of the human understanding; the nominalists, that they were *subjective, i. e.* existent only in the mind.—*Note by the Translator.*

(268) their own system. Among their professors was John
A Huss, who wrote against indulgences, notwithstanding the
repeated prohibitions of the Archbishop of Prague and the
pope. Huss appeared before the council, and in direct
violation of a safe conduct granted to him by Sigismund,
was condemned as a heretic, and delivered up to the emperor, who commanded him to be burnt, and charged the
elector palatine with the execution of the sentence. His
friend, Jerome of Prague, at first recanted, but subsequently
withdrew his recantation, and suffered the same punish-
B ment. (3) *A thorough reform of the Church.* This plan
almost entirely miscarried through the dissensions of the
different nations; a few only of the more pressing demands
being met by concordats with each nation separately.
The Hussite war (1420—1436). The disciples of
Huss (who had also adopted the opinion of Professor
Jacob of Meiss, that the Holy Communion ought to be
administered in both kinds to the laity) chose Huss's liege
lord, Nicholas of Hussinecz, to be their leader, and demanded of Wenceslaus permission to celebrate their service
C in all the churches. This being refused, they assembled
on a mountain, to which they gave the name of Tabor,
placed themselves under the command of a brave knight
named John Ziska, and stormed the council-house of
Prague. In the midst of these disorders, Wenceslaus died
of apoplexy, and was succeeded in his hereditary dominions by his brother Sigismund. The opposition of the
Hussites to their new sovereign was even more violent
than it had been to his predecessor, because it was to him
that they attributed the murder of their master, Huss. The
D pope commanded the preaching of a crusade against them;
but the Hussites (although divided after Huss's death into
four parties, viz., the Taborites, Orphans, Horebites, and
Pragueites) maintained their position in the mountains,
until they had extorted from the council of Bäsle permission to receive the Holy Communion in both kinds, it being
at the same time distinctly taught that its reception under
one form was equally efficacious. The embarrassments in
which Sigismund was involved, compelled him not only to
pledge and alienate many of the privileges and possessions
of the empire, but even to sell his own hereditary margra-

vate of Brandenburg, with its electoral dignity, to the Bur- (268)
grave Frederick of Nürnburg, for 400,000 ducats (in the A
year 1415).

C. Kings of the house of Austria (from 1438).

1. Sigismund was succeeded on the German throne, as 269
well as in Bohemia and Hungary, by his son-in-law, Albert of Austria (1438, 1439), who revived the question of the division of Germany into circles, which was again brought forward by his cousin and successor,

2. Frederick III. (1440—1493), who undertook the 270
guardianship of Ladislaus, the infant son of Albert II. B
But the want of unanimity among the nobles rendered such a measure impracticable, and also prevented, at a subsequent period, the accomplishment of a plan for the establishment of an imperial chamber of justice. Proclamations, it is true, were issued from time to time, strictly enjoining peace throughout the empire; but the feuds of her nobles still continued to exhaust the energies of Germany. In C
conjunction with Zürich (which had quarrelled with Schwyz respecting the county of Toggenburg), Frederick at the head of an army of French mercenaries, the Armagnacs, entered Switzerland, in the hope of recovering the Austrian provinces which had been wrested from Leopold, but was compelled, after sustaining two defeats, to confirm the confederates in the possession of the conquered territory. The council of Bäsle, which had attempted to reduce the power and revenues of the papal see, was vehemently resisted by Pope Eugenius IV., who summoned another council to meet at Ferrara. In consequence of this proceeding, the D
council of Bäsle elected a rival pope (Felix V.); but the conclusion of the concordat of Aschaffenburg, or Vienna, by Frederick II. (through his private secretary Æneas Sylvius Piccolomini, afterwards Pius II.) with Pope Nicholas V., the successor of Eugenius IV., restored to the pope most of the rights of which he had been deprived by the council, which soon afterwards dissolved itself, and also persuaded its creature, Felix V., to abdicate. A crusade against the Turks, who had taken Constantinople, and now threatened the western empire, was in vain proclaimed by the pope and emperor. Frederick, the last emperor

(270) who received the imperial crown at Rome, increased his
A hereditary possessions by (1) sharing with his brother Albert the dukedom of Austria, vacant by the death of the young Ladislaus (son of Albert II.). After his brother's death, Frederick became sole duke of Austria; but the Bohemians and Hungarians elected two native kings, the former George Podiebrad, and the latter Matthias Corvinus, both of whom successfully resisted the attempts of the emperor to reduce them to submission. In the year 1485, Corvinus took possession of Austria, which he
B retained until his death (in 1490). 2. But the most important acquisition of territory was that of the Netherlands and Burgundy, by the marriage of his son Maximilian with Mary, daughter of Charles the Bold, duke of Burgundy (1477). The possession of these territories was successfully maintained by Maximilian in a war with France.

§ 61. *The States of Italy.*

A. In Upper Italy.

271 4. Venice, which had been raised by the crusades to
C the rank of a first-rate commercial and naval power, and possessed most of the islands and maritime towns of the Byzantine empire, was engaged for 125 years in a war with Genoa (1256—1381) respecting the trade of the Black Sea. At the end of that period a peace was concluded at Turin, on terms advantageous to Venice. The most palmy days of the republic were in the first half of the fifteenth century, when a monopoly of the Indian trade, by way of Egypt, was secured to her by a treaty with the Sultan of Egypt, an increase of territory obtained in Upper Italy and Dalmatia (partly by treaties and partly by conquest), and the islands of Corfu aud Cyprus added to her
D possessions. Most of these Greek dominions were afterwards wrested from them by the Turks; and the discovery of a new passage to the East Indies destroyed their monopoly of the Indian trade, and completed their ruin. The sovereign authority was in the hands of a *great council* of 480 members, who at first were chosen annually by the people out of the entire body of citizens, but at a later period (1297) the right of sitting in the council being con-

fined to the actual members and their families, an hereditary A
aristocracy was created.

2. In Milan, the struggle between the Ghibelline no- 272
bles, headed by the family of Visconti, and the Guelphic
burghers, supported by the family of Della Torre, was
terminated by Henry VII., who expelled the Torre, and
nominated Matteo Visconti imperial lieutenant (vicar) of
Milan (1310). The conquest of several neighboring cities
enabled Visconti to increase the possessions of his house,
which under John Galeazzo Visconti (who obtained the
grant of an hereditary dukedom from Wenceslaus) was
owner of almost the whole of Upper Italy. After the B
extinction of the male line of the Visconti, the supreme
authority was conferred on Francesco Sforza, a mercenary
soldier in the Milanese service, who made the dukedom
hereditary in his family.

3. The republic of Genoa acquired some maritime 273
towns and considerable commercial advantages in consequence of the restoration of the Greek empire. The
conclusion of a struggle of 200 years with Pisa, placed at C
their disposal the greater part of Corsica and Sardinia;
but their long war with Venice, and still more their own
intestine feuds, so weakened them, that they were compelled to submit sometimes to Milanese, sometimes to
French domination.

B. In Central Italy.

1. In Florence the people, or guilds, after a long strug- 274
gle with the nobles, obtained the ascendency, conquered the
neighboring districts, and divided themselves into three
classes, *viz.* higher and lower guilds, and commons, *i. e.*
persons not belonging to any guild. The members of the D
higher guilds were, generally speaking, bankers; hence
arose an aristocracy of wealth, headed in the fifteenth century by the rich and powerful family of the Medici. The foundation of their importance was laid by John di Medici, the wealthiest banker of Florence. His son Cosmo (1429—1464) was driven into exile by the jealousy of the other bankers, but within a year he was recalled, and honored with the title of father of his country, a distinction richly merited by his political sagacity and liberal

(274) patronage of the fine arts. Not only in Florence and
A Tuscany, but in Umbria, Venice, and even in Jerusalem,
the most magnificent works of architecture, sculpture, and
painting, bore witness to his exquisite taste. His son
Peter died soon after his father (1469), to whom he bore
little resemblance, and was succeeded by Lorenzo, whose
munificent patronage of the arts and sciences elevated
Florence to the rank of a second Athens (1469—1492).

275 2. States of the Church. During the residence of
B the popes at Avignon (1305—1376) several cities, principally in the March of Ancona, threw off the papal yoke, and placed themselves under the control of tyrants. Even Rome itself was distracted by frequent revolutions (in one of which a plebeian named Cola Rienzi assumed the title of tribune), and by the feuds of the Colonna (Ghibellines) and Ursini (Guelphs). It was not until the end of this period that the States of the Church were re-united. Avignon was added to them by purchase in 1348.

C. In Lower Italy.

276 1. In Naples, the house of Anjou occupied the throne
C until 1442, when the country was conquered by Alfonso V. of Arragon, who already possessed Sicily. At his death Alfonso bequeathed Naples, as a separate kingdom, to his natural son Ferdinand, whose posterity continued to reign until the year 1504.

277 2. Sicily remained a distinct kingdom under the sons of Peter III. of Arragon and their successors, until the extinction of the family, when it was united to Arragon.

§ 62. *France.*

A. Under the last Capets (1270—1328).

278 10. Philip III. (1270—1285), after the death of his
D father, withdrew his army from Tunis, married his son Philip to Johanna, heiress of Navarre, and died on his return from an unsuccessful expedition against Arragon.

279 11. Philip IV., Le Bel (1285—1314), king also of Navarre, in right of his wife Johanna. This monarch, the distinguishing features of whose character were ambition,

cunning, avarice, and cruelty, obtained possession of Gui- (279)
enne (which he afterwards restored) during a war with A
England, occasioned by a quarrel between some English
and French sailors. A successful insurrection of the Flemings, at that time allies of England, compelled him to
abandon Flanders, which had also fallen into his hands.
Pope Boniface VIII., who had excommunicated Philip for
extorting contributions from the clergy for the prosecution
of this war, was seized by the king's servants, and died of
grief. The next pope but one, Clement V. (Archbishop
of Bourdeaux), established himself at Avignon, which continued to be the papal residence from 1305 to 1376. A B
cruel persecution was carried on against the Knights Templars, whose wealth had excited the cupidity of Philip.
After a long but most unfair trial, many members of the
order were condemned to be burnt, on the evidence of
perjured witnesses, or after confessions extorted by the
rack. The order itself was entirely suppressed by Pope
Clement V. (at the council of Vienne).

After the death of Philip IV. the crown was worn in 280
rapid succession by his three sons, Louis X., Philip V. C
(who persuaded the estates of his kingdom to pass an act
excluding females from the throne), and Charles IV., who
died without male issue, and was succeeded by his cousin,
Philip of Valois. Navarre was settled on Johanna, daughter of Louis X., and was not re-united to France until the
accession of the Bourbons in 1589.

B. Under kings of the house of Valois

(1328—1589).

281
D

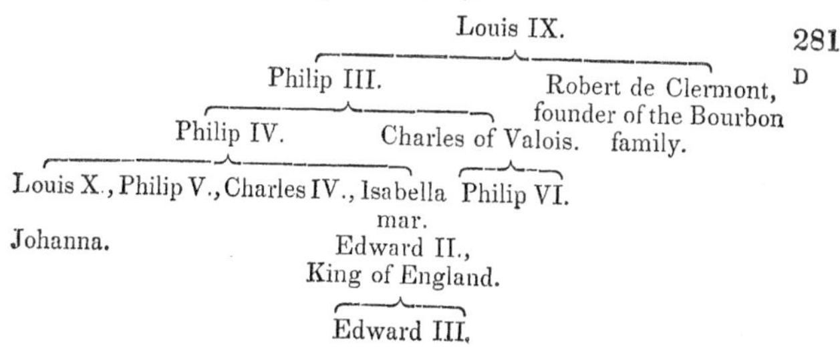

282 I. Philip VI. (1328—1350). The claims to the
A throne of France advanced by Edward III., as grandson of Philip IV., on the ground that his mother alone, and not her male issue, was excluded from the succession, occasioned *a war between England and France, which lasted more than a hundred years* (1339—1453). Edward III. (who had assumed the title of King of France) formed an alliance with the Flemings, under Artevelde, a brewer of Ghent, and the Count of Artois, who had been expelled from France for forgery, and obtained a splendid naval
B victory off Sluys (1340); then landed in Normandy with his son, Edward the Black Prince, defeated the French at Cressy (1346), and took Calais, which was entirely colonized by the English, and remained in their possession until the year 1558. Philip added Dauphiné, Champagne, and Brie, to the possessions of the French crown. The right of voting grants of the public money was conceded by him to the estates of the realm. He died during an armistice with England.

283 2. John the Good (1350—1364) was defeated by
C the Black Prince at Maupertuis, near Poitiers (1356), where he was taken prisoner with his youngest son Philip, and conveyed to London. During his captivity a democratic party was formed at Paris by Marcel, president of the Parisian guild of merchants, whilst almost at the same time a disturbance broke out in the north of France, among the peasants (Jaquerie), who were grievously oppressed by the nobles. After defeating these undisciplined bands, the nobles tendered their services to Prince Charles, who obtained quiet possession of Paris after the assassination
D of Marcel. A peace was concluded at Bretigny (near Chartres), on the following terms,—Edward III. received Guienne, Poitou, Calais, &c., as *souverain* possessions, in return for his renunciation of the title of King of France, and of the provinces formerly held by England. On the other hand, King John agreed to pay a considerable ransom for his liberation: but this not being forthcoming, he returned to London, where he died a prisoner, after bestowing the vacant dukedom of Burgundy on his youngest son, Philip the Hardy.

284 3. Charles V., the Wise (1364—1380). His distinguished general, Bertrand du Guesclin, cleared the kingdom

of marauding bands of mercenaries, whom he led into Spain, (284)
where a disputed succession to the Castilian throne had A
occasioned a civil war. The same general, in a war which
soon afterwards broke out between France and England,
wrested from the English crown all its possessions in France
except Calais and a part of Guienne.

4. Charles VI. (1380—1422) at first, on account of 285
his minority, and afterwards of his imbecility,[1] was placed B
under the guardianship of his uncles the Dukes of Berry
and Burgundy, whose right to this office was vehemently
contested by the Duke of Orleans, brother to the king.
These conflicting claims occasioned the formation of two
parties, one of which sided with Burgundy, whilst the other
(headed by the Compte d'Armagnac) supported the Duke of
Orleans. After the assassination of Orleans, a bloody civil
war raged between the two factions, during which the
English again entered France and gained the victory of
Azincourt (1415). The Burgundian party obtained pos- C
session of the city of Paris, which they held until the death
of the Duke of Burgundy, who was assassinated by the
attendants of the Dauphin, on the bridge of Montereau (on
the Yonne). His son, Philip the Good, of Burgundy, implored the assistance of Henry V. of England, who entered
Paris, married Catherine, daughter of Charles VI., and was
proclaimed heir-presumptive to the throne of France; but
died before Charles, leaving an infant son. Two months
after his decease Charles died also, and was succeeded by
the Dauphin as

5. Charles VII. (1422—1461), whilst at the same 286
time Henry VI. of England was proclaimed king in the north D
of France. After sustaining two defeats, Charles was compelled to cross the Loire, and the city of Orleans was on the
eve of surrendering to the English, when a peasant girl
named *Joan of Arc, the Maid of Orleans*, a native of Dom
Remy, near Vaucouleurs, in Champagne, placed herself at
the head of the French army, and compelled the English to
raise the siege (1429). Then she conducted Charles VII.
in triumph to the city of Rheims, where he was crowned;
but falling (1430) into the hands of her enemies during

[1] Cards were invented, it is said, for the amusement of Charles VI.

(286) the siege of Compiegne, she was tried for witchcraft, and
A burnt at Rouen, on the 30th of May, 1431. A reconciliation was effected between the Duke of Burgundy and Charles VII., the city of Paris surrendering to the king, whilst the English, deprived of Normandy and Guienne, were compelled, after a fruitless struggle, to content themselves with the possession of Calais and the Channel Islands. The war was terminated, without any formal conclusion of peace, in consequence of the struggles between the factions of the red and white roses in England. The organization of some companies of cavalry, and of the francs-archers, or free sharpshooters, as a body of infantry,
B laid the foundation of a standing army. The influence exercised over the mind of the king by his mistress, Agnes Sorel, occasioned an estrangement between Charles and the Dauphin, who sought an asylum at the court of the Duke of Burgundy, after an unsuccessful attempt to deprive his father of the crown.

287 6. Louis XI. (1461—1483) attempted to establish the absolute power of the crown by the following measures: 1. All the servants of his father were dismissed, and their places supplied by persons who were indebted for their advancement solely to Louis himself. 2. The estates of the different provinces were convoked instead of the great council of estates of the realm. 3. Measures were adopted for humbling the princes of the blood, and two great vassals
C of the crown, the Dukes of Burgundy and Brittany. The result of this policy was the formation of a league, termed "la ligue du bien public," between the disgraced ministers of the crown and the two dukes, who compelled the king, after an indecisive battle at Montlheri, to make important concessions, which he afterwards refused to ratify. The league was soon afterwards dissolved through the intrigues of Louis, by whom the Liegeois were urged to make
D repeated incursions into the Burgundian territory. During one of these inroads, Louis, who had rashly visited the Duke of Burgundy at Peronne, was detained a prisoner, and only released on condition of granting several important immunities to his powerful vassal. In revenge, Louis, during the absence of Charles the Bold (who was engaged, as protector of the Archbishop of Cologne, in reducing the revolted city of Neuss), stirred up the inhabitants of Lor-

raine and the Swiss to make war on Burgundy. After re- (287)
ducing Lorraine, Charles marched into Switzerland, where A
he was defeated at Granson and Murten, in 1476.
The Duke of Lorraine, who had been deprived of his
dominions, was restored by the Swiss; and Charles, in an
attempt to avenge this insult, lost his life before Nancy
in 1477. The dukedom of Burgundy lapsed, as a void B
male fief, to the crown of France; but the numerous German seignories which had been incorporated with Burgundy by marriage, purchase, and inheritance, and even some of the smaller French fiefs, were afterwards acquired by Austria, through the marriage of the Archduke Maximilian with Mary of Burgundy, daughter and sole heiress of Charles the Bold. The death of his brother enabled Louis to annex Guienne and Normandy to France; and when the house of Anjou became extinct, he inherited Anjou, Provence, and Maine, together with the claims of that family to the Neapolitan throne. His son,

7. Charles VIII. (1483—1498) conquered Naples, 288
but was compelled to abandon his conquest by the united C
forces of the pope, the Emperor Maximilian, Ferdinand the Catholic, the Duke of Milan, and the Republic of Venice. With him expired the elder line of the house of Valois.

§ 63. *England and Scotland.*

A. Kings of the house of Plantagenet.

5. Edward I. (1272—1307) annexed Wales to the 289
English crown. His son Edward assumed the title of D
Prince of Wales, which has ever since been borne by the heir-apparent. The extinction of the dynasty of the house of Kenneth (1286) was followed by the disputes of thirteen claimants to the Scottish throne, among whom the most powerful were Balliol and Bruce. Edward, as feudal sovereign of Scotland, decided this dispute by placing John Balliol on the throne; but the new king immediately renounced his allegiance to the crown of England, and was deposed by Edward, who subdued Scotland, but died during a campaign against Robert Bruce, who had been crowned by the insurgent Scots.

(289) 6. Edward II. (1307—1327), son-in-law of Philip IV.
A of France. The feeble government of this monarch, who
was a mere tool in the hands of unworthy favorites,
encouraged the nobles to resist the authority of the crown,
whilst at the same time the Scotch not only maintained
their independence, but even made frequent incursions into
England, and at length compelled the king to grant an
armistice. His wife Isabella, who had visited France, in
the hope of putting an end to a war which had broken out
between Edward and her brother Charles IV., conspired
with her paramour Mortimer against the unfortunate king,
and having landed in England at the head of some Netherlandish troops, and gained over a majority of the nobles
and the rabble of London, she compelled the parliament
to depose Edward (who was soon afterwards brutally
murdered) and to proclaim his son

290 7. Edward III. (1327—1337), who emancipated him-
B self from all control by hanging Mortimer, and banishing
his mother from court. After the death of the Scotch
king, Robert Bruce († 1329), his son David was called to
the throne, but was soon compelled by the English to
abdicate in favor of Edward Balliol, who consented to
recognize the supremacy of Edward III. The disputes
respecting the right to the Scottish throne continued until
C the accession of the Stuarts in 1371. The frequent pecuniary embarrassments, occasioned by the expenses of a war
with France, compelled Edward to convoke his parliament
seventy times. During this reign the great council of the
nation was first divided into the Upper House (prelates
and barons), and the Lower (inferior nobles and representatives of cities).

291 8. Richard II. (1377—1399), son of the Black
D Prince, suppressed an insurrection of the people, occasioned by the oppressive system of taxation; but afterwards became the slave of unworthy favorites, and was
deprived of almost all his authority by his uncle the Duke
of Gloucester and a commission of regency. The reins of
government were again placed in his hands by the parliament, and a second time wrested from him by Henry,
duke of Lancaster (a grandson of Edward III., who
had been banished by Richard). The unfortunate king

was taken prisoner, and compelled by the parliament to (291)
abdicate in favor of his rival. A

B. Three kings of the house of Lancaster, *a collateral branch of the house of Plantagenet.*

(1399—1461.)

1. Henry IV. (1399—1413.) His reign was dis- 292
turbed by repeated conspiracies, all of which were rendered B
abortive by the courage and sagacity of the king. His brave son,

2. Henry V., obtained a brilliant victory over the 293
French at Agincourt, and conquered Normandy. He married the daughter of Charles VI., and was nominated successor to the French throne after the death of his father-in-law, but died before him, and was succeeded by his infant son.

294 A

The houses of Lancaster and York.

Edward III.

- Edward, the Black Prince.
  - Richard II.
- Lionel, duke of Clarence.
  - Anne Mortimer, wife of Richard, earl of Cambridge.
- John, duke of Lancaster.
  - Henry IV.
    - Henry V. mar. Catherine. of France.
      - Henry VI.
        - Edward, prince of Wales.
  - John.
    - John.
      - Margaret of Lancaster, mar. Edmund Tudor.
        - Henry VII. m. Elizabeth,
- Edmund, duke of York.
  - Edmund, duke of York.
  - Richard, earl of Cambridge.
    - Richard, duke of York.
      - Edward IV.
        - Elizabeth, Edward V.
      - George, duke of Clarence.
      - Richard, duke of Gloucester, afterwards Richard III.

3. Henry VI. (1422—1461), who assumed the title 295
of King of France, but was soon deprived of all his pos- A
sessions in that country, with the exception of Calais and the Channel Islands. These losses, added to the disgust occasioned by the conduct of the king's favorites, produced an opposition in parliament, headed by his cousin, Richard duke of York, who claimed the crown as a descendant of the *second* son of Edward III., the house of Lancaster tracing its descent from the *third*. This dispute occasioned the wars of the red (Lancaster) and white (York) roses. Richard was nominated protector during the insanity of the king, but refused to resign the office
on his recovery. Two battles were then fought (at St. B
Alban's in 1455, and Northampton in 1460), in each of which the king was taken prisoner, but released; and finally, he agreed to abdicate in favor of Richard. The war having been renewed by the queen, Margaret of Anjou, Richard was slain in the battle of Wakefield. His son Edward then assumed the title of king, and defeated the Lancastrian party near Towton.

C. Three kings of the house of York.

(1461—1485.)

1. Edward IV. (1461—1483.) After an ineffectual 296
attempt to replace her husband on the throne by means of C
French troops, Margaret formed an alliance with the Earl of Warwick (who had been ill-treated by Edward, and had taken refuge in France), and with his son-in-law, the Duke of Clarence. Warwick returned to England, deposed Edward, and reseated Henry on the throne (1470); but in the following year, Edward, who was supported by his brother-in-law, Charles the Bold, of Burgundy, reappeared in England, and defeated the forces of Warwick and Margaret. Henry VI. died suddenly in the Tower (possibly by the dagger of Richard, duke of Gloucester), and the house of Lancaster became extinct, with the exception of Henry Tudor, who fled to Brittany.

2. Edward V. (1483), soon after his father's death, 297
was set aside by his guardian and uncle, Richard of Glou- D
cester, who ascended the throne as

298 3. Richard III. (1483—1485.) In the year 1485 he
A was slain at the battle of Bosworth, and Henry Tudor (earl of Richmond) as King Henry VII., reconciled the conflicting claims of the two houses, by a marriage with Elizabeth of York.

§ 64. *The Pyrenæan Peninsula.*

299 The only possession which still remained (in 1237) in the hands of the Moors, was the little kingdom of Granāda, generally dependent on Castile, but enjoying considerable political, agricultural, and commercial prosperity, until its union with Castile (in consequence of a disputed succession) in 1492.

300 The two Christian kingdoms—*Arragon* (to which
B Sardinia, and afterwards Sicily, and, for a short time, Naples, were annexed, and which was partly governed by a peculiar magistracy (the Justitia), acting as a mediator between the king and the estates of his realm) and *Castile*, were united in 1479, by the marriage of Ferdinand of Arragon with Isabella, the heiress of Castile. Each kingdom retained the constitution by which it had been governed previously to the union. *Granada* was added in 1492. *Navarre*, which had been annexed at an early period to France, was settled in 1316 on Johanna, daughter of Louis X., and became thenceforward a separate independent
C kingdom. In *Portugal*, after the extinction of the legitimate Burgundian line in 1383, a new dynasty was founded by John I., a natural son of Peter I. In the fifteenth century Madeira, the Azores, the Cape Verd Islands, and the coast of Guinea, were discovered by Henry the Voyager (third son of John I.). In 1486, Bartholomew Diaz reached the cabo tormentoso, afterwards named by John II. cabo de bonna esperanza (Cape of Good Hope).

B. The East.

§ 65. *The Byzantine empire under the Palæolŏgi.*

(1261—1453.)

301 Under the dynasty of the Palæolŏgi, the fragments of the
D ancient Byzantine empire were re-united, with the exception

of a few small independent seignories, which had been (301)
established by the Latin knights; but the government of A
sovereigns, of whom the majority were feeble-minded and
incapable, and whose administration was frequently embar-
rassed by civil wars, ecclesiastical disputes, and court-
intrigues, opposed but an ineffectual barrier to the advancing tide of Ottoman encroachment. An unsuccessful
attempt was made to obtain assistance from the West, by a
union of the Greek and Latin Churches, and the empire
was now on the verge of destruction, when an invasion of
the Mongols withheld their enemies for a time; but the
respite was of short duration, for on the 29th of May,
1453, Constantinople, after a short siege, surrendered to
Mohammed II. The empire, also, of Trebizond, and all B
the smaller Greek states in the islands, the Morea, Epirus,
and Attica, fell into the hands of the conqueror. The
kingdom of Cyprus alone became a dependency of the republic of Venice.

§ 66. *The Osmans.*

An independent empire was founded in the fourteenth 302
century on the ruins of the Seldschuk kingdom of Iconium, C
by Osman, emir of a nomadic tribe. Its boundaries,
which at first comprehended only Bithynia, were rapidly
extended, until they embraced the greater part of Asia
Minor and Thrace. Adrianople became the imperial residence in 1365. The Osmans had already compelled
Macedonia, Bulgaria, Wallachia, and Moldavia, to acknowledge their supremacy, and were advancing into
Styria, after a victory over Sigismund, king of Hungary,
near Nicopolis in 1396, when they were themselves defeated in the East by the great Mongol conqueror, Timur D
Lenk (Tamerlane). Notwithstanding, however, this check,
the power of the Osmans was speedily re-established, and
in the year 1453, Mohammed II. became master of the
Byzantine empire and the empire of Trebizond (see § 65),
Servia, Wallachia, Bosnia, Albania, and several settlements
of the Genoese on the Black Sea.

§ 67. *The Mongols.*

The Mongols became again a formidable power under 303
Timur Lenk, or Tamerlane, a descendant of Dschingis

(303) Khan (1369—1405), who founded a kingdom at Samar-
A cand, in great Bucharia, and thence carried on successful wars against Persia, a portion of India, and Natolia; sacked Moscow and Asof in Russia, and died on an expedition against the Chinese. After his death, this mighty empire, which extended from the wall of China and the Ganges to the shores of the Mediterranean, was split into a number of petty principalities.

C. The north-east of Europe.

§ 68. *Scandinavia.*

304 Denmark, at the commencement of this period, was
B divided (among the sons of Eric IV.) into several principalities, which were re-united by Waldemar III., after the loss of Esthonia. Margaret, daughter of this sovereign, married Haco VIII., King of Norway, and after the deaths of her father and husband, governed the two kingdoms as guardian of her son Olaf, whose early decease
C placed both Denmark and Norway at her absolute disposal. In Sweden, which at an earlier period had been united to Norway (from 1319 to 1365), the estates, disgusted at the avarice of their king (Albert, a prince of Mecklenburg), offered the crown to Margaret of Denmark. Thus the three Scandinavian kingdoms of Sweden, Denmark, and Norway, were united (by the treaty of Calmar, 1397) under one sovereign, each, nevertheless, retaining its own parliament and code of laws. Margaret was succeeded by Eric of Pomerania, her sister's grandson, and his
D nephew Christopher of Bavaria. The throne of Denmark and Norway was then filled by Christian I. (of the house of Oldenburg), who had married Christopher's widow. Schleswig and Holstein were soon added by inheritance to the possessions of the new royal house, which was either not recognized at all in Sweden, or compelled to intrust the administration of that kingdom to a native viceroy, or president.

§ 69. *Russia.*

305 Russia, where the grand principality of Wladimir (which comprised also Novgorod) was united to Moskwa, or Moscow, in 1328, was deprived by the Lithuanians and Poles

(during the period of its dependence on the Mongol empire) (305)
of several of its western provinces, such as Volhynia, Kiev, A
Podolia, Red and White Russia; but after several long and bloody struggles (during which a brilliant victory was obtained on the Don, by Demetrius Donski, and successful resistance was offered to the attacks of Timur), the Russians under Ivan the Great emancipated themselves from the tyranny of the (so called) golden Horde in Kaptschak. The Khanate of Kaptschak was then divided into four kingdoms (Crim, Astrachan, Kasan, and Turan). Ivan the B
Great, the real founder of the Russian empire, extended his dominions to the borders of Lithuania, exacted tribute from the Khanate of Kasan, laid the foundation of an improved constitution, and was the first Russian sovereign who assumed the title of Czar.

§ 70. *Poland.*

1. Under the Piasts (840—1386), who re-assumed the 306
title of king in 1320, Great Poland (on the Lower Warthe), C
and Little Poland (on the Upper Vistula, or Cracow and Sendomir) were united, Cracow being the place appointed for the coronation of the Polish kings. Casimir the Great, the last king of the Piast male line, was deprived of Silesia by Bohemia, and of Pomerella by the knights of the Teutonic order; but on the other hand, Galicia, or Red Russia, Podolia, and the feudal sovereignty of Masovia, were acquired by this monarch, who greatly improved the condition of his people by the establishment of a supreme court of justice and a university at Cracow, and by a succession of benefits conferred on the citizen and peasant estates (hence his title of the "peasant's king"). Casimir was succeeded by his sister's son, Lewis the Great, king of Hungary, who secured the succession for one of his daughters, by granting various important privileges to the nobility. Lithuania, which since the Mongol invasion had D
become an independent government, was re-united to Poland by the marriage of Hedwig (youngest daughter of the king of Poland) to Jagello, duke of Lithuania, who was baptized (with all his subjects), and assumed the name of Wladislaw II.

2. Under the descendants of Jagello (1386—

307 1572), Wladislaw II. was compelled to recognize the right
A of election claimed by the estates, and to allow the Lithuanians grand dukes of their own, subject to the supremacy
of the Polish crown (— 1502). In the year **1410** Wladislaw defeated the Teutonic order at Tannenberg, and
obtained possession (by the peace of Thorn) of Samogitia,
to which by a second peace, concluded at the same place
(in 1466), Casimir II. added West Prussia, and the feudal
sovereignty of East Prussia. Thus the kingdom of Poland
extended from the Black Sea to the Baltic.

§ 71. *Prussia under the Teutonic order.*

308 The Teutonic order, which since the year 1309 had
B been settled at Marienburg, had acquired, partly by conquest and partly by purchase, Pomerella, Esthonia, Neu-
mark, and Samogitia, so that its empire at last comprehended the entire coast of the Baltic from Dantzic to
Narva, with the islands of Gothland and Oesel. The
golden period of this dynasty was from **1351** to **1382**, under the Grand Master Winrich von Kniprode; but a single
defeat at Tannenberg, in **1419** (which terminated the
war between the Lithuanians and Poles), completely shattered its power, although the brave defence of Marienburg,
by Henry von Plauen, obtained for it (at the peace of
Thorn, in **1411**, see § 70) more favorable terms than could
C reasonably have been anticipated. The insufferable
tyranny of the order was soon afterwards resisted by a
confederacy of nobles and cities (at Marienwerder), which
publicly repudiated its authority, and sought the protection
of Poland. After a twelve years' war with the confederation and Poland, a second peace was concluded at Thorn
in **1466**, the order ceding Western Prussia to Poland, and
D consenting to hold Eastern Prussia as a Polish fief. The
head-quarters of the order were transferred to Königsberg.
Until the year 1513 Livonia, Esthonia, and Courland,
were governed by the provincial grand master of the Order of the Sword, subject to the supreme authority of the
Teutonic order.

§ 72. *Hungary.*

309 Scarcely had Hungary (including Transylvania, Scla-
vonia, Croatia, and Bosnia) begun to recover from the

effects of the Mongol invasions, when the extinction of (309)
the Arpad dynasty occasioned fresh struggles, which ter- A
minated at length in the accession of a prince of the House of Anjou, Charles Robert (1308—1342), a great-grandson of Stephen V., whose vigorous government, followed by the wise administration of his son Lewis the Great, raised Hungary to a position which she had never before occupied. *Lewis the Great* (1342—1382), by the acquisition of Dalmatia, the feudal supremacy of Servia, Bulgaria, Wallachia, and Moldavia, and finally of the crown of Poland (as nephew and heir of Casimir III.), became the most powerful monarch of
Europe. He was succeeded, after a short struggle be- B
tween rival candidates, by his son-in-law Sigismund, a prince of the house of Luxemburg (1387—1437), who was too feeble either to maintain the prerogative of the crown against rebels at home, or to protect the kingdom from foreign enemies. The short reigns of his son-in-law Albert of Austria, and the King of Poland, were followed by the accession of Albert's posthumous son Ladislaus, who was succeeded by a native prince, *Matthias Corvinus* (son of the brave Hunyad, regent of the kingdom
during Albert's minority). His violation of the conditions C
to which he had solemnly pledged himself at his election so offended the electors, that they offered the crown to the Emperor Frederick III.; but the claims of this new candidate were successfully resisted by Matthias, whose victories over the Osmans, Bohemians, and the emperor, procured for himself and his kingdom a reputation, which was maintained by the establishment of a standing army, the encouragement which he afforded to artists and learned men, and the great improvement effected (though not without the imposition of heavy taxes) in every branch of the administration.

§ 73. *Religion, Arts, Sciences, &c., during the Fourth Period.*

1. The Church. Lithuania, the last heathen nation of 310
Europe, had embraced, as we have seen, the Christian D
religion, and discoveries on the western coast of Africa were preparing the way for its reception in a quarter of the globe still more barbarous. During this period the influ-

(310) ence of the papacy, although never lost, was grievously
A endangered by the disputes of the pope with Philip IV. of France and Louis the Bavarian, as well as by the teaching of Wickliffe and Huss, and more than all, by the seventy years' residence of the popes at Avignon, the forty years' schism, and the contest between the council of Bâsle and Eugene IV. The great object of that council, as well as of the council of Constance, had been the limitation of the papal power; but the hopes of ecclesiastical reform, which thousands had cherished at the opening of the latter, had vanished long before the termination of its session. A terrible pestilence, termed the "Black Death," which devastated western Europe in the fourteenth century, occasioned the formation of societies of both sexes for the care
B of the sick and the burial of the dead. Renewed attempts to re-unite the Greek and Latin churches were successful to a certain extent, a convention having been executed by representatives of the two parties, at a synod held at Florence; but the proceedings of the synod were never recognized either by the people, or those of the clergy who remained at Constantinople.

311 2. Political Constitution. The spirit of political
C combination, which had been awakened in the preceding century, continued to spread, particularly in Germany, where confederacies of cities, nobles, &c., manifested the extent of its influence. In France, the power of the king was steadily augmented by the acquisition of crown lands, whilst the reverse was the case in Germany, where the narrow-minded personal ambition of the emperors led them to seek the aggrandizement of their own families at the expense of the imperial prerogative, which was weakened by their reckless grants of immunities and revenues to cities and nobles, in return for some personal benefit.
D By this policy the German empire was split into a number of petty principalities, forming a sort of federal republic, with an elective president at its head. In Italy, a system of political counterpoise was maintained, chiefly by means of Florence, which occupied a middle position between the commonwealth of the north (Venice and Milan), and the absolute monarchies of the south (States of the Church and Naples). The constitution of the east was a military despotism. At this period the most remarkable pecu-

liarity in the administration of justice, was the existence of (311)
the Free Court, or *Vehmgericht* of Westphalia, a dark and A
mysterious tribunal, which judged in secret, and soon spread over the whole of Germany. The origin, character, limits, and regulations of this institution, are involved in impenetrable obscurity.

3. In the Sciences, three causes united to produce 312
new life: (1) the rapid *increase* in the *number of universities*, of which more than fifty were founded at this period (in Germany: Prague, 1348; Vienna, 1365; Heidelberg, 1386; Cologne, 1388; Erfurt; and in the fifteenth century, Würtzburg, Leipzic, Rostock, Greifswalde, Freiburg, Trèves, Ingoldstadt, and Mainz): (2) *the revival of the*
study of classical literature. The attempted reconciliation B
between the Eastern and Western Churches, and still more, the conquest of the Byzantine empire by the Turks, had inundated Italy with a host of learned Greeks, who brought with them their literary treasures, and were installed as professors of their native language at the universities, or found an honorable asylum in the palaces of the Medici
and other noble Italian families. Thus a better taste in C
literature was introduced and propagated through the exertions of these illustrious foreigners and their native disciples, Joh. Boccaccio, Laurentius Valla, Marcilius Ficinus, &c.; and the German writers, Agricola and Reuchlin. At the same time academies, or learned societies (*e.g.* that of the Platonic philosophy founded at Florence, by Cosmo di Medici); new schools and libraries (the Vatican, &c.), were established in different parts of Europe: (3) the invention of printing, by John Gänsfleisch, of Sulgeloch (Sorgenloch), commonly called Gutenberg of Mainz, who had already tried many experiments, during a sojourn of twenty [?] years at Strasburg, and on his return (1445) to his native town, brought his plans to perfection, with the assistance of Peter Schöffer, and a rich goldsmith
named John Fust (1450). The first printed book was Gu- D
tenberg's Latin Bible (finished in 1456). In the scholastic Aristotelic philosophy (which was not superseded by the new Platonic philosophy until the end of the mediæval period), the distinction continued to exist between the Realists (who maintained that general ideas were *things*), and the Nominalists (who contended that they were only

(312) *words*). Both these schools were opposed to the Mystics.
A The use of the vernacular language in historical writing became more common. Geographical science was promoted by the travels of missionaries, ambassadors, and merchants, and the discoveries of the Portuguese; the study of mathematics and medicine by translations of the best Greek treatises on those subjects.

313 4. Art. (*a*) *Poetry* flourished most in Italy, where the
B Florentine Dante Alighieri (†1321) won for himself the title of "Father of Italian poetry," by the publication of his "Divina Commedia" (Wanderings in Heaven, Hell, and Purgatory). The sonnets of Francesco Petrarca (Petrarch), on Laura of Sade (†1374), and the Decamerone of Giovanni Boccaccio (†1375), are also works of no ordinary merit. The Tuscan dialect, in which Boccaccio wrote, became thenceforward the language of Italian literature. In Germany, as in France, the drama owed its development to the mysteries and Shrovetide mummeries
C (as they were called) of the Romish Church. The sermons of John Tauler are the earliest attempt at German prose composition. The father of English poetry was Geoffrey Chaucer (†1400). (*b*) *Architecture.* In addition to the Gothic, which was occupied partly in completing the works commenced in the preceding century, and partly in constructing new edifices (the church of St. Mary, at Nürnburg; the cathedrals of Ulm, Antwerp, and Milan), there arose in Italy a new school, which professed to copy the monuments of classical antiquity. The best architects in this style were at Pisa and Florence.
D (*c*) *Painting* was brought to great perfection (*a*) in Italy by the Tuscan or Florentine school (which numbered among its professors Leonardo da Vinci (†1519), the inventor of perspective), as well as by the Roman and other schools: (*b*) in Germany, by the earlier Cologne (Meister Wilhelm) and Flemish schools (the two brothers van Eyck). (*d*) *Sculpture* in clay, bronze, and marble (by Donato of Florence and others) emulated the perfection of ancient art. (*e*) *Copperplate printing* was invented in Germany in the fifteenth century. (*f*) *Music* was improved by the invention of singing in parts, the addition of pedals to the organ, and various important alterations in the construction of other instruments.

5. Trade, Navigation, and Manufactures. (*a*) In (313)
the south, the *maritime trade* was almost exclusively in the A
hands of the Italians. The command of the Mediterranean
was at first divided between Venice and Genoa, the former
possessing the East Indian, Syrian, and African trade, the
latter the trade to the Black Sea, Byzantium, and the
Levant; both republics having also settlements in the
islands, and even in Greece and the Tauric Cherso-
nesus. But the long war (see § 61), which ended in the
triumph of Venice over her rival, placed at her disposal
the trade to the Levant and the Black Sea, in addition to
her former commercial advantages. (*b*) All the coasts of B
western and northern Europe belonged to the German
Hansa. This union of nearly eighty Netherlandish,
North-German, and Prussian cities, for the protection of
their commerce from piracy and violence, had gradually
been formed (since the thirteenth century) out of several
smaller Hansas or associations, and was at first divided
into three branches: (1) the Wendish-Saxon; (2) the
Westphalian-Prussian; and (3) the Gothlandish towns;
i. e. the Germans in Gothland, Livonia, and Sweden; and
at a later period into four, *viz.* the Westphalian, of which
Cologne was the centre; the Prussian, which had Dantzig;
the Wendish, Lübec; and the Saxon, Brunswick, for
their respective commercial capitals. The Hansa had C
dépôts at Bruges, Novgorod, in all the seaports of the
Baltic and German Ocean, and even in Spain. It maintained also a considerable navy, held diets, and carried on
wars. After a long struggle with Cologne, Lübec was
recognized as the chief city of the Union. The overland
trade between the east and west, as well as between the
north of Europe and Italy (from Dantzic and Kiev to
Venice), was in the hands of the Viennese, Ratisboners,
Nürnburgers, and Augsburgers; but a considerable inter-
change of commodities between the north (Prussian and
Slavish provinces), and South (Constantinople and Venice),
was effected through the agency of Breslau merchants.
Towards the end of the mediæval period, the fairs held D
at Frankfort-on-the-Maine were in general repute. The
principal emporium of the French overland trade was at
first Troyes, and at a later period (1445) Lyons.

CHRONOLOGICAL TABLE.

THE MIDDLE AGES.

First Period.—*From the fall of the western empire to the accession of the Carlovingians and Abbasides*, 476—750.

A. D.

476—493. The Italian empire of Odoacer.
486. End of the Roman supremacy in Gaul. Syagrius defeated by Clovis near Soissons.
493—555. Empire of the Ostrogoths in Italy.
496. Battle of Zülpich.
507. Southern France wrested from the Visigoths by Clovis.
527—565. Justinian I. Legislation. Nika. Architectural works.
531—712. Elective Visigothic monarchy in Spain.
533. Kingdoms of Thuringia and Burgundy united to Spain.
534. Empire of the Vandals overthrown by Belisarius.
535—555. War between the Ostrogoths (under Totilas and Tejas) and the Byzantines (under Belisarius and Narses). Rome taken five times.
555—568. The whole of Italy subject to the Byzantine government.
558—561. The Frankish monarchy re-united under Chlotar I.
568—774. Kingdom of the Lombards in Upper and Central Italy, founded by Alboin.
585. Union of the empire of the Suevi with that of the Visigoths.
613. The Frankish monarchy re-united under Chlotar II.
622. Flight of Mohammed from Mecca to Medina.
632. Death of Mohammed.
632—661. Four caliphs of the race of Kureish, viz. Abu Bekr, Omar, Othman, and Ali. Conquest of Syria, Palestine, Phœnicia, Egypt, the northern coast of Africa, Cyprus, and Rhodes.
661—750. The thirteen Ommaijad caliphs. Great extension of the Arabian empire.
687. Pepin of Heristal sole Major-Domus of the Frankish empire (after his victory at Testri).
711. Victory of Tarik over the Visigoths at Xeres de la Frontera.
712. The whole of Spain, except Asturia, in possession of the Arabians.
716—754. Bonifacius in Germany.

A. D.

732. Charles Martel defeats the Arabians between Tours and Poitiers.

750. Assassination of the Ommaijades.

SECOND PERIOD.—*From the accession of the Carlovingians and Abbasides to the Crusades, about the year* 1100.

750—1258. The Abbaside caliphs.

752—911 (987). THE CARLOVINGIANS

752—758. Pepin the Short. Two expeditions into Italy for the protection of the pope against the Lombard King Aistulf.

756—1028. Cordova an independent caliphate.

768—814. CHARLEMAGNE.

771. Charlemagne becomes sole ruler by the death of his brother Carloman.

772—804. War with the Saxons.

773—774. Conquest of the Lombardic kingdom.

778. War in Spain. Defeat of the Mohammedan governors on this side the Ebro. Disastrous retreat.

787—788. Defeat and removal of Duke Tassilo of Bavaria.

791—799. War with the Avares. Extension of the empire to the banks of the Theiss. Subjugation of the Slavish tribes on the eastern frontier of the empire.

800. Charlemagne receives the imperial crown.

814—840. LEWIS THE PIOUS. Partition of the empire among his three sons. Birth of Charles the Bald, and consequent redivision of the empire. The elder sons make war on their father. Plans for a further division.

827—1016. Monarchy of the West-Saxon kings in England.

840—1370. The Piasts in Poland.

840—843. Lewis the German and Charles the Bald make war on their brother Lothar.

843. Partition of the Frankish empire by the CONVENTION OF VERDUN.

864—1598. The Rurik dynasty in Russia.

867—1056. Macedonian emperors at Constantinople.

871—901. Alfred the Great.

885—887. The Frankish monarchy re-united under Charles the Fat, by the exclusion of Charles the Simple.

887. Charles the Fat deposed. Final division of the Frankish empire into five portions.

887—987. THE LAST CARLOVINGIANS IN FRANCE.

887. ARNULF OF CARINTHIA. Defeat of the Normans near Louvain. Arnulf forms an alliance with the Magyars against Zwentibald, king of the Moravians.

888—962. Italy under native sovereigns.

889—1301. The Arpads in Hungary.

About 900. Four Scandinavian kingdoms.

900—911. LEWIS THE CHILD. Germany invaded by the Hungarians.

911—918. CONRAD OF FRANCONIA. His authority disputed by the nobles. Lorraine annexed to France. Irruptions of the Hungarians.

A. D.
919—1024. SAXON EMPERORS.
919—936. HENRY I. The empire re-united. Lorraine restored to Germany. Nine years' truce with the Hungarians. Military improvements. Subjugation of Bohemia and the Wendish tribes as far as the Oder. Defeat of the Hungarians (at Merseburg). The northern frontier of the empire extended to the (so-called) Danawirk.
936—973. OTHO (I.) THE GREAT. Insurrection of the dukes. Expedition to Jutland.
951. First Italian campaign. Berengar a vassal of the German crown.
955. Final defeat of the Hungarians on the banks of the Lech. The Sclavonians subdued.
962. Second Italian campaign. Otho crowned at Rome. Berengar taken prisoner.
966—972. Third Italian campaign. War with the Greeks in Lower Italy.
973—983. Otho II. War with Lothar of France for the possession of Lorraine. Otho defeated in Lower Italy. His death.
983—1002. Otho III. Rebellion of Henry, duke of Bavaria. Otho crowned at Rome.
987—1328. THE CAPETS IN FRANCE.
1002—1024. HENRY II. Wars with the Italians, Poles, and Bohemians.
1002. Massacre of all the Danes in England.
1016—1042. The Danes conquer all England. Canute.
1024—1125. FRANCONIAN EMPERORS.
1024—1039. CONRAD II. Burgundy annexed to the German crown. The March of Schleswig ceded to Canute. A law passed rendering the smaller fiefs hereditary.
1039—1056. Henry III. Greatest extension of the empire. The "Treuga Dei," or God's truce.
1042—1066. Restoration of the Anglo-Saxon kings in England.
1056—1106. HENRY IV. Regency of the Empress Agnes. Influence of the Archbishops of Cologne and Bremen.
1057—1185. The Byzantine empire under the Comneni and Dukas.
1066—1154. Norman kings in England.
1073—1075. The Saxons renounce their allegiance.
1073—1085. Disputes between Henry and Pope Gregory VII. respecting the right of investiture.
1077. Henry visits the pope at Canossa.
1087. The Arabian empire in Spain united to Morocco.
1094. The county of Portugal, at first a Castilian fief, afterwards independent.

THIRD PERIOD.

1096—1273. AGE OF THE CRUSADES.
1096—1100. THE FIRST CRUSADE. Peter of Amiens. Councils of Piacenza and Clermont. Storming of Nicæa and Antiochia. Edessa and Antiochia Christian principalities.

A. D.

1099. THE CRUSADERS TAKE JERUSALEM. Godfrey de Bouillon elected king. Battle of Antioch.

1099—1187. KINGDOM OF JERUSALEM.

1100. Death of Godfrey de Bouillon.

1106—1125. HENRY V.

1122. The dispute respecting investiture terminated by the Concordat of Worms.

1125—1137. LOTHAR THE SAXON. Bavaria and Saxony united under the house of Guelph. Struggles with the Hohenstaufen.

1130—1194. The sovereignty of the Two Sicilies in the hands of the Normans.

1138—1254. THE HOHENSTAUFEN.

1138—1152. Conrad III. Henry the Proud deprived of both his dukedoms. Siege of Weinsberg.

1147—1149. THE SECOND CRUSADE. Edessa taken by the Turks. Unsuccessful campaign of Conrad III. and Louis VII. in Palestine.

1152—1190. FREDERICK (I.) BARBAROSSA. His first Italian campaign. Destruction of three of the Lombard cities. Execution of Arnold of Brescia. Bavaria restored to Henry the Lion.

1154—1399. England under the house of Plantagenet.

1158—1162. Frederick's second Italian campaign. The Milanese humbled. Diet on the Roncalian plain. Milan destroyed.

1166—1168. Frederick again visits Italy for the purpose of placing Paschal III. on the papal throne. Returns without his army. Alexandria built.

1174—1178. Fifth Italian campaign. Defection of Henry the Lion.

1176. Frederick defeated at Legnano.

1183. Peace concluded at Constance between Frederick and the Lombards. Henry the Lion placed under the ban of the empire, and his estates divided.

1186. Sixth Italian campaign. Frederick's son Henry marries Constance, heiress of Apulia and Sicily.

1185—1204. The Byzantine empire under the house of Angelus.

1187. Defeat of the Christians at Hittin. Jerusalem re-taken by the Turks.

1189—1193. THIRD CRUSADE. Death of Frederick Barbarossa. The Teutonic order instituted in the camp before Acre. Misunderstanding between Philip II. and Richard Cœur de Lion. Truce with Saladin. The kingdom of Cyprus. Captivity of Richard.

1190—1197. HENRY VI. His cruelties in Apulia and Sicily.

1194—1266. Kingdom of the Two Sicilies under the Hohenstaufen.

1198—1208. PHILIP OF SWABIA AND OTHO IV. Ten years' dispute terminated by the assassination of Philip, by Otho of Wittelsbach.

1203—1204. THE FOURTH (so-called) CRUSADE. The Crusaders visit Constantinople for the purpose of replacing the Emperor Isaac on the throne. They quarrel with the emperor. Constantinople taken.

A. D.
1204—1261. THE LATIN EMPIRE. Division of the empire. Sovereignties of Nicæa and Trebizond.
1206. Temudschin becomes Tschingis-Khan. Religious wars in the south of France. The Cathari and Waldenses.
1208—1215. OTHO IV. sole emperor. He quarrels with the pope.
1212 The Childrens' Crusade.
1215. Magna Charta Libertatum in England.
1215—1250. FREDERICK II. His disputes with the pope respecting the union of the German and Sicilian crowns, and the crusade.
1224. Victory of the Mongols on the Kalka.
1228. CRUSADE OF FREDERICK II. Treaty with Sultan Camel. Jerusalem restored to the Christians.
1230—1283. War between the Teutonic order and the Prussians.
1237. Frederick defeats the Lombards at Cortenuova. Second irruption of the Mongols. Russia subject to them for more than 200 years.
1241. Victory of the Mongols at Wahlstatt. They invade Hungary. Henry of Thuringia elected emperor in opposition to Frederick. He dies at the end of a year. Election of William of Holland.
1248. THE SIXTH CRUSADE. Louis IX. in Egypt.
1250—1256. CONRAD IV. († 1254) and William of Holland rival emperors.
1256—1273. The INTERREGNUM in Germany. Richard of Cornwall and Alfonso of Castille.
1258. END OF THE ARABIAN CALIPHATE IN BAGDAD.
1266. Charles of Anjou defeats Manfred near Benevento. Conquers Italy and Sicily.
1268. Conradin defeated near Scurcola, and executed at Naples.
1270. THE SEVENTH CRUSADE. Lewis IX. dies before Tunis.

FOURTH PERIOD.

1273—1492. FROM THE END OF THE CRUSADES TO THE DISCOVERY OF AMERICA.
1273—1291. RUDOLF OF HABSBURG. War with Ottocar of Bohemia. The house of Habsburg acquires Austria, Styria, and Carinthia.
1282. Sicilian vespers. Expulsion of the French from Sicily.
1291. The Christians lose Acre, the last of their possessions in Palestine.
1292—1298. ADOLPHUS OF NASSAU. War with the sons of Albert the Degenerate (of Thuringia). Adolphus slain in the battle of Worms.
1298—1308. ALBERT I. OF AUSTRIA.
1305. The papal see transferred to Avignon.
1307. THE SWISS CONFEDERATION.
1308. Albert assassinated by his nephew.
1308—1313. HENRY VII. OF LUXEMBURG. Bohemia re-annexed to the German crown.

A. D.

1309. Head-quarters of the Teutonic order transferred to Marienburg.

1312. Extermination of the Knights Templars in France.

1313—1347. } LEWIS IV. THE BAVARIAN, with FREDERICK OF
1330. } AUSTRIA.

1315. Leopold of Austria defeated by the Swiss at Morgarten.

1322. Battle of Mühldorf. Frederick taken prisoner. Lewis and Frederick reign conjointly. Lewis quarrels with Pope John XXII.

1328—1498. ELDER LINE OF THE HOUSE OF VALOIS IN FRANCE.

1338. The electoral diet at Rhense declares the emperor independent of the pope.

1339—1453. War between England and France in consequence of the claims of the King of England to the French throne. The English victorious at Sluys, Crecy, Maupertuis, and Agincourt. Charles of Bohemia elected king in opposition to Louis; and (after the death of Louis) Count Günther of Schwarzburg in opposition to Charles.

1347—1437. GERMAN KINGS OF THE HOUSE OF BOHEMIA.—LUXEMBURG.

1347—1378. CHARLES IV.

1348. FIRST GERMAN UNIVERSITY FOUNDED AT PRAGUE.

1356. THE GOLDEN BULL.

1378—1400. WENCESLAUS. Repeated attempts to establish a universal peace throughout Germany.

1397. The union of Calmar.

1399—1461. The house of Lancaster in England.

1400—1410. RUPERT OF THE PALATINATE.—Unsuccessful expedition against Wenceslaus.

1414—1418. COUNCIL OF CONSTANCE. Termination of the papal schism. Four concordats instead of a real reform in the Church. Martyrdom of John Huss and Jerome of Prague.

1417. The March of Brandenburg granted as a fief to the Burgrave, Frederick of Nürnberg, of the house of HOHENZOLLERN.

1419—1436. THE HUSSITE WAR. John Ziska († 1424). Five unsuccessful campaigns of the imperial army against the insurgents in Bohemia. The war terminated by a convention between the insurgents and the council of Bâsle.

1429—1431. JOAN OF ARC, THE MAID OF ORLEANS.

1438—1806. EMPERORS OF THE HOUSE OF AUSTRIA.

1438—1439. ALBERT II. Unfortunate expedition against the Turks.

1440—1493. FREDERICK II.

1453. CONSTANTINOPLE TAKEN BY THE TURKS.

1459—1485. War of the red and white roses in England.

1461—1485. England under the house of York.

1466. West-Prussia incorporated with Poland. East-Prussia a Polish fief.

1476. Charles the Bold of Burgundy defeated at Murten and Granson.

1477. Charles of Burgundy slain at Nancy. Austria acquires the Netherlands and Burgundy by the marriage of Maximilian with Mary of Burgundy.

1486. Diaz discovers the Cape of Good Hope.

1492. COLUMBUS DISCOVERS AMERICA.

QUESTIONS.

§ 1. *Geography of Germany in the First Century after Christ.*

[1] In what part of Germany were the principal Roman settle-
A ments at the commencement of the first century? By what
works were these settlements protected? To whom did the
territory southward and westward of this frontier belong? In-
B to how many provinces was it divided, and what were their
names? By what people was the rest of Germany inhabited?

[2] By what Roman writers is the soil of Germany described?
What account do they give of it? What forest is particularly
mentioned, and what was its extent? How was the climate
A affected by these peculiarities of the soil? What animals
were produced in Germany? Describe the vegetable and
mineral productions of the soil.

[3] Into how many nations were the Germans divided at this
B period? Name the first of these divisions, and the various
tribes of which it was composed, with their respective positions.

[4] Name the second division with its tribes.

[5] Name the third division. To what nations is this general
C term applied by Tacitus? How many of these tribes are especially mentioned by the historian? Why are they thus
particularized? Name and describe each of them. Of how
many smaller tribes was the second of these composed? What
D deity did they worship? Name the other tribes belonging
to the same stock, but not especially mentioned by the historian. What circumstances indicate the common descent of
all these tribes from a distinct and unmixed race?

§ 2. *Religion, Manners, and Customs in the First Century of the Christian Æra.*

[6] Under what names was the Supreme Being worshipped by
A the Germans? Where were sacrifices offered to these deities,
and from what occurrences were auguries derived? What
was their idea of a future state? Describe the peculiarities
of a German chief's funeral.

[7] What distinction existed between freemen and serfs? At
B what seasons did their great national councils assemble, and
for what purposes? How were the assent and disapprobation
of the assembly expressed? To what privileges were their
young men admitted at these assemblies? From what classes
were their princes and dukes chosen? What was the extent
of their authority?

[8] Describe their arms offensive and defensive. In what fig-
C ure was their order of battle formed, and how was it protected?
What religious ceremony was performed before and during
the battle? To whom were they frequently indebted for victory after the failure of their first attack?

[9] Describe the habitations of the ancient Germans. Explain
D the terms *mark*, *zent*, and *gau*. Describe the ordinary sum-
A mer and winter dress of men and women. What were the
two chief employments of their lives? By whom was the soil
cultivated? How did they pass most of their leisure time?
What subjects were frequently discussed at their feasts?
B What were the distinguishing virtues of the Germans? In
what manner was atonement made for violations of the
law?

§ 3. *History of the Germans to the Period of the Migrations.*

[10] To whom were the shores of the Baltic probably known
from the remotest antiquity? With what events do our first
distinct accounts of the Germans commence? Mention some
C instances. Who were the most formidable of these invaders,
and what Roman post did they attack? Describe the next
migration. Who was their leader? By whom and at what
D place was he defeated? What nations were subdued by Cæsar? By whom was the subjugation of Gaul completed?
A What decisive victory did he gain? What emperor formed
a body-guard of Germans? What nations were subdued by
his step-sons? What measures were adopted by Drusus for
B the subjugation of the Low German tribes? How far did he
advance? Name the two first unions of German tribes.

[11] By whom was the war in Germany continued after the
death of Drusus? What empire did he threaten, and of what
tribes was it composed? By whom was this empire founded?
C What occurrence put an end to the war? What was the position of the Romans in Germany at this period? What circumstances occasioned a confederation of the Low German
tribes? Who was the Roman governor, and what was his
D conduct? By whom was he resisted? Where were the Romans attacked, and what was the result of the battle? What
measures were adopted by Augustus in consequence of this
A disaster? By whom was the slaughter of the Roman legions
avenged? In what battle? What prevented the re-establishment of Roman supremacy in Germany?

[12] What German tribes renounced their allegiance to Marbod
B at this period? By whom were their places supplied? What
was the result of these secessions? What became of Marbod?
What was the fate of Herman? [Arminius.]

[13] After the dissolution of these confederacies, what was the
C result of the Roman policy in Germany? Were not some
attempts made to throw off the Roman yoke? With what
success?

[14] On what occasion do we first hear of the Vandals and
D Alans? By whom were several campaigns undertaken against

A these barbarians, and where did he die? By whom and on what conditions was peace granted to several German tribes?
[15] Of what tribes was the confederacy in Western Germany
B composed?
[16] How many confederacies existed in Eastern Germany?
C To what circumstances may the origin of these confederacies be traced? In what countries did the Goths first appear, and where did they carry on their warfare? Who re-established
D the frontier wall between the Rhine and Danube? What transplantation of German tribes took place at the same time? Trace the progress of the Alemanni and Franks. How were
A these encroachments met by the Romans? By what general and where were the Alemanni defeated? By whom were they finally expelled from Gaul?

§ 4. *Destruction of the Gothic empire by the Huns.*

[17] What portions of Europe were occupied by the Ostrogoths
D and Visigoths in the fourth century? By whom were they governed?
[18] What German tribe first embraced Christianity? Was
C their belief orthodox or heretical? At what council was a Gothic bishop present? Who was his successor and what book did he translate into the Gothic language?
[19] What quarter of the globe did the Huns originally inhabit? To what empire had they rendered themselves formidable?
D What barrier was erected against their encroachments? Into how many kingdoms was the Hunnish empire divided at a later period? By whom was their Northern kingdom overthrown? By what tribe were they encountered between the Volga and the Don? What was the result of the contest between the Huns and Goths?
[19] Where were the Visigoths permitted to settle? What in-
A duced them to revolt? What auxiliaries did they call in and what was the result of their expedition into Thrace? What became of Valens? By whom was he succeeded? What
B terms did the new emperor make with the Goths? Who was chosen king of the Visigoths, and for what reason? What country did they invade? By whom were they compelled to retire? What command was conferred on Alaric?

§ 5. *General immigration of the Barbarians into the Countries of the West.*

[20] What country was next invaded by Alaric, and with what
C success?
[21] What German chief led his forces into Italy? What was their fate?
[22] In what direction did the grand movement take place from
D the interior of Germany? What countries were respectively occupied by the Burgundians, Alani, Vandals, and Suevi?
A What portion of the Spanish Peninsula remained in the hands of the Romans?
[23] How often was Rome besieged by Alaric? What was the

result of the last attack? How were the inhabitants pun-
B ished? Where did Alaric die, and where was he buried?
By whom was he succeeded? What countries did he invade?
Who was the next Gothic sovereign? What nations did he
conquer? Where did he fix the seat of government?

[24] What new empire was established by the Vandals? By
C whom were they led? What was the capital of the Vandalic
empire? What islands did it comprehend?

[25] What was the condition of the Britons at this time? To
D whom did they apply in vain for protection? What German
tribes accepted their invitations? By whom were they commanded? What kingdoms did they establish in Britain?
What became of the original inhabitants?

§ 6. *Dissolution of the Hunnish empire.*

[26] What became of the Huns after the conquest of the Ostro-
A goths? Under whose command did they again become for-
B midable? With whom did he share the throne? By whom
was Attila persuaded to invade the Eastern empire? What
emperor was defeated by him? Under what circumstances
was the siege of Constantinople raised? Where and by what
C generals was Attila defeated? By what peculiarity was this
battle distinguished? For what reason, and with what success, did Attila invade Italy? What became of the inhabit-
D ants of the Lombard cities? At whose instance was peace
granted to the Romans? What happened to the Hunnish
empire after the death of Attila? What was its extent in his
lifetime? By what nations were new kingdoms formed?

§ 7. *Dissolution of the Western Roman empire.*

[27] By what circumstances was the progress of the Germanic
A tribes favored? By whom was the capital of the Western
empire plundered? Over what countries did the Visigoths
extend their empire? What tribes spread over Gaul? By
whom were the attempts of the Romans to reconquer Africa
B rendered abortive? Who was Odoăcer? What sovereign did
he depose, and by whom was he proclaimed King of Italy?
By whom was the last Roman governor compelled to evacuate
Gaul?

§ 8. *Empires in Italy.*

[28] By whom was the Italian empire established in 476? Who
A was Theodoric, and what plan did he propose to the emperor
Zeno? What religion did he profess? What victories did
he gain, and what Italian city did he besiege and take? What
B was the fate of Odoăcer? By what surname is Theodoric
generally distinguished?

[29] By whom was he recognized as king of Italy? Over what
countries did he extend his empire? Where did he establish
the imperial residence? By what name is he commonly
C known in Germany? To what circumstances do you attribute
A the prosperity of Italy during his reign? Among what
princes did he succeed in maintaining peace? Which of the

German sovereigns opposed his plans? To whom was the
Visigothic throne secured? What circumstances occasioned
B the death of Theodoric? By whom was he succeeded? In
whose name did she govern? What was her fate? Under
what pretence did Justinian revive the claims of the Eastern
emperor to the throne of Italy? What was the result of this
demand? What was the name of the Byzantine general, and
what advantages were gained by him? How were these ad-
C vantages lost? Under what leader were the Goths victorious?
What German tribes fought as mercenaries against their
countrymen, and under what leader? What was the fate of
Totila? What became of one portion of the Goths? By
D whom were the remainder overthrown? What form of government was now established in Italy?

[30] By whom were the Romans compelled to relinquish their
sovereignty over the whole of Italy? How long had they
A exercised this authority? To what territories were they now
restricted?

[31] What nation was subdued by the Langobardi on their return
from Italy? By whom were they commanded? By what
nation were they assisted? What portion of Italy did they
wrest from the Byzantines? What name was given to this
B portion? What city was made the capital of this new kingdom? What was the fate of Alboin? By whom was he succeeded? What was the extent of the Lombard empire during
his reign? What was his fate, and what form of government
C was established after his death? Who was chosen king when
the restoration of monarchy was found necessary? By whom
were many of the Lombards converted to the orthodox faith?
D Within what limits was the exarchate confined by succeeding
Lombard kings? By whom were the Lombards compelled
to cede a portion of the coast of the Adriatic to the pope?
A What was the effect of this concession? What circumstance
occasioned the incorporation of the Langobardic empire into
that of the Franks?

§ 9. *Empire of the Vandals in Africa.*

[32] What was the extent of the empire in Africa? What
islands in the Mediterranean did it also comprehend?

[33] By whom was Geiseric [Genseric] invited into Italy? What
B was the result of this invasion? What became of Eudoxia?
What measures were adopted for clearing the Mediterranean
C of Vandal pirates? What was the result? By what circum-
stances was the decline of the Vandal empire accelerated?
In what manner did Justinian avail himself of this position
D of affairs? What sovereign occupied the Vandal throne at
this time? What was the issue of the attack on Carthage,
A and by what important consequences was it followed? What
became of Gelimer and his Vandal soldiers?

§ 10. *Empire of the Suevi in Spain.*

[34] By what nation had Bœtica been occupied since the departure of the Vandals? Who was their first Christian sove-

reign? By whom, and for what reason, was he attacked?
B What was his fate? By whom was a new Suevic kingdom
established, and into what empire was it finally incorporated?

§ 11. *Empire of the Visigoths.*

[35] What was the extent of the Visigothic empire in Gaul?
C What portion remained in their hands after the battle of
D Vouglé? Describe their possessions in Spain at different periods. What African territory belonged to them?
[36] Who was the founder of the Visigothic empire, and by
A whom was he succeeded? What conquests were achieved by
this sovereign, and what was his fate? What nations were
subdued by Theodoric II. and Euric? Who succeeded Euric
on the throne? With whom did the Visigothic Catholics
form an alliance? Under what pretence did he attack Alaric
II.? Where was the battle fought, and with what result?
What was the fate of Alaric? What portion of their posses-
B sions in Gaul were the Visigoths allowed to retain? In whose
reign, and for how long a period, were the Visigothic and Ostrogothic empires united? To what place was the imperial
residence transferred after the death of Amalric? By whom,
and under what circumstances, was he slain?
[37] By what people was the Visigothic empire still further cir-
C cumscribed? By whose invitation did they invade the country? What tribes were reduced to submission by Leuwigild?
[38] To what object was the attention of the Visigothic kings
D directed after the expulsion of the Greeks from Spain? What
foreign conquest was achieved during this period? By whom,
and under what circumstances, were the Arabians invited
over from Africa? By whom was their army commanded?
A Who was king of the Goths at this time, and where did he
encounter the invaders? How long did the battle last, and
what was the result? By whom were the Moorish generals
recalled? What division of the Pyrenæan peninsula took
place after their departure? By whom was Arabian Spain
governed, and until what period?

§ 12. *Empire of the Burgundians in Gaul.*

[39] What name was probably given by Tacitus to the Burgun-
B dians? In what part of Europe did they first appear in the
first century? What disaster compelled them to retire west-
C wards? Where did they next settle? What was their form
of government? For what reasons were their kings set aside?
By whom, and under what circumstances, was their kingdom
D conquered and divided? What privileges were the Burgun-
dians permitted to retain?

§ 13. *Empire of the Franks under the Merovingians.*

[40] How did the Franks obtain settlements in Gaul? Into how
A many principal branches were they divided? By what mon-
B arch was the Roman supremacy in Gaul destroyed? What

people did he subdue? By whom was he assisted? Why
did he embrace the Catholic religion? By whom was he
C crowned? What nations were reduced by him to the condition of tributaries? Did they ever recover their independence? Under what pretence did he attack the Visigoths?
Where was the battle fought, and what was the result? To
D what city did he now transfer his residence? By whom were
the Frankish clans united into one kingdom? By what
means was this arrangement facilitated? Into how many
portions was the Frankish empire divided after the death of
Clovis? By whom were these new kingdoms governed, and
where did they respectively fix their residences? What conquest was achieved by the king of Metz? With whom did
A he share the Burgundian territory? By what accession of
territory was the empire of the Franks further augmented?
What privilege were the Bavarians permitted to retain?
[41] Under what sovereign was the Frankish empire reunited?
Into how many portions was it divided after his death? How
long did this arrangement continue? What was the next di-
B vision? Describe these kingdoms, and give the names of
C their respective capitals.
[42] What city continued to be the common capital of the three
kingdoms?
[43] What was the character of Clothaire's successors? By
whose misconduct were these calamities chiefly occasioned?
D Under what sovereign was the empire a second time united?
What change took place in the administration of the Frankish empire during the reign of Clothaire II.?
[44] How many of these officers were there, and what district
A was assigned to each? What were their duties? By whom
was the Frankish monarchy united for the third time? Who
became major domus of the whole empire? What nation
soon separated itself from the empire? What was the character of the Frankish kings, and what authority was exercised by the majores domus during this period? On whom
was the title of duke and prince of the Franks conferred?
B After what victory? By whom was the successor to the office
of major domus disputed after his death? In whose favor
was the dispute finally decided? What conquests were
C achieved by him? By whom was the Merovingian dynasty
supplanted? How had he conciliated the clergy?

§ 14. *Religion, Manners, and Customs of the West, particularly of the Frankish empire.*

[45] By what German tribes were Arianism and Catholicism re-
D spectively adopted? What tribes were afterwards persuaded
A to renounce Arianism? What was the religion of the Germans at the commencement of this period? Into what had
the pure adoration of nature which they originally professed
B degenerated? Prove this by an instance. What nations remained in a state of heathenism after the conversion of Clovis? At what period did the Burgundians embrace the
C Catholic religion? By whom was the Gospel most effectually

propagated in Germany? By what title was he generally known? What offices did he fill in the Church? What was his fate?

[46] What was the origin of the Christian monastic life? Who
D was the chief of the Egyptian monks? By whom were they
A assembled within the walls of one building? What names were given to this house? What was the title of their president? By whom was a new form given to this institution in
B the West? For what convent was his "rule" originally framed? What were its provisions? What was the general character of these monks between the sixth and ninth centuries, and what results were produced?

[47] What circumstances rendered the excommunication of the
C Church and the ban of the empire inseparable? Mention some instances in which the privileges of the Church were violated by the kings. In what causes did the bishops exercise a peculiar jurisdiction? What was the heaviest ecclesiastical punishment?

[48] Of how many sorts were the warlike enterprises of the an-
D cient German states? Who was the leader in each of these
A instances? What proportion of the land belonging to the
B vanquished was generally claimed by the conquerors? In what manner was the German throne at once hereditary and elective? How was the successful candidate inaugurated?
C What offices in the royal household were held by the nobles of the kingdom? What addition was made to this order after the introduction of Christianity? In what did the power of the kings consist? What circumstances indicate their de-
D pendence on the Roman emperors? In what other particulars was the influence of Rome perceptible?

[49] What division was made of the territory obtained by con-
A quest? What name was given to these allotments? What privilege was enjoyed by the possessors of them? What was the origin of vassalage? On what terms were the fiefs held?
B Who was the chief of these vassals, and what was his office?
C How did these fiefs become hereditary? Under what circumstances were many of the allodes converted into feudal estates? What revolution took place in their military system? Of whom was the army now composed? Describe the manner in which these parties respectively were called into active service. How often, and in what place, was the Frankish army reviewed?

[50] Among what nations, and at what period, were written laws
D first introduced? In what language were all these codes drawn
A up? Was there not one exception? Under what circumstances were they probably compiled? What laws are found in the statute books of the eastern and western Goths and Bur-
B gundians? What remarkable difference existed between the punishments inflicted on serfs and on freemen? How many
C sorts of courts of justice had they? How many sorts of proof? By what circumstances was agricultural improvement in some measure retarded?

[51] What obstacles also existed to the advancement of *manu-*
A *facturing and commercial industry?* To what causes do you

attribute the little influence exercised by Christianity during
this period?
[52] In whose hands was scientific knowledge at this time? Describe their system of education. What do you understand
by the terms Trivium and Quadrivium? Where were the
B best educational establishments? Mention some of their most
distinguished scholars. In what language were all the works
of this period written?
[53] Enumerate the most important of these works. What
C specimens have we of the transition from the ancient to the
modern style of architecture?

§ 15. *The Eastern Roman (or Byzantine) empire.*

[54] What were the limits of the Byzantine empire from A. D.
D 395 to 534? What additions were made to the empire in
A subsequent years? What losses did it sustain in the seventh,
eighth, and ninth centuries? What military arrangement
was adopted during this period?
[55] What portion did Arcadius receive at the partition of the
B empire by Theodosius? What was his character? Mention
the names of some of his favorites. By what concessions
were the Huns and Visigoths conciliated? By whom was
Arcadius succeeded? Who was his guardian? What further
C concessions were extorted from him by the Huns? Was not
this loss counterbalanced by an accession of territory? By
whom, and under what title, was the first digest of laws published? What provinces were added to the empire by his
D immediate successors? Name the first emperor crowned by
the patriarch of Constantinople. Against what nation did he
undertake an expedition, and with what success? Who was
placed in his hands as security for the fulfilment of a treaty
by the Ostrogoths? Where was he educated? How did he
A afterwards distinguish himself? Under whose auspices?
What military work was undertaken and completed by Anastasius? By whom was he succeeded?
[56] With whom did the new emperor share his throne? How
long did they reign conjointly? By whom was Justinian governed? What was his first and greatest work? Were any
B other works on jurisprudence published during his reign?
C What was the Nika? How was it suppressed? What buildings were restored after the suppression of the insurrection?
D By what measures did Justinian secure his northern and
eastern frontiers? What great work did he next undertake?
By what general was the empire of the Vandals destroyed?
By whom was the Ostrogothic empire conquered and annexed
A to the Byzantine empire? What Persian king renewed the
B war? On what terms was peace concluded? By whom was
the imperial exchequer left full, and how was it exhausted
during this reign?
[57] Who succeeded Justinian on the throne? What important
C military operations were commenced or renewed in his reign?
What heavy losses were sustained by the Emperor Heraclius?
D By what tribes were the suburbs of his capital attacked?

What plan was proposed by the emperor in this extremity?
By whom was he persuaded to abandon it? What was the
result of this change of policy? What losses did the empire
A sustain soon afterwards? By the encroachments of what na-
tions were the limits of the empire still further circumscribed?
By whom and how often was the city of Constantinople itself
B besieged? How were the besiegers repulsed? What was
C the intestine condition of the empire at this time? To what
D cause do you attribute the religious feuds of this period?
A Mention the most remarkable of these controversies. By
what council was the worship of images condemned? By
B whom was their restoration at last effected? What act pre-
pared the way for the separation of the Greek and Roman
Churches? What was the fate of Michael III.?

[58] From what emperor did the Roman empire receive a con-
C stitution? By whom were the emperors crowned? What
title did they assume? How did they endeavor to conceal
their real weakness? Of what description of persons was the
supreme deliberative council composed? What change took
D place in the mode of reckoning time? By what sort of persons were the provinces governed?

[59] What languages were spoken by the court after its removal
to Constantinople? To what species of composition was po-
A etry restricted? In what cities do we find the most flourishing
schools of philosophy? Where was the most renowned school
of jurisprudence? Where was medicine most successfully
studied? What was the character of the Byzantine historians?

[60] By what favorable circumstances was new life given to art?
B What were the distinguishing features of ancient Christian
architecture? Where are these peculiarities seen in the
C greatest perfection? To what descriptions of work were
sculptors confined? In what age do we find the earliest
specimens of Christian sculpture? Into what western countries did the Byzantine style of architecture find its way?

[61] By what artists was a knowledge of painting generally dif-
D fused? By what obstacles were the operations of commerce
A impeded? In what manner was trade carried on with the
shores of the Mediterranean and with India? What city was
the principal emporium for western as well as eastern produce? To what circumstances do you ascribe the success of
manufacturing industry?

[62] By whom, and from what country, were silk-worms brought
B to Constantinople? What was the moral condition of the
people at this period?

§ 16. *Geography of Arabia.*

[63] What is the extent of the Arabian peninsula? What is
C the character of the soil? What name was given by the an-
cients to the south-western portion? By what description of
D persons is it inhabited? Name their most celebrated cities.
What was their religion before the time of Mohammed? By
what name was their national sanctuary distinguished? By

what family was it superintended? What rites were practised
by the Arabians in common with the Jews and Egyptians?

[64] To whom do the Arabians trace their origin? To what
A people was one of the districts of Arabia for a short time subject?

[65] Where and in what year was Mohammed born? By whom
B was he brought up? What fortunate circumstance enabled
him to gratify his taste for seclusion? Where did he pass
one month in every year? Of what commission did he pro-
C claim himself the bearer? To whom was this doctrine exclusively preached at first? By whom was he opposed? What
was the effect of this persecution? From what event do the
Arabians date their æra? Where did he assume the authority of king? Whom did he marry? By what means were
his doctrines propagated? In what city did he establish the
national sanctuary? What conquests did he achieve? What
D potentates did he invite to embrace Islamism? Where did
he die? What issue did he leave behind him?

[66] Who was the first caliph? What celebrated work did he
compile? What wars were begun by his general? By whom
was he succeeded?

[67] What city was taken by his generals? Were any other
A conquests achieved by them? For what purpose did he visit
Palestine? On what terms was toleration granted to the
Christians? What fortunate event enabled the Arabians to
take rank as a naval power? By whom was Egypt subdued?
What account of the destruction of the Alexandrian library
is supposed to be incorrect?

[68] By whom was Omar succeeded? What conquests were
B completed by him? What famous work of art was sold?
What was the fate of Othman?

[69] By whom was he succeeded? By whom was the new caliph
placed on the throne? Why was he not generally recog-
C nized? What measures did he adopt for the purpose of
strengthening his authority? By whom was he resisted?
What conspiracy was entered into, and what were its results?
In whose favor was Ali compelled to abdicate?

[70] From whom is the name of Ommaijad derived? To what
place did the first caliph of this race transfer the royal resi-
A dence? What other important change did he effect? Under
what sovereigns were the Arabian dominions most extensive?
By whom were they invited into Africa? What conquests
B did they achieve in that quarter of the globe? By whom
were they invited into Spain? Where did they engage the
Goths, and with what success? By whom were the Arabian
C generals recalled? How was the bravery of Musa rewarded?
What privileges were the Spanish Christians permitted to re-
tain? By whom was an attempt made to wrest Gaul from
the Frankish kings, and with what success? Where were
D battles fought? What eastern countries were subdued by
the Arabians? What was the effect of their success in India?
In what struggles were the reigning dynasty engaged during
the progress of these events? By whom was the throne of

A the Abbasides firmly established? What sanguinary measures were adopted for the destruction of the Ommaijad dynasty? Which of the Ommaijad princes escaped, and where
did he establish himself?

[71] In what light was Islamism viewed by its founder? Name
B the different branches of the Mohammedan system. What
C are its principal articles of faith? What duties are enjoined
by the moral law? What sins are permitted? Of what writings do the sacred books of the Mohammedans consist? Was
D any other work subsequently published? To what sects did
the publication of this work give birth? To what circumstances do you attribute the rapid propagation of Mohammedanism?

[72] In whom was the supreme authority vested? What share
A had the people in the administration? At what period did
the power of the caliphs become completely despotic? To
what circumstances do you ascribe the gradual increase of
luxury? What authority was possessed by the lieutenants
of the provinces? What effects resulted at a later period
from their possession of this authority?

[73] What specimens of early Arabian poetry are extant?
B Where are the names of their authors inscribed? What circumstances prevented the cultivation of science during the
reign of the Abbasides? With the erection of what works
C did the golden age of Arabian architecture commence? Why
were painting and sculpture utterly neglected?

[74] Why were trade and manufactures in high estimation
among the Arabians? How far did their maritime trade ex-
D tend westward and southward? By what means was their
land traffic carried on? Where were the principal markets
A for eastern and western produce? On what shores did commerce especially flourish?

§ 17. *The modern Persian empire.*

[75] By whom was the Persian empire founded? What was its
extent under Chosroes I. and II.? Into how many provinces
B was it divided? What name was given to the capital city
with its suburbs?

[76] With what nations were the Persians generally at war?
C What is recorded of Chosroes I.? Before whom was he compelled to retreat? On what conditions did he renounce his
claims on Colchis? How long did he reign? By what
D measures did he promote the prosperity of the empire? To
what offices was the government of the four provinces intrusted? How did he encourage agricultural enterprise?
What plans did he adopt for the promotion of learning?

§ 18. *The Sclavonians.*

[77] By what names were the eastern neighbors of Germany dis-
A tinguished until the beginning of the fifth century? For what
name was the last of these exchanged? By whom were these
tribes incorporated into the Gothic and Hunnish empires?
What territory did they retain after the dissolution of these

B kingdoms? Into how many tribes were they divided? Who
was recognized as king by most of the Slavish tribes? What
happened to the Slavish confederacy after his death? Mention
some of the new empires which arose from its ruins. Under
whose dominion did the southern Slaves remain?
[78] Mention some particulars in which a similarity is discernible
C between the Slavish and Germanic tribes. What traces do we
D find of physical and moral difference? Did their languages
A at all resemble one another?

§ 19. *Other nations in the East of Europe.*

[79] In what countries did the Avari establish themselves?
B What was the extent of their empire in the year 600? By
the secession of what states were its limits circumscribed in
the following century?
[80] What countries had been occupied from time immemorial
C by the Bulgarians? In what century did they invade the
D Byzantine empire? What barriers did they surmount? To
whom were they indebted for deliverance from the tyranny
A of the Avars? How long had they been tributary to that
nation? What portion of his empire was inherited by his
third son?
[81] Of what countries were the Chazares masters in the seventh
century? With what nations were they engaged in almost
perpetual warfare? By whom, and for what purpose, was
the Caucasian wall erected?

§ 20. *The Frankish empire under the Carlovingians.*

[82] What kingdoms were governed by Pepin the Short? By
B whom, and under what circumstances, was Pepin invited into
Italy? What title was conferred on him by the Pope? Against
what nation was he enjoined to undertake a crusade? What
possessions were wrested from the Lombards? To whom
A were they presented? What grievous crime had been committed by the Frieses? What other nations were subdued
by Pepin?
[83] Where and in what year was Charlemagne born? With
whom did he share the throne? By what event was he made
sole king of the Franks? Whom did he exclude from the
succession?
[84] In what manner did this act of injustice eventually occasion
B the invasion of Lombardy? In what city was Desiderius besieged? What was the issue of this war? How did Charlemagne frustrate an attempt of the Lombard nobles to reinstate
Desiderius on the throne?
[85] Into how many provinces was the Saxon nation divided?
C With whom had they been engaged in hostilities from the
A earliest times? How was the preaching of the Frankish missionaries received by the Saxons? What measure was determined on at the diet of Worms? What fortress was
stormed by Charlemagne in the first campaign? Against
whom did Charlemagne march after his first Italian campaign?
B What success attended this movement? What happened

during his second campaign in Italy? Of what act of treachery were the Saxons guilty, and how was it punished? What
C was the immediate effect of this severity? What became of
the Wittekind and Alboin? How were the Saxons finally
subdued?

[86] At whose instance did Charlemagne invade Spain? What
D name was given to the district annexed to the Frankish em-
A pire? What celebrated commander was slain at Roncesvalles?

[87] By whom was Duke Tassilo abetted in his rebellion against
B Charlemagne? How was he punished? What punishment
was inflicted on his confederates? By what sovereign was
the whole of their country afterwards ravaged? By what
name was it now distinguished?

[88] What was the result of the war carried on by Charle-
C magne's son against the Danes and Wilzes? What river was
recognized as the boundary between the Danish and Frankish
territories?

[89] What measures were adopted for the defence of the different
frontiers?

[90] By whom and with what object was Charlemagne invited
A to visit Rome? What dignity was conferred on him in return
B for these services? What was the character of the new relation between the pope and the emperor? In what manner
was this supremacy mutually recognized?

[91] What bishoprics were founded by Charlemagne in Saxony?
C By whom was Charlemagne assisted in the establishment of
D schools? What measures were adopted for restoring the re-
spectability of the clergy? What proofs have we of the
A affection of Charlemagne for his mother tongue? What plan
was adopted for the improvement of church music?

[92] To what nations were codes of laws given? In what man-
A ner was a code formed for the empire in general? By what
measure was the execution of the laws facilitated?

[93] Were any important changes effected in the constitution by
B Charlemagne? What sort of opposition did the emperor
encounter in establishing the feudal system? What division
C of estates was still retained? Which of the court offices
was abolished, and for what reason? Who were the emperor's vicegerents in spiritual and in temporal matters?

[94] How many general assemblies were held in the course of
the year? What name was given to the first of these meet-
D ings, and for what purpose was it convened? At what place
was the second meeting held? What sort of questions were
decided at it? What plan did Charlemagne adopt for obtain-
A ing a more accurate knowledge of each province? From
what classes of persons were these officers selected? What
were their duties? From what description of persons was
B military service required? What indulgence was granted to
those who possessed less than the legal qualification? By
whom was the militia of each province commanded? What
fine was imposed on those who neglected to appear at the
C place of rendezvous? Were any persons exempt from this
service? On whom was the punishment of death still inflicted?
From what sources were the imperial revenues derived?

[95] What measures were adopted for the encouragement of
commerce? How had it been crippled? Among whom did
D Charlemagne divide his empire? Who succeeded him in the
imperial and royal dignities? From whom did he receive his
crown? To whom was the kingdom of Italy granted, and on
what condition? When and where did Charlemagne die, and
where was he buried?

[96] What was the character of Lewis the Pious? What new
A regulations did he promulgate? Among whom did he divide
his empire? Which of his sons was raised to the imperial
throne? What portions of the empire were granted to the
others? On what prince was an atrocious act of cruelty perpetrated?
Who succeeded him as king of Italy?

[97] What was the name of the emperor's second wife, and what
B issue had he by her? What provocation occasioned the rebellion
of the emperor's sons? Where was a battle fought,
and what name was given to the field? What was the result
C of this engagement? By whom was Lewis restored? What
became of Pepin and his sons? Among whom, and by whose
advice, were the dominions of Lewis divided? What district
was allotted to each?

[98] What circumstances occasioned the battle of Fontenay, and
A what was its result? What famous treaty was concluded at
[99] the end of this war?
[100] Describe the districts severally allotted to the three sons of
[101] Lewis the Pious?
B Whence do you derive the name of Lorraine?

[102] By what untoward circumstance were these three king-
C doms thrown into confusion? Who were the Normans, and
in what part of France did they carry on their predatory warfare?
Did any other pirates visit Italy? What depredations
did the Normans commit in Germany? By what tribes was
the eastern frontier of his kingdom disturbed during the
reign of Charles the Bald?

[103] Among whom did Lothar I. divide his kingdom? By
A whom was Lorraine seized after the death of Lothar II.

[104] Who succeeded Lewis II. as king of Italy and Roman emperor?
Among whom was the kingdom of Lewis the German
divided? Which of these became sole occupant of the throne
B after the death of his brothers? By whom, and in consequence
of what events, was the Frankish monarchy reunited?
What provinces were excluded from this arrangement?
C What cities were destroyed by the Normans? For what
reasons was Charles the Bald deposed by his subjects? Into
how many portions was the Frankish empire divided after
his death?

[105] To whom was the Western Frankish empire assigned?

[106] Who reigned in Germany?

[107] Into how many portions was Germany divided, and by
whom were they governed?

[108] Between whom was the sovereignty of Italy disputed?

[109] To what circumstances do you ascribe the origin and influ-
A ence of the temporal and ecclesiastical aristocracy under the
successors of Charlemagne? By what practices were these

usurpations facilitated? What was the policy of the kings
during this period? Mention one instance of their weakness.
C In what provinces were the suppressed dukedoms restored?
To what circumstances do you attribute the increased influence of the clergy during this period? What were the decretals of S. Isidore, and what effect was produced by them?

§ 21. *The East Frankish empire under the two last Carlovingians.*

[110] By whom and in what manner were Italy and Burgundy
A reunited to the German empire? By whom were the Nor-
mans utterly defeated? To what circumstances do you as-
B cribe their perseverance in acts of piracy after this defeat?
By whom were the Moravians expelled from their country?
[111] Who were the guardians of Lewis the Child? In what
C countries, and for what purpose, were national dukedoms
established? Where was the ducal dignity re-established?
How many national dukes were in Germany at this period?

§ 22. *Empire of the East Franks under Conrad I. of Franconia.*

[112] By what nations was an attempt made to establish indepen-
A dent kingdoms after the extinction of the Carlovingian race?
By whom was Otho the Illustrious elected emperor, and on
what grounds did he refuse the crown? Who was then
chosen? Was not the election more unanimous on this than
B on the former occasion? What became of Lorraine? How
was Conrad occupied during the whole of his reign? By
what marauders were the provinces infested? What was the
C conduct of the Duke of Bavaria? Whom did Conrad recom-
mend as his successor? How many German dukedoms were
there at this time?

§ 23. *The German empire under kings of the house of Saxony.*

[113] By what surname was Henry I. distinguished? How did
he carry into effect the plans of his predecessor? What
D province did he reunite to the empire? For how long a period, and on what terms, did he conclude an armistice with
the Hungarians? How was this time employed? What for-
A tresses did he build? What surname did he obtain from
this circumstance? Against what nations was the army exercised in warfare? What advantage was obtained by the
conquest of the Sclavonians? How many margravates were
B established for the defence of the frontiers? Where did Henry engage the Hungarians, and with what success?
[114] By whom was he succeeded? What remarkable circumstance distinguished his election? Where was the ceremony
of coronation performed from this time? With whom was he
C engaged in disputes during the first years of his reign? In
what manner did Otho attempt to diminish the influence of
the dukes? How was his own authority strengthened? On
whom, and for what service, did he confer his own dukedom
D of Saxony? Into how many districts did he divide Lorraine?
By what measures was the constitution in church and state
materially improved?

[115] What was the issue of his war with the Danes? What
A happened to the duke of Bohemia? What circumstances occasioned Otho's first campaign in Italy? Whom did he mar-
B ry? On whom did he bestow the sovereignty of Italy? Where were the Hungarians defeated, and what important event followed? What effect was produced by a victory over
C the Wendish Sclavonians? What title was revived by Otho I.? How long was this title borne by the German kings? By what measures did Otho endeavor to improve the condi-
A tion of his cities? What advantages did he gain in his third Italian campaign? To whom did he marry his son?

[116] What events occurred during the war between Otho II. and the King of France? How was this war terminated? What circumstance furnished Otho with an excuse for enter-
B ing Lower Italy with an army? By whom and where was he attacked, and with what result? Where did he die?

[117] By whom was he succeeded? Who were the guardians of the young king? What province was erected into a seventh duchy? By what party was an attempt made to emancipate Rome from the German yoke? What measures were adopted by Otho in consequence of this rebellion? What favorite pro-
C ject was he unable to carry out? By what peculiarity was the election of his successor distinguished?

[118] What surname was given to him? What conditions were required from him, which had never been imposed on any of his predecessors? What attempts were made by some of the
A provinces during his absence in Germany? How were these attempts defeated by Henry? What circumstance occasioned his second visit to Italy? What event terminated the contests between native and German princes for the possession
B of the Italian crown? What advantages were gained in a third Italian campaign? To whom was Henry in a great measure indebted for his victory? How were they rewarded?

§ 24. *The German empire under the Franconian emperors.*

[119] By whose suffrages was Conrad II. elected? Where was he crowned? What was the first act of his reign? What country was added to the German empire, and under what circumstances? Over what countries was the supremacy of
C Germany re-established? To whom did Conrad cede a portion of his dominions? What was the effect of this cession? What law was passed by Conrad during his second visit to Italy? By what measure was his family influence extended?

[120] What was the first act of Henry's administration? In
A what manner did he establish the imperial authority, without the intervention of any secondary power, over the whole of southern Germany? Was the same effect produced in any other countries? What foreign prince was reduced to submission? How was the feudal sovereignty over Hungary secured? What kingdoms and dukedoms did the German
B empire comprise at this time? What measures were adopted for the better maintenance of peace in Alemannia, Bavaria, and Carinthia? What was the condition of Franconia at this time? What was the "Treuga Dei?"

[121] What was Henry's next project? What were the two most
glaring ecclesiastical irregularities at this time? In what
manner did Henry endeavor to re-establish unity in the
C Church? How was he rewarded for these services? What
sort of ecclesiastical laws were enacted? Who resisted his
D plans for subjecting the Church to the temporal power?
What benefit did Henry confer on the Normans? By what
tenure were they afterwards content to hold their possessions?

[122] At what age was Henry IV. called to the throne? Who
A was his guardian? By whom was the administration of the
kingdom usurped? Who wrested it from his hands? What
sentence was passed on Adalbert? By whose threats was
B Henry compelled to adopt this measure? What German
prince was unjustly deprived of his dukedom, and on whom
was it conferred? What was the conduct of Henry after the
C death of Adalbert? Against what country did he particularly carry on his operations? Whom did he detain a prisoner?

[123] What circumstances occasioned the Saxon insurrection?
D Before what city did the Saxon army first appear? Whither
did Henry fly, and how was he received by the citizens?
A Where and on what terms was peace concluded? Who
refused to ratify this peace? What was the effect of their
refusal?

[124] What offices had been held by Hildebrand before his
elevation to the papal throne? What was his favorite pro-
B ject? How did he prepare the way for its ultimate success?
C What important ally was secured? What title did Hildebrand assume, and for what reason? What measures did he
adopt for securing the independence of the clergy? What is
D meant by "investiture?" What was the conduct of Henry
A under these circumstances? How did Gregory punish his
audacity? Why did Henry cross the Alps, and how was he
treated by the Pope on his arrival in Italy? On what conditions did he obtain a reversal of the sentence of excommuni-
B cation? Who had been chosen emperor during his absence?
On what terms was the new emperor elected? What was his
C fate? Whom did Henry place on the papal throne in the
room of Gregory VII.? To whom did he leave the prosecution
of the war in Germany? From what pope did he receive the
imperial crown? After what important victory? What be-
D came of Gregory VII.? Where did he die? Who had been
elected emperor during Henry's absence in Italy? By what
nations was he chosen? How long did he reign?

[125] By whom and at whose instigation, was the crown of Italy
A assumed? How was he punished for this act of treason? To
whom was the succession secured, and on what conditions?
B How was this compact violated? Of what act of violence
were the conspirators guilty, and what was its effect?
Where did Henry IV. die? Where was his body afterwards
buried?

[126] What twofold object had Henry V. in view? How was the
C first of these objects promoted? What proposal was made by
the pope, and how was it received by the German clergy?

D To what conditions was he compelled to accede? On what grounds was this decree annulled? How long did the contest
A last, and how was it terminated? What were the conditions of this compact?

Changes in the Constitution during the Saxon and Franconian period.

[127] What practice disappeared with the extinction of the Car-
B lovingian line? Was the hereditary right of succession entirely abolished? When did the election of the successor to the throne take place? At whose election was the elective
C character of the monarchy fully established? How were the limits of the royal authority defined?

[128] Whose functions were usurped by the dukes after the
D death of Charlemagne? How was their authority crippled? By whom were they nominated? In whose reign were most of the dukedoms made hereditary?

[129] In whose reign was the number of margraves increased?
A What powers did they possess?

[130] What were the duties of the counts palatine? Who was the most important among them?

[131] Were the counties hereditary or elective under the Fran-
B conian kings? What was the most important duty of the count?

§ 25. *Italy.*

[132] How long was Italy governed by kings of its own? By whom was it reunited to Germany? What was its condition
C after the death of Arnulf? By whom was the country ravaged during this period?

[133] By whom was a fruitless attempt made to deprive Henry
A II. of the Italian crown? What was the condition of Italy under the Othos? What privileges were conferred by them on the priesthood? What measures were adopted by the Emperor Conrad for restraining the power of the great feudal lords? What important privilege was at the same time secured to the people? What revolutionary measure was adopted by the Lombard cities during the reigns of Henry IV. and Henry V.

[134] By whom were the Venetian Islands originally peopled?
B How were they governed in the first instance? To what nations were they successively subject? At what period was the form of government changed? When, and for what cause, was their connection with the Byzantine empire dissolved?
C What island became the seat of government and centre of a maritime city? By what conquests did the Venetian republic enlarge its dominions? To what advantageous circumstances was it indebted for its importance?

[135] Who laid the foundation of the pope's temporal power?
D What provinces were settled on the papal see, and by whom was this endowment confirmed? By what name was this territory distinguished? What addition was made to it by Henry III.? What concession was made by the pope in return for this benefit? Through whose liberality was a still

more important accession of territory obtained? On what terms were Apulia and Calabria held by the Normans? Of what nature was the pope's authority within the walls of Rome, and throughout the dukedom in which it was situated?

[136] What sort of government was established in Lower Italy
B on the ruins of the Lombard empire? What was its condition
at first, and subsequently? What provinces separated from
it, and formed independent principalities? What districts
were retained by the Greeks? By what people were these
districts perpetually molested?

[137] To whom did the whole of Lower Italy become a prey in
C the fourteenth century? When did they first visit Italy?
What city did they build? What Norman noble was invested
by the pope with the dignity of duke, and what fiefs were
D granted to him? Under what pretence did he raise an army?
Where did he obtain a victory? Against what city did he
A advance? By what circumstances was he compelled to re-
turn? Where did he die? By what prince were Apulia and
Calabria united with Sicily? What name was given to the
new kingdom?

[138] By whom was Sicily taken from the Byzantines, and to whom were the conquerors compelled to surrender it?

[139] To whom did Sardinia belong from the year 850 to 1022?

[140] To whom was Corsica at first subject? What two nations afterwards contended for the possession of it, and how long did the struggle continue?

§ 26. *France under the last Carlovingians.*

[141] By whom, and under what circumstances, was Otho elected king of France?

[142] Were the anticipations of the electors realized?

[143] Who succeeded Otho? What dignities did he confer on Rollo? What was the effect of this arrangement? Of what province did Charles take possession after the extinction of the Carlovingian race in Germany?

[144] By whom, and for what reason, was Robert elected? What was his fate?

[145] By whom was he succeeded? What became of Charles?
A By whom was Lorraine reunited with Germany?

[146] Who succeeded Rudolph? What surname did he bear?

[147] Against whom, and with what results, did his successor
B carry on war? How long did Lewis V. reign, and by whom
was he succeeded?

[148] Why was his uncle Charles excluded from the succession? Whence did Hugo derive his surname of Capet?

[149] What was the political condition of France at this time?
What provinces were under the immediate control of the Car-
lovingians? Name the immediate fiefs of the crown? What
was the foundation of the distinction between Northern and
Southern France? By what peculiarities of character were
A the inhabitants of these two districts distinguished? What
distinct legal codes were established in the North and in the
South of France?

§ 27. *France under the four first Capets.*

[150] By whom was the dukedom of Francia annexed to the
crown? What measures did he adopt for conciliating the
clergy and lay nobles? After whose death was he generally
B recognized as king? What was the extent of his authority?
[151] By whom was he succeeded? What territory was added
by the new sovereign to the possessions of the crown? On
whom was it conferred? Of what royal family was he the
ancestor?
[152] By what authority was the Treuga Dei established?
[153] What remarkable event occurred in England during the
C reign of Philip I. of France?

§ 28. *England under the West Saxon kings.*

[154] By whom were the seven Anglo-Saxon kingdoms united
under one crown? What name did he give to the island of
D Britain? By what foreign invaders was the kingdom ravaged
during the reign of Egbert?
[155] What was the condition of England at the accession of
A Alfred the Great? Where was he compelled to pass a winter?
How did he obtain information respecting the Danes? In
what manner did he avail himself of this knowledge? What
concessions were extorted from the Danish leader?
[156] What measures were adopted by Alfred for the security
B of his kingdom? How was the administration of justice facilitated?
What plans were adopted for the advancement of
C learning? Against what enemies was Alfred now compelled
to take the field? By what Anglo-Saxon king was tribute
paid to the Danes, and what was the effect of this compro-
D mise? What cruel act was perpetrated by Ethelred, and how
was it avenged?

§ 29. *Supremacy of the Danes in England.*

[157] With whom did Canute at first share his throne? Into
A how many provinces did he divide England? What important
reforms did he effect? Of what other dominions did he
B become possessed by negotiation or conquest? Among whom
was his empire divided after his death? Who succeeded
Harold on the English throne?

§ 30. *Restoration and extinction of the Anglo-Saxon dynasty.*

[158] By whom was Edward the Confessor governed? What
C innovations excited discontent among the Saxon inhabitants?
D By whom was he succeeded? What was the fate of Harold
II.? What surname was given to William in consequence of
this victory?

§ 31. *Scotland.*

[159] By what races was Scotland inhabited? By whom, and
A under what name, were the two kingdoms united? What
enemies were successfully resisted by the Scots? By what
English monarch was Cumberland granted to the king of
Scotland? On what conditions? By whom were Scotland

and Cumberland conquered? On what terms were they permitted to retain their kings?

§ 32. *Ireland.*

[160] Into how many states was Ireland divided at the period of
B its conquest by the English? Name these states. In what
century, and by whom, were the Irish converted to Christi-
C anity? By what unfavorable circumstances, and for how long
a period, was the progress of civilization retarded in Ireland?

§ 33. *Spain.*

[161] Under what Caliphs, and for how long a period, did the
D Arabian portion of the Peninsula enjoy uninterrupted prosperity? By what river was Arabian separated from Christian
A Spain, and what was the amount of its population? Describe
its capital city. What were the chief employments of the
population? To what extent were the arts and sciences cultivated?

[162] After what event, and under what circumstances, was
B Arabian Spain annexed to the empire of Morocco?

[163] How many Christian kingdoms were there in Spain at the conclusion of this period?

[164] To which of these kingdoms did Portugal belong? In what
C, D year was it separated?

§ 34. *The Byzantine empire under the Macedonian emperors.*

[165] What countries did the empire comprehend at the com-
A mencement of this period? By whom, and under what title,
B was the code of Justinian republished? What countries
were wrested from the Arabians, and by whom? By what
emperor was Bulgaria conquered? Who were raised to the
throne after the extinction of the Macedonian male line? By
whom was the last of these rulers deposed?

[166] What position did the Byzantine empire occupy at this
C period among the kingdoms of the Christian world? By
what name did the Byzantines designate themselves, and what
D appellation did they reject with scorn? In whom were the
legislative and executive authorities united? By whom was
the senate deprived of its last vestige of power?

§ 35. *The Arabians under the Abbasides.*

[167] To what city was the seat of government transferred soon
A after the accession of the Abbasides? By whom was this city
built? Of what Christian sovereign was the Caliph Harun
al Raschid a contemporary and friend? By which of the
B Caliphs were the arts and sciences fostered? Mention the
causes which eventually produced the dissolution of the Caliphate. How did the first of these causes operate in Spain,
Africa, and Asia? By whom, and at what period, were most
of the Asiatic possessions of the Caliphs united under one
C crown? After what event was this union dissolved? What
portion of the empire remained in the hands of the Caliphs?
D What power was exercised by the Turkish body-guard?
What formidable sects existed at this period? To whom did

the Caliphs intrust the affairs of government, and what office did they reserve to themselves?

§ 36. *Scandinavia.*

[168] What was the political condition of Norway until the ninth
A century? Who founded the Norwegian kingdom, and what
islands were added to it by conquest? What became of the
chieftains who refused to submit to his authority? What
B kingdom did they found? By whom was Christianity introduced? Who conquered and divided Norway?

[169] By whom was its independence re-established? By how
C many races was Sweden inhabited? How were the latter subdivided? Who placed the different tribes under one sovereign? Where did he reside? By whom, and at what period,
were the Swedes converted to Christianity?

[170] By whom were the Danish islands and Jutland united into
one kingdom? From what fabulous hero did he trace his
A descent? How long did his male descendants occupy the
throne? What countries were conquered by Sweyn? By
whom was he succeeded in England? By whom was Schleswig annexed to the kingdom of Denmark? By a convention
B with what emperor? What kingdom was again reduced to
submission? In what manner did Canute endeavor to promote Christianity? To whom was Denmark subject after his
death? By whom was it emancipated?

§ 37. *Russia.*

[171] By what tribes were the southern, northern, and central
C parts of Russia inhabited? By what chieftain and at what
period, was the grand duchy of Russia founded? What was
its capital? To what city was the government afterwards
D transferred? Under what circumstances was Christianity introduced into Russia? What Russian sovereign first embraced Christianity? What district was conquered by this
sovereign? In what manner did he endeavor to civilize his
A subjects? By what title was Kiev popularly designated?

§ 38. *Poland.*

[172] By what name were the Slaves on the middle Vistula generally known? Whom did they first choose for their duke,
and what was the date of his election? How long did his
family reign in Poland? Which of their dukes first embraced
B Christianity? Whom did he recognize as his feudal sovereign? By whose assistance did his son exterminate the
remnants of heathenism? In what cities did he found bishoprics? Against what nations did he carry on wars, and with
what success? What dignity did he assume a short time
before his death? Under what circumstances did Poland
again become a dukedom?

§ 39. *Hungary.*

[173] By what other name were the Hungarians known?
C Whence did they come? Under what leader? What country

did they enter? Of what countries did the Hungarians ob-
D tain possession? By whom were they driven back? In
what century was Christianity introduced among them? By
what king were several bishoprics founded? By whom, and
A in what year, was he crowned? What became of his son?
By whose assistance did he recover his throne? By whom
was tranquillity eventually restored?

§ 40. *Religion, arts, sciences, &c., during the first period.*

[174] In what light was the increasing influence of the clergy
B viewed by the temporal power? What privileges belonged
to the pope? In what cases had he judicial authority over
laymen? What territories did he possess? How were the
C monks generally employed? To what causes do you attribute
D the laxity of monastic discipline at this period? By what
circumstance was a partial reformation effected? By what
rule were the new convents governed? Who endeavored to
introduce this rule into the convents of England? What new
A orders were founded in the eleventh century? At what period were cathedral chapters founded? By whom were they
generally established?
[175] In what manner was the cultivation of the arts and sciences promoted by the Caliphs during this period?
[176] What learned establishments existed in the Arabian pro-
B vinces? What is the general character of Arabian literature?
C In what sciences were the labors of their learned men most
D successful? Why was the study of anatomy omitted? How
A was this defect in some measure supplied? What works
were produced by the Arabian school of architecture, and
what were its characteristics? Who was the most renowned
B of the Persian poets? What was the state of Greek litera-
ture at this period? Mention the chief philosophical writers.
C In what condition were sculpture and painting? Mention the
historical works published in the West of Europe. Describe
D the scholastic philosophy taught in the church schools during
this period. Name the most distinguished professors of phi-
A losophy. Where were jurisprudence and mathematics most
successfully studied? At what period did the Latin cease to
B be a living language? Mention the earliest specimens of
German literature. What architectural works were produced
during this period? In what condition were painting and
music? In what countries did trade and manufacturing industry principally flourish?
[177] To what ports was the commerce of Byzantium gradually
C, D transferred? What German city was the emporium of the
trade between the East and West, and between the North and
South? To what ports did the cities of the North and South
of France trade? By what circumstances was manufacturing
industry chiefly promoted?

§ 41. *The First Crusade.*

[178] What practice had existed for many years among the
A Christians of the Roman empire? By whom were the pil-
B grims persecuted, and what was the effect of this intolerant

measure? By whom were the complaints of the eastern
C Christians seconded? What was the immediate effect of his
preaching? Describe the commencement of the Crusade.
A What was the fate of the first detachment of crusaders? By
whom was an expedition on a larger scale undertaken? Who
was the commander-in-chief, and what was the amount of the
B force under his command? What Asiatic cities first fell into
the hands of the crusaders? What extraordinary circumstances attended the siege of Antiochia? On what general
C was the principality of that district conferred? By whom
was another principality established? Describe the capture
of Jerusalem. What dignity was offered to Godfrey de
D Bouillon? By whom, and under what circumstances, was the
Caliph of Egypt defeated? By whom was Godfrey succeeded?
[179] What cities were added to the kingdom of Jerusalem by
A the new sovereign? Into how many districts was the kingdom now divided?

The Second Crusade.

[180] What circumstance occasioned the second Crusade? By
B what sovereigns was it undertaken, and at whose instance?
C What fate befell the German division of the army? What
was the result of this expedition?

The Third Crusade.

[181] By what monarch were the claims of Egypt to Syria and
D Palestine revived? What was the result of his operations?
[182] What circumstance occasioned the third Crusade? By
A what sovereigns was it undertaken? How did Frederick I.
lose his life?
[183] What order of knighthood was instituted by his son? On
B what occasion was the banner of Austria insulted, and by
C whom? On what terms was a truce concluded with Saladin?
What became of the island of Cyprus? What happened to
Richard on his return from Palestine?

The (so-named) Fourth Crusade.

[184] By what sovereign were fresh bands of crusaders sent out?
D Of what cities did they regain possession? By what nations
was the fourth crusade undertaken? Did they reach Jeru-
A salem? What empire did they found? Who was elected
emperor, and what territories were assigned to him? What
portions were assigned severally to the Venetians, French,
and Lombards? What noble obtained the largest share, and
B what kingdom did he found? By whom was a Greek empire
established at Nicæa? Was any other independent empire
founded in Asia? By whom was the Latin empire destroyed?

The Crusade of Frederick II.

[185] What unsuccessful attempts to regain Palestine had been
C made previously to the Crusade of Frederick II.? What oc-
D currence induced the pope to urge on Frederick the necessity

of fulfilling the promise made at his coronation? What circumstance compelled him to defer the expedition, and in what
A light was his conduct viewed by the pope? Did he revisit Palestine?

The Sixth Crusade.

[186] What causes occasioned the sixth Crusade? By what
B sovereign was it undertaken? Where did he first land, and
C what success attended his operations in that country? What check did he receive, and on what conditions was he released from captivity? How was he employed after his liberation?

The Seventh Crusade.

[187] By whom, and under what circumstances, was the seventh
D Crusade undertaken? What was his fate? In what year did the last of the Christian possessions in Palestine fall into the hands of the Mamelukes? What was the name of this fortress?

Results of the Crusades.

[188] In what manner was the hierarchy affected by the Cru-
A sades? Mention another circumstance by which the authority of the pope over the clergy was augmented. By what circumstances was the wealth of the clergy increased? Mention an important result of the wars against the infidels as re-
[189] gards the extension of Christian influence.
B How was the position of the European sovereigns affected by the Crusades?
[190] What were the consequences of the Crusades to the nobili-
C ty? Describe the development of the knightly power. In what manner were the distinctive forms of nobility created?
D Mention the degrees of chivalry. Describe the institution of the order of Knights Hospitallers. Were they known by any other name? Into how many classes were they divided, and what were the duties of each class? Into what sections was
A the order again subdivided? In what countries did the Knights Hospitallers establish themselves after the loss of
B Palestine? By whom were they deprived of the last of their settlements? Describe the origin of the order of Knights Templars. Whence did they derive their name? In what country did they seek an asylum after the loss of the Holy
C Land, and what was their fate? At what period was the Teutonic order founded, and by whom? For what benevolent purpose was it established? Of what country were all the knights natives? What was the title of their president? By whom was the residence of the order removed from Jerusalem, and to what place was it transferred? What country was conquered by the knights, and in what city did they es-
D tablish their residence after that conquest? What effect had the establishment of these orders on European society? What service did they render in Palestine?
[191] What effect had the Crusades on the Burgher order? To what circumstances do you ascribe the growth and prosperity

A of their cities? How was the peasant order affected by the
Crusades?

Consequences to Trade and Manufactures.

[192] By what nations were important commercial privileges ac-
B quired during the period of the Crusades? In what countries did the Venetians establish colonies during the fourth
C Crusade? At what period, and by whom, were they expelled
from Constantinople? What circumstances rendered this
disaster comparatively unimportant?

[193] To what route had the overland trade been confined in
D former days, and into what other channels was it directed
during the period of the Crusades?

[194] When was this commercial intercourse fully developed?
A What manufactures were introduced into Europe, and to what
countries was European produce exported during this period?
What was the result of this manufacturing prosperity?

[195] By what circumstances was the mass of geographical in-
B formation augmented? To what traveller was Europe indebted
for information on this subject?

§ 42. *The German Empire under Lothar [Lothaire] the Saxon.*

[196] Who were nominated as his successors by Henry V., and
C on whom did the choice of the electors fall? What concessions did he make to the pope? On whom did Lothar bestow
the hand of his daughter and the dukedom of Saxony?
D What service did his son-in-law render to Lothar? How often
did Lothar visit Rome, and what was his object on each of
these occasions?

§ 43. *The German Empire under the Hohenstaufen.*

[198] Who ascended the German throne after Lothar's death?
A What became of Henry the Proud? On whom was his dukedom of Bavaria conferred? By whom was the war carried on
B after Henry's death? What remarkable circumstance attended the capture of Weinsberg? What name was given to the
hill in commemoration of this event? To whom was the
dukedom of Saxony restored? In what respect was Conrad
inferior in dignity to his predecessors? Had this happened
on any previous occasion?

[199] By whom was Conrad succeeded? In what manner was
C he connected with each of the rival houses? How did he endeavor to effect a reconciliation between the two factions?
On whom was Bavaria bestowed, and how was the Margrave
of Austria indemnified for the loss? What was the great object of the new emperor's policy? How many times did he
visit Italy?

[200] What cities were taken in his first campaign? For what
A, B purpose was he summoned to Rome, and what measures did
he adopt on entering that city? What homage did Frederick
render to the pope? What calamity compelled him to return
to Germany? By what marriage did he reunite the kingdoms
of Germany and Burgundy? What duke was elevated to the
rank of king?

[201] To what city did Frederick lay siege in his second Italian
C campaign? What were the principal conditions of the capitulation signed by the inhabitants? At what diet were the
D relations of Italy to the emperor settled? What attempt on the part of the Milanese occasioned a fresh war? What was
A the fate of Milan? Which of the two popes elected by the college of cardinals was supported by Frederick?

[202] What occurred during Frederick's third visit to Italy?

[203] What pope was placed on the papal throne in Frederick's
B fourth Italian campaign? What disaster compelled him to recross the Alps? What circumstance occasioned the revolt of the Lombard cities, and what were the results of that movement?

[204] By whom was Frederick abandoned in his fifth campaign?
C What were the consequences of this defection? At what place was a formal peace concluded with the Lombards? What were the conditions of this new treaty?

[205] What measures were adopted by Frederick on his return
D, A to Germany? What became of Henry the Lion? In what court did he seek an asylum? On whom were Bavaria and Saxony bestowed? What occurred at the diet of Mainz?

[206] How was Frederick received by the Italians on his sixth visit to Italy? To whom did he marry his eldest son Henry? Where was the marriage celebrated?

[207] What office had Henry filled during the absence of his
B father in Palestine? What was the result of his visit to Naples? Who was placed on the Sicilian throne? Where did
C Henry receive the imperial crown? Whence did he derive funds for a second campaign in Italy? What was the result
D of that campaign? What acts of cruelty were perpetrated by Henry, and how was he punished by the pope? What cherished plan of Henry's was rendered abortive, and by
A what circumstance? Where did he die, and what feelings were excited by his death?

[208] What was the fate of Henry the Lion?

[209] What two princes were elected to fill the vacant throne?
B By what party was each of them supported? To whose arbitration was the disputed election referred, and how did he decide? What was the fate of Philip?

[210] What was the first act of Otho's reign? By what means
C did he effect a reconciliation with the house of Hohenstaufen?
D What insult did he offer to the pope, and how was it avenged?
A Where did Otho die, and under what circumstances?

[211] What promises were made to the pope by Frederick II. on
B his accession? Were these engagements fulfilled? In what condition did Frederick find Apulia on his return from Palestine? Through whose intervention did he effect a reconciliation with the pope? What important reform was effected in
C Apulia? What was the fate of Frederick's son Henry? On whom, and subject to what conditions was the duchy of Brunswick Lüneburg conferred? For what purpose, and with what result, did Frederick visit Italy? Who acted as
D regent during his absence? What circumstance retarded the surrender of Milan?

[212] What success attended the endeavors of the pope to place a rival sovereign on the German throne? By what tribes was the North-East of Europe overrun at this time? How far did they penetrate, and where did they engage the Germans?

[213] By whom was Gregory IX. succeeded, and what was the
B policy of the new pontiff? Who was elected in opposition to Frederick, and by what nick-name was he distinguished?
C How long did he survive his election? Who was then chosen, and by what electors? Who was left to oppose the usurper in Germany? By what generals was Frederick assisted in the Lombard war? Where did Frederick die?

[214] What circumstance induced Conrad to quit Germany?
D, A What issue did he leave? By what public acts was the reign of William of Holland distinguished? What was his fate?

§ 44. *The Interregnum in Germany.*

[215] On whom did the choice of the electors fall after William's
B death? What was the condition of the empire at this period? Which of the rival sovereigns was afterwards set aside by the electors, and on whom did their choice then fall?

§ 45. *The kingdom of the Two Sicilies.*

[216] By whom was the kingdom of the Two Sicilies founded?
C Who were his immediate successors? By whom, and for how long, was the Sicilian throne usurped?

[217] What reforms were effected by Frederick I. (Hohenstau-
A fen)? Who was Manfred, and what was his fate? Who was Conradin?

[218] By whom was he assisted, what battle did he fight, and
B what was his fate? To whom did he bequeath his claims? Who wore the Sicilian crown at this time? How was the murder of Conradin avenged? What division of the Sicilian empire now took place?

§ 46. *France.*

[219] By what surname was Louis VI. distinguished? By what
C measures was the sovereign authority consolidated during his reign? By whom, and subject to what conditions, was Normandy held at this time? Were any attempts made to alter this arrangement?

[220] By whom was Louis VII. persuaded to take part in the
D second Crusade? Who administered the affairs of his king-
A dom during his absence? What portion of France was annexed to England during his reign, and under what circumstances?

[221] With whom did Philip II. quarrel, and what attempt did he make in consequence of this dispute? What punishment was inflicted on John, king of England, and for what crime? What advantage did the king of France gain by this arrange-
B ment? By whom, and under what circumstances, was the crown of England offered to Philip? On what terms was an arrangement subsequently effected? What advantage was
C gained by Philip, and what use did he make of it? What
D religious war raged during the progress of these events?

A What steps were taken by the pope to check the progress of
heresy? What changes took place at this time in the political and ecclesiastical condition of France?

[222] By whom was a fresh crusade against the Albigenses undertaken?

[223] By what surname is Louis IX. known in history? Under
B whose guardianship did he commence his reign? What became of the Albigenses? On what terms was peace esta-
C blished with England? What measures were adopted for the preservation of peace at home?

§ 47. *England.*

[224. A] Trace the pedigree of Henry II. and Stephen.

[225] What changes were made by William the Conqueror in
B the constitution of England? What measures did he adopt for the security of his throne? Under what title does the register of the lands of England still exist?

[226] By whom was William I. succeeded, and whom did he ex-
C clude from the succession?

[227] How did Henry I. obtain the crown? Did he commit any other act of usurpation? What cruel punishment was inflict-
D ed on Robert? To what public bodies were privileges granted by Henry? Who was recognized as his successor by the nobles? What change did this recognition effect in the constitution of England?

[228] By whom was the succession disputed? What was the
A result of this opposition?

[229] What dominions were inherited by Henry II. from his father and mother? Did he not also hold certain provinces in right of his wife? By whom were the attempts of Henry
B to restrict the privileges of the clergy successfully resisted? What was his fate, and how was Henry punished for his participation in this bloody act? To what unhappy circumstance do you attribute the death of Henry?

[230] What prerogative of the English crown was alienated by
C Richard I.? How long did he remain in Palestine, and what befell him on his journey homewards?

[231] Why was John deprived of his French fiefs? By what
D pope, and for what offence, was he excommunicated? On
A what terms was a reconciliation with the pope effected? What important public instrument did he endeavor to set aside, and with what success? By what disease was his death occasioned?

[232] How old was Henry III. when he ascended the throne? Was there not a rival candidate? By whom was he compelled to renounce his claims? How was the incapacity of
B Henry manifested? What was the result of the discontent occasioned by his misgovernment? By whom was this insur-
C rection headed? What measures was the king compelled to adopt? What occasioned the battle of Lewes? On what conditions was the king liberated? Was any other member of the royal family taken prisoner? What important change was effected in the constitution during this reign? By whom

D was this measure introduced? Who commanded the royal-
ists at the battle of Evesham? In what year was that battle
fought, and with what results? What person of note was
slain?

§ 48. *Spain.*

[233] With what empire did the Arabian kingdom of Spain con-
A tinue in close connection until the end of this period? From
what event do you date the gradual decline of Moorish power
both in Africa and the peninsula? To what circumstances
do you ascribe the gradual preponderance of Christianity over
Islamism in Spain?

[234] By whom, and into how many sovereignties, was the king-
B dom of Leon and Castille divided? By whom were they re-
united? What provinces were added to them? By whom
was the conquest of these provinces principally achieved?
C What Spanish sovereign was elected King of Germany?
When did Navarre cease to be an independent kingdom?
What provinces were added to the kingdom of Arragon? By
D whom, and under what circumstances, were these provinces
annexed? What Spanish monarch became King of Sicily?
By whom had he been nominated heir to the Neapolitan
crown? What event placed him on the throne?

§ 49. *Portugal.*

[235] Whence does Portugal derive its name? To whom was a
grant of territory first made in that country? What were its
A boundaries? What was its capital? Who first assumed the
title of King of Portugal? By what fortunate events was he
enabled to extend the boundaries of his infant kingdom?
How did he obtain the recognition of his title by the pope?
From what public body did he procure a constitution for his
new kingdom? What city did he wrest from the infidels?
By whom was he aided in this exploit? How did he further
enlarge his kingdom?

§ 50. *The Byzantine empire.*

[236] By whom was Isaac Comnenus placed on the imperial
B throne? Did he retain the crown long? Whither did he
retire? Who was then invested with the purple? To whom
did he bequeath the imperial dignity, and on what conditions?
C What was the conduct of the empress? By whom was her
husband defeated and imprisoned? In what state did he find
the capital on his return? What dreadful punishment was
D inflicted on him? In what condition was the empire when
the Comneni again ascended the throne? By what emperors
of that race were the encroachments of the enemies of the
empire successfully resisted? From what quarters, and by
A whom, were these attacks made? To what circumstances do
you attribute the feebleness of the empire at this time? What
was the fate of Alexius II.? How long did the last of the
Comneni reign, and by whom was he superseded?

[237] Who was the first emperor of the house of Angelus, and

by whom was he set aside? For what reason? What cruelties were inflicted on him? By whom, and for what purpose, was the fourth (so-called) Crusade undertaken?

[238] Give some account of the Latin empire, and those of Nicæa and Trebizond.

§ 51. *The Abbasides.*

[239] By what people and in what year was the caliphate of the
C Abbasides extinguished? What city was taken by the invaders? What cruel punishment was inflicted on the last of the caliphs? What member of the royal family escaped the general destruction? In what country and during what period did the descendants of this prince continue to exercise
D authority? What was the nature of their supremacy? What African dynasties became extinct during this and the preceding period? By what dynasties was the whole of Arabian Africa now shared?

§ 52. *The Seldschuks.*

[240] Who were the Seldschuks? What countries did they sub-
A due, and under what commander? Where did they establish their head-quarters? Of what other countries did they make
B themselves masters? Into how many governments was this empire divided after the death of Malek? What was the extent of their empire in its most prosperous days? Into whose hands did these small governments fall during the Crusades? Which of them continued to exist, in what condition, and how long?

§ 53. *The Mongols.*

[241] Who were the Mongols, and what countries did they in-
C habit? Who was the most renowned of their chieftains? What title did they confer on him? What countries did he
D conquer? What Russian prince was overthrown by him? What countries were overrun by the sons of Dschingis-Khan? What bloody victory did they gain? Where were they defeated, and what measures did they adopt in consequence of this check? Was this operation rendered necessary by any
A other circumstance? What dynasty did they extinguish, and in what year? In what century had their empire reached its widest limits? Describe its boundaries. Where did the great khan reside? To whom was the administration of the provinces committed?

§ 54. *Scandinavia.*

[242] How long did Iceland remain independent, and by whom
B was it at last subjugated? By what peculiarity were its manners, language, and literature distinguished? Is there any exception to this general remark?

[243] Who was the last of the legitimate descendants of Harold Harfagr? and what was the condition of Norway after his death? What islands were annexed to the Norwegian crown? Was any portion of their empire alienated, and to whom?

[244] By what circumstances were the disturbances in Sweden

C during this period chiefly occasioned? What was the frequent
result of these disputes?
[245] What countries were comprehended under the name of
D Denmark? What additions were made to the Danish empire
A by conquest? To whom, and under what circumstances, was
the greater part of this conquered territory afterwards surrendered?
To what circumstance do you ascribe the cessation of intercourse between Denmark and England? With
what country was an intimate connection formed, and what
were its results?

§ 55. *Russia.*

[246] Which were the two great principalities of Russia? How
B many inferior principalities were there? By what people was
the whole of Russia occupied in 1238? What cities did they
destroy? Which of the Russian states retained its independence?
What important position did it occupy in 1267? On
what conditions were the grand principalities permitted to
C remain? What country was conquered during this period of
dependence, and by whom? What brilliant victory was
gained by his son, and what surname was given to him in
consequence of this success?

§ 56. *Poland under the Piasts.*

[247] To what favorable circumstance do you attribute the rapid
improvement of Poland during this period? What countries
did she now comprehend? What was the capital of Eastern
Pomerania? Were there any obstacles to her advancement?
Into how many new sovereignties was the dukedom divided
D after the death of Boleslav III.? Name them. What priv-
A ilege was enjoyed by the eldest son? By whom were the
knights of the Teutonic order called in, and how were they
rewarded? What were the results of the invasion of Poland
and Silesia by the Mongols?

§ 57. *Prussia.*

[248] Who were the Prussians, and what country did they in-
B habit? What measures did they compel Conrad, duke of
Masovia, to adopt? How long did this struggle continue?
By whom were the Teutonic knights supported? What cities
did they found in Prussia? By whom was the government
of the conquered territory administered? Where was the
order finally established, and in what year?

§ 58. *Hungary under the Arpads.*

[249] By how many kings of the Arpadic family was Ladislav
C the Saint succeeded? In what year did this family become
extinct? With what nations were the Hungarians engaged
D in war during this period? By what monarch was a charter
granted to the Hungarians? What terrible calamity was experienced
by the nation? Who was king of Hungary at that
time, and how did he behave?

§ 59. *Religion, Arts, Manufactures, &c., during the Third Period.*

[250] What attempts were made by Gregory VII., and by whom
A were they followed up? What effects were produced by their
B exertions, towards the end of this period? By what arrange-
ments was the ecclesiastical authority of the popes strength-
C ened? Name the religious orders of chivalry established in
Palestine, Spain, and Livonia? What fresh orders were cre-
D ated from time to time? What was the result of attempts to
reunite the Greek and Latin Churches? What religious
communities were partially reconciled to the Church of Rome?
By whose teaching in the twelfth century was a variety of
A sects produced? Name these sects. What measures were
adopted for their suppression?

[251] Mention the distinguishing political characteristic of this
B and the following period. What results were produced by
C this spirit? In what practice do we find the germ of chival-
D ry? To whom is it indebted for its development? Describe
the degrees of chivalry. What were its chief duties? How
A was the knight rewarded for the faithful discharge of these
duties? What was the origin of tournaments? At what period did those exercises begin to assume a systematic character? In what part of the empire was the establishment of a
B free Burgher order most general? To what circumstance do
you attribute this? Where did Frederick I. hold a diet during his second Italian campaign? What was the result?
Who were appointed to execute the emperor's decrees? By
whom, and for what reason, were those officers superseded?
In whose hands had the government hitherto been? By
whom were the Patricians compelled to receive a more democratic constitution? What name was given to the chief popular magistrate? Of whom was he the constant opponent?
C What measure was adopted, whenever it was necessary
that the contending parties should act in concert? By what
name did they designate the supreme political authority?
What do you understand by the term "Condottiere?" What
code and system of taxation was adopted by these cities? In
what reign, and by what means, did the German cities acquire
similar privileges? Mention some of the most important of
D these privileges. To what officer was the conservation of
them intrusted? By whom was he assisted? What violent
change was effected in the fourteenth century? By whom
were political privileges granted to the French cities? By
A what motives were they induced to make these concessions?
How was the executive authority divided in Arragon? At
what period and after what model were cities founded in the
north and east of Europe? What advantage was obtained
by existing communities? Was the attempt to emancipate
the cities from the authority of their feudal sovereign gener-
B ally successful? In what country especially was this authority
maintained? In what country did delegates from the cities
first appear at diets? Was this practice imitated in other
countries?

[252] From what materials were the written codes of this period

generally compiled? Mention some of them which were the
C work of private individuals. Give examples of charters
granted by kings to their subjects. What changes took place
in the administration of justice towards the conclusion of this
period?

[253] By whom had the sciences hitherto been exclusively cultivated? Under whose auspices was education more generally
D diffused? How was this object mainly promoted? To what
circumstance do the most ancient of these foundations owe
their origin? Where were the most celebrated theological,
philosophical, and legal schools established? Who were the
most renowned lecturers at these schools? In what countries,
A and after what model, were other universities founded? Name
some of the most remarkable. By whom was the scholastic
mode of treating theological subjects introduced? By what
writer were the dogmas of Abelard condemned as heretical?
In what estimation were the writings of Peter Lombard held
by the Church? What discovery was made in the thirteenth
century, and what was its effect on the scholastic literature
B of that period? Who were the most distinguished professors
of philosophical scholastics? What studies were considered
next in importance to theology and philosophy? In what
language was history written in central and western Europe?
By whom was the first historical work in the vernacular language published? From what sources was mathematical
science derived? Who was the most celebrated student in
this department? Was he famous for proficiency in any other
science? To what circumstance do you ascribe the perfection to which mechanics were brought? What important
C discovery was made during this period? To what subjects
was Byzantine literature confined? Name some of the most
distinguished Byzantine and Arabian writers.

[254] What was the character of the poetry of this period? Un-
D der what dynasty did epic and lyric poetry attain their highest degree of excellence in Germany? How many sorts of
A epic poetry were there? Name some of the most distinguished
professors of lyric poetry. What specimen do we possess of
the poetical contests of those days? What sort of poetry
was cultivated in the south of France? What name was given
to its professors, and at what courts did they recite their compositions? Name the different sorts of poetry cultivated at
different periods in the north of France. By whom was it
professed? Into what countries did the minstrelsy of the
B Troubadours travel? Mention the most fruitful subject for
romance in the history of Castille. Where was Scandinavian
poetry most successfully cultivated? What was the Edda?

[255] From what country was the German or new Gothic style
of architecture imported? By whom was it introduced?
What were its characteristics? At what period did it attain
C its highest perfection? Mention some of the most magnificent specimens of Gothic architecture commenced in this
century. Were secular buildings erected on a similar scale
of grandeur?

[256] Mention some of the other arts which were more especially

D cultivated during this period. To what do you attribute this
preference? In which century was painting on glass invented? When and by whom were sculpture and painting
elevated to the rank of independent arts? In what century
were companies or unions of painters formed?

[257] By what countries was the Mediterranean trade chiefly
A carried on? With what eastern seaports? In what towns
B did the commerce of the north of Europe principally flourish?
C What were the chief stations of the inland trade? Between
what German and Italian cities was a commercial league
formed, and what was the natural result of this policy? In
what respects did the spirit of the age manifest itself among
merchants? Where was this especially the case? For what
purpose were Hansas established? What privileges did they
D enjoy in foreign countries? What was the object of provincial unions? What great commercial union was formed out
of these two elements? Of what nature were the enactments
A respecting maritime enterprise and commerce during this period? Were any branches of commercial adventure forbidden by the Church? With what success?

[258] What circumstances were favorable to agriculture during
this period? In what part of Europe was the cultivation of
the vine most successful? Where were mining operations
B carried on most vigorously? By what circumstance was the
importance of manual crafts greatly augmented? What was
their mode of carrying on business? Mention the principal
sorts of manufacture, and state in what countries they were
carried on most successfully. Where were the best articles
C of hardware produced? By what city was the trade in glass
monopolized? Mention the circumstances which contributed
to the advancement of commercial prosperity during this
period.

§ 60. *Germany and Switzerland.*

[259] Name the seven electorates, distinguishing between the
D spiritual and temporal. Mention the duchies (with their cap-
A itals) in the west, south, and north. Enumerate the Princi-
B palities, Margravates, Landgravates, Burgravates, Counties,
C Archbishoprics, and Bishoprics. How many imperial cities
were there? Mention the most considerable. Between what
sovereigns was the kingdom of Burgundy divided after its
dismemberment?

[260] In what century was the right of election transferred from
D the dukes to the great officers of the imperial household?
A Name these officers. Who was elected King of Germany after the death of Richard of Cornwall? By whom was he proposed? Who refused to recognize Rudolf? For what reason?
B How was he punished for his contumacy? What was his
fate? On whom did Rudolf confer his forfeited principalities? What seems to have been from this period the grand
object of the German kings?

[261] Through whose influence was Adolphus of Nassau placed
on the throne? By what measures did he strengthen the in-
C fluence of his family? How did these proceedings ultimately

occasion the removal of Adolphus from the German throne?
Who was elected in his place? What was the fate of Adolphus?

[262] What success attended the plans of Albert I. for the aggrandizement of his house? What claims did he revive, and
D with what success? What circumstance afforded him an opportunity of placing his son on the throne of Bohemia? How
A was this connection dissolved? What attempt of Albert was resisted by the three forest cantons of Switzerland? By whom were the Swiss oppressed? Who laid the foundation
B of the Swiss confederacy? What happened to the two governors? What was the fate of Albert I.?

[263] By whom was he succeeded? On whose motion was the new sovereign elected? What success attended the attempts of Henry to extend the influence of his family? To what circumstances was he chiefly indebted for this good fortune?
C What did he restore? How was he enabled to effect this? What project was interrupted by his death?

[264] By whom was he succeeded? By what parties were the
D new kings respectively elected? With what nation did the house of Habsburg engage in war? What were the results of the battles of Morgarten and Mühldorf? What arrange-
A ment was made between the two kings? By what pope, and for what offence, was Louis excommunicated? To whom was the German crown offered? What respect was paid by Louis to this sentence? What dignity did he assume at Milan? By whom was he crowned at Rome? Whom did he place on the papal throne? Why did he return to Germany? Where was the first electoral diet held? What important resolution
B was passed at it? Which of the electors was absent? How
C did Louis increase the possessions of his family? Which of these measures disgusted the German nobles? What was the effect of this distaste? On whom did the choice of the electors fall? Who was elected after the death of Louis? By what party? How was the contest terminated?

[265] From whose hands, and through whom, did Charles IV.
D receive the imperial crown? To what subjects did he devote
A his chief attention? What measures did he adopt for the promotion of this object? What were the provisions of this instrument? What mode of proceeding did it prescribe on the death of an emperor? Where was the coronation to take
B place? What rank was assigned to the electors? What plans of family aggrandizement were pursued by Charles? What provinces were annexed to his hereditary dominions? Where was the first German university founded? What
C other plans of improvement were adopted? How did he obtain the funds necessary for his operations? Mention some of the most important privileges granted to the imperial cities.
D What additions were made to the aristocratic order? Enumerate the confederacies of towns and those of the nobility.

[266] By whom was Charles succeeded? What sovereignties
A did he retain? What addition was made to his dominions? What union was formed in Swabia? Under whose auspices? What measure was adopted by Wenceslaus in consequence

of this proceeding? By what circumstances was the dissolu-
B tion of the confederacies of cities occasioned? Between what
parties, and with what result, was the battle of Sempach
C fought? To whom were the conquerors chiefly indebted for
their victory? What was the effect of a second victory? In
what light was Wenceslaus regarded by his subjects? Where
did he usually reside? What measures were adopted in consequence of his incapacity?

[267] How did Rupert forfeit the confidence of the nation?
D What measures did he adopt on his return to Germany?
Who were elected after his death? How many kings had
Germany at this time?

[268] What was the great object of Sigismund's reign? What
practice had been adopted for many years by the Roman and
B French colleges of cardinals? Where was a council held,
and with what results? How many rival claimants to the
popedom were there at this time? What measure was adopted for the removal of these irregularities? Where was the
council assembled, and in what year? What were its three
C principal objects? How was the first of these objects attained?
Who were the Bohemian reformers, and where had they
D learnt their doctrine? To what circumstance do you ascribe
A the ready reception of these doctrines by the Bohemian theologians? What was the fate of the two reformers? To what
B circumstance do you attribute the miscarriage of the third
plan? Who was chosen as their leader by the disciples of
Huss? What demand was made by them, and how did they
act when it was refused? What name did they give to their
C camp? Who commanded them? What act of violence did
they commit? Who succeeded Wenceslaus in his hereditary
dominions? How was he received by the Hussites? What
was the cause of this opposition? Into how many parties
D were they divided after Huss's death? What permission did
A they extort from the council of Bâsle? To whom did Sigismund sell the electorate of Brandenburg?

[269] Who succeeded Sigismund on the German throne? What
question did he revive?

[270] By whom was this question again brought forward? Of
B whom did he undertake the guardianship? How was such
a measure rendered impracticable? What other plan failed
from the same cause? What was the condition of Germany
at this time? With what Swiss canton did Frederick form
an alliance? By what foreign troops was he supported?
C What was the result of his Swiss campaign? What measures
were adopted by Pope Eugenius IV. with reference to the
council of Bâsle? By whom was he succeeded? Through
whose intervention was a concordat concluded between the
emperor and the pope? What effect had this proceeding on
D the council and the rival pope? What success attended the
proclamation of a crusade against the Turks? What reasons
A were assigned for this proclamation? Who was the last emperor crowned at Rome? How did Frederick increase his
B hereditary possessions? What opposition did he encounter
in Bohemia and Hungary? By what alliance did Frederick

acquire the Netherlands and Germany? Against what country did Maximilian successfully maintain possession of these territories?

§ 61. *The States of Italy.*

[271] By what circumstances had Venice been raised to the rank
C of a first-rate commercial and naval power? What islands
and seaports had she acquired? With what state, and for
how many years, was she engaged in war? Where was peace
concluded, and on what terms? To what circumstances do
you chiefly attribute the prosperity of Venice? When were
D her most palmy days? By what power was she afterwards
deprived of most of her Greek dominions? What circumstance
completed her ruin? In whom was the sovereign authority
lodged? By whom were they chosen? What change
was introduced at a later period?

[272] By whom were the struggles of the Milanese parties termi-
A nated? Who were the heads of these parties? What measures
were adopted by Henry VII.? What noble family became
the possessor of almost the whole of Upper Italy? By
what means? On whom was the supreme authority conferred
after the extinction of the Visconti? What change did he
effect in the tenure of the dukedom?

[273] What advantages did Genoa obtain by the restoration of
B the Greek empire? How long was she engaged in war with
Pisa, and with what results? To what causes do you attribute
her weakness?

[274] What was the result of the struggle between the people of
C Florence and the nobles? Into how many classes were the
commons divided? What business was carried on, generally
speaking, by the members of the higher guilds? By what
family was this aristocracy of wealth headed in the fifteenth
D century? Who laid the foundation of their importance?
How was his son treated by the other bankers? What distinction
was afterwards conferred on him? How did he merit
A this distinction? What cities did he embellish? By whom
was he succeeded? To which of the Medici is Florence most
indebted?

[275] What happened in the March of Ancona, and other parts
of the States of the Church, during the residence of the popes
B at Avignon? What was the condition of Rome at this time?
What title was assumed by a plebeian in one of these revolutions?
At what period were the States of the Church reunited?
What city was afterwards added to them?

[276] By what family was the Neapolitan throne occupied until
C 1435? Who conquered the country in that year? To whom
did he bequeath Naples? How long did his posterity continue
to reign?

[277] To what kingdom was Sicily annexed? When, and under what circumstances?

§ 62. *France.*

[278] From what country did Philip III. withdraw his army
D after the death of his father? To whom did he marry his
son? What unsuccessful expedition did he undertake?
[279] By whom was he succeeded? Had the new monarch any
other kingdom? What was his character? Of what English
A province did he obtain possession? What occasioned the
war? Why did Philip abandon Flanders? For what offence
was he excommunicated, and how did he avenge himself?
Where did the next pope but one establish his residence?
B How long did the pope continue to reside there? By whom
was the order of Knights Templars suppressed?
[280] Who succeeded Philip IV.? What act was passed in the
C reign of Philip V.? By whom was Charles IV. succeeded?
On whom was Navarre settled? When was it reunited to
France?
[281, D] Give the pedigree of Philip of Valois.
[282] What occasioned the war between England and France?
A How long did it continue? With whom did Edward III. of
England form an alliance? By whom were they commanded?
B Where were the English victorious? Who commanded the
English army? What important town fell into his hands?
How long did it remain in possession of the English? What
provinces were added by Philip to the possessions of the
French crown? What right was conceded to him by the estates of the realm?
[283, C] By whom was he succeeded? What misfortune befell
him? Who commanded the English in this battle? What
happened in France during his captivity? By whom were
the insurgents commanded? What was his fate? On what
D terms was peace concluded between England and France?
What concession was made by Edward III.? On what terms
was liberty offered to the king of France? Where did he die?
On whom did he bestow the dukedom of Burgundy?
[284] What distinguished services were rendered to Charles V.
A by his general Bertrand du Guesclin?
[285] Under whose guardianship was Charles VI. placed? What
B was his character? By whom was the right of his guardians
contested? What was the effect of these conflicting claims?
What was the fate of Orleans? What important victory was
C gained at this time by the English? By whom was the Duke
of Burgundy assassinated? To whom did his son apply for
assistance? Whom did Henry V. of England marry? What
important advantage did he gain by this marriage? What
issue did he leave?
[286] By whom was Charles VI. succeeded? What foreign
D monarch was now proclaimed king of France? Who compelled the English to raise the siege of Orleans? Where was
A Charles VII. crowned? What became of Joan of Arc? On
what terms was a reconciliation effected between Charles VII.
and the Duke of Burgundy? What losses of territory were
sustained by the English? To what circumstance do you ascribe the termination of the war? How was a standing army

B first organized in France? What occasioned the estrangement between Charles and his son? At whose court did the
Dauphin seek an asylum?
[287] By what measures did Louis XI. attempt to establish the
C absolute power of the crown? What was the result of this
D policy? What occasioned the dissolution of the league? Of
what rash act was Louis guilty? On what terms did he re-
A gain his liberty? How did he avenge himself? Who were
victorious at the battles of Granson and Murten? Where did
B Charles of Burgundy lose his life? What became of the
dukedom of Burgundy? What territories were afterwards
acquired by Austria? By what means? What provinces
were annexed to France?
[288] What conquest was achieved by Charles VIII.? By whom
C was he compelled to abandon it? What line expired with him?

§ 63. *England and Scotland.*

[289] What province was annexed to the English crown by Ed-
D ward I.? What title was assumed by his son? By whom,
and in whose favor, was the disputed succession to the throne
of Scotland decided? How was the new king's breach of
A faith punished? Who was crowned by the insurgent Scots?
Who succeeded Edward? What was his character? What
advantage was taken of his weakness by the English nobles
and by the Scots? Who conspired against Edward? What
continental troops were brought against him? What was his
fate?
[290] How were the conspirators punished by Edward III.?
B Who succeeded Robert Bruce on the throne of Scotland? In
whose favor was he compelled to abdicate? By what concession had Balliol secured the favor of Edward? How long did
C the disputes respecting the right to the Scottish throne continue? How often, and for what purpose, did Edward convoke his parliament? What division of the great council of
the nation took place in this reign?
[291] Whose son was Richard II.? How did he commence his
reign? Did he continue to reign wisely? By whom was he
D deprived of almost all his authority? Who placed the reins
of government again in his hands? By whom were they a
A second time wrested from him? What became of Richard?
[292] How was the reign of Henry IV. disturbed? Were these
B attempts successful? By whom was he succeeded?
[293] What brilliant victory did Henry V. obtain? What province did he conquer? Whom did he marry? What important advantage did he gain by this marriage? What circumstance prevented his availing himself of it?
[294] By whom was he succeeded? Give the genealogical table
of the houses of York and Lancaster.
[295] What title did the new king assume? What became of
A his possessions in that country? Was there no exception?
What effect had these losses on the minds of his subjects?
What was the immediate result of their discontent? By whom
was this opposition headed? On what grounds did he claim

the crown? What wars were occasioned by this dispute?
B Who was nominated protector, and during what period?
Where did the two armies meet, and with what results? To
what terms did Henry eventually consent? By whom was
the war renewed? What was the fate of Richard?

[296] By whom was the title of king then assumed? With whom
C did Queen Margaret then form an alliance? What was the
result of this measure? By whom was Edward supported in
his attempt to recover the English crown? What was the
fate of Henry VI.? What became of the house of Lancaster? What member of that house escaped, and where did
he seek an asylum?

[297] By whom was Edward IV. succeeded? What was his fate?

[298] Who next ascended the throne? In what battle was he
A slain? What claims were reconciled by the accession of
Henry VII.?

§ 64. *The Pyrenæan Peninsula.*

[299] What possession still remained in the hands of the Moors in 1237? On what kingdom was it generally dependent? What was its condition?

[300], B] Name the two Christian kingdoms in Spain. How was
Arragon governed? In what year, and by whose marriage,
were the two kingdoms united? What kingdom was added
in 1492? From what event do you date the independence of
C Navarre? By whom was a new dynasty founded in Portugal?
By whom were Madeira and the Azores discovered? Did he
make any other discoveries? By whom, and in what year,
was the Cape of Good Hope discovered? What was its first
name?

§ 65. *The Byzantine Empire under the Palæologi.*

[301] By whom was the Byzantine empire reunited? With what
D exception? What was the character of the sovereigns of this
A dynasty? What attempt was made to obtain assistance, and
with what success? By what circumstances were the Ottomans withheld for a time? To whom, and in what year, did
B Constantinople surrender? What other states fell into the
hands of the conqueror? Of what nation did the kingdom of
Cyprus become a dependency?

§ 66. *The Osmans.*

[302, C] Who was Osman? On the ruins of what kingdom did
he found an empire? What were its original boundaries?
How were they afterwards extended? What city became
D the imperial residence? By whom were the Osmans defeated?
What conquests were achieved by Mohammed II.?

§ 67. *The Mongols.*

[303] Under whom did the Mongols again become a formidable
A power? Of whom was he a descendant? What kingdoms

did he found? Against what countries did he carry on successful wars? What was the extent of the empire at his death?

§ 68. *Scandinavia.*

[304] By whom were the several Danish principalities reunited?
B Whom did the daughter of this sovereign marry? What
kingdoms were placed at her disposal? By what circum-
C stances? To whom did the estates of Sweden offer the
Swedish crown? By what treaty were the three Scandinavian kingdoms united? What privileges were retained by
D each? By whom was Margaret succeeded? By whom was
the throne of Denmark and Norway then filled? What provinces were added to the possessions of the new royal house?

§ 69. *Russia.*

[305] What grand principalities were united to Russia? Of
A what provinces was it deprived? By whom, and during what
period? Under which sovereign did the Russians emancipate
B themselves? From the tyranny of what horde? Into how
many kingdoms was the Khanate of Kaptschak divided?
Who was the real founder of the Russian empire? How far
did he extend his dominions? From what nation did he exact tribute? What title did he assume?

§ 70. *Poland.*

[306] Under what dynasty were Great and Little Poland united?
C Of what territories was Casimir the Great deprived, and by
whom? What new possessions did he acquire? What title
was given him, and for what reason? By whom was he succeeded? By what means did he secure the succession for
D his daughter? What province was reunited to Poland? By
whose marriage? What name was assumed by the new sovereign?
[307] What concessions were extorted from Wladislaw II.? Af-
A ter what victory did he obtain possession of Samogitia?
Where was peace concluded? What territories were added
by a second peace? In whose reign? What was then the
extent of Poland?

§ 71. *Prussia under the Teutonic Order.*

[308, B] Where was the Teutonic order settled? Since what
year? What countries had it acquired by conquest? Under
what grand master was the order most flourishing? By what
defeat was its power shattered? What war was terminated
by this battle? By whom, and with what result, was Marien-
C burg defended? By whom was the tyranny of the order resisted? Where was a second peace concluded? What con-
D cessions were made by the order? Whither were its head-
quarters transferred? By whom were Livonia, Esthonia, and
Courland governed until 1513?

§ 72. *Hungary.*

[309] What was the result of the struggles occasioned by the ex-
A tinction of the Arpad dynasty? Under what kings was the
political condition of Hungary greatly improved? What Hun-
garian sovereign became the most powerful monarch of Eu-
B rope? By what conquests? By whom was he succeeded?
Of what family was the new king a member? Name the
C three next kings. By whom was he succeeded? How did
he offend the electors? To whom did they offer the crown?
To what circumstances do you ascribe the great renown of
Matthias Corvinus?

§ 73. *Religion, Arts, Sciences, &c., during the Fourth Period.*

[310] What circumstances were preparing the way for the recep-
D tion of Christianity in Africa? How was the influence of the
papacy endangered during this period? What was the great
object of the councils of Bâsle and Constance? Was this object attained? What terrible pestilence devastated Europe
in the fourteenth century? What was the result of renewed
attempts to reunite the Greek and Latin Churches? Who
refused to recognize the proceedings of this synod?
[311, C] How was the spirit of political combination manifested
in Germany? By what means was the power of the French
D kings augmented? What was the result of an opposite policy in Germany? What system was maintained in Italy?
A By means of what state? What was the constitution of the
East? What was the most remarkable peculiarity in the administration of justice at this period?
[312] Mention the three causes which united to produce new life
B in the sciences. To what circumstances do you ascribe the
C revival of the study of classical literature? By whom was a
better taste in literature introduced and propagated? By
whom was the art of printing invented? By whom was he
D assisted? What was the first book printed? What distinc-
A tion existed in the scholastic Aristotelic philosophy? By
what circumstances were the studies of geography, mathematics, and medicine severally promoted?
[313, B] In what country did poetry most flourish? Name a few
of the most distinguished Italian writers. What dialect be-
C came the language of Italian literature? Who was the earliest German prose writer? Who was the father of English
poetry? What new school of architecture arose during this
D period? Where were the best architects? Who was the
inventor of perspective? Who were the most distinguished
masters in the earlier Cologne and Flemish schools? In what
A country, and when, was copper-plate printing invented? In
whose hands was the maritime trade of the South? Between
what nations was the command of the Mediterranean at first
B divided? What advantages were obtained by Venice during
the long war? To what confederation did the coasts of western and northern Europe belong? Of how many cities did
this union consist? Name its three branches. What divi-

C sion took place at a later period? Where were its principal
dépôts? What city was at last recognized as the chief of the
D Union? In whose hands was the overland trade? What
fairs were in general repute towards the end of this period?
Where was the principal emporium of the French overland
trade?

APPENDIX.

REFERENCES FOR A FULLER COURSE.

In preparing the following references, I have confined myself to such works as are generally found in every good library, without aiming at even a partial bibliography of the Middle Ages, which will be given in another place. The student will also find some useful hints in Smith's Lectures, although the references in that work to Continental and French history are very imperfect even in the last edition.

(The Arabic numerals refer to the Sections in the text.)

FIRST RERIOD.

§ 1. The original sources for the ancient Germans are Tacitus Germania (V. the valuable notes, though too brief, in Tyler's edition) and Cæsar de Bello Gall., L. VI.

Moderns. V. Greene's Historical Series, v. 3, ch. 1; also Hist. Geography, ch. 2; Gibbon, ch. 9 and part of 10 (Milman's edition); Sismondi, Fall of the Roman Empire, ch. 3.

§ 8. V. Greene's Hist. Series, ch. 2; Gibbon, ch. 39, 41, 43, 45; Sismondi, ch. 9, 10, 11; Lord Mahon's Bellisarius.

§ 9. Hist. Series, ch. 1, 84; ch. 5, 73; Gibbon, ch. 33, 36, 37, 41; Sismondi, ch. 6, 7, 8, 10.

§ 10. Hist. Series, 33.

§ 11. Hist. Series, ch. 11, § 11; Gibbon, ch. 31, 35, 36, 38, 51; Sismondi, 6, 7, 8, 15.

§ 12. Hist. Series, 51, 52, pass.; Gibbon, ch. 25, 31, 38; Sismondi, 8.

§ 13. Hist. Ser., ch. 4, part 1; Gibbon, ch. 35, 38; Sismondi, 8, 9, 11, 12.

§ 14. Hist. Ser., ch. 4, part 2; ch. 6, pass; Gibbon, by Index.

§ 15. Hist. Ser., ch. 5; Gibbon and Sismondi, by Index.

§ 16. Hist. Ser., ch. 7; Gibbon, ch. 50, 51, part of 52; Sismondi, 13, 14. part of 15; Irving's Mahomet and his Successors; Hallam's Middle Ages, ch. 6; Bush, Life of Mahomet (Fam. Lib.).

§ 17. Hist. Ser., ch. 5, pass.; Gibbon, ch. 8, part of 18, 24, 25, 42, 46; Sismondi, 3, 10, 12, 14.

§ 18. Hist. Ser., ch. 17; Gibbon, by Index.

§ 19. Hist. Ser., ch. 17; Gibbon, by Index.

SECOND PERIOD.

§ 20. V. Hist. Ser., ch. 8, 9; Gibbon, 49; Sismondi, 16, 17, 18, 19, 20; Hallam's Middle Ages, ch. 1, p. 1; James's History of Charlemagne.

§ 21. Hist. Ser., ch. 11; Gibbon, ch. 49; Sismondi, pass.

§ 22. Hist. Ser., ch. 11.

§ 23. Hist. Ser., ch. 11; Gibbon, ch. 49; Sismondi, 23; Hallam, parts of ch. 5.

§ 24. Hist. Ser., ch. 11; Gibbon, 56; Hallam, ch. 5, part of ch. 7.

§ 25. Hist. Series, ch. 10, 11; Sketches of Venetian History (Family Library); Gibbon, by Index, and ch. 56; Sismondi, Italian Republics (Cab. Cyc.), ch. 1.

§ 26. Hist. Ser., ch. 9; Hallam, ch. 1, part 1.

§ 27. Hist. Ser., ch. 9.

§ 28. Hist. Ser., ch. 3; Hume (Alfred), Lingard id. Turner Anglo Saxons, pass.

§ 29. Hist. Ser., ch. 3; Hume, Lingard, Turner, by Index.

§ 30. Hist. Ser., ch. 10; Thierry's History of the Norman Conquests; Hume; Lingard; Turner.

§ 32. Hist. Ser., 89.

§ 33. Hist. Ser., ch. 7, part 2; Hallam, ch. 4.

§ 36, 37, 38, 39, Hist. Ser., ch. 17.

THIRD PERIOD.

§ 41. Hist. Ser., ch. 12; Gibbon, ch. 58, 59, part of 60; Mill's History of the Crusades; James's do.

§ 42, 43, 44. Hist. Ser., ch. 11, § 4, id. nos. 217, 218; Hallam, ch. 3, p. 1, ch. 5; Sismondi, Ital. Repub., ch. 1, 2, 3.

§ 45. Hist. Ser., ch. 14; Sismondi, Ital. Repub., pass.

§ 46. Hist. Ser., ch. 15, § 1.

§ 47. Hist. Ser., ch. 16, § 2.

§ 48, 49. Hist. Ser., ch. 18; Hallam, ch. 4.

§ 50. Hist. Ser., ch. 12.

§ 52. Gibbon, ch. 57.

§ 53. Gibbon, ch. 64.

§ 54 et sq. Hist. Ser., ch. 17.

§ 59. Hallam, ch. 9.

FOURTH PERIOD.

§ 60. Koch, Revolutions of Europe, period 5th, part of 6th; Hist. Ser., pass.

§ 61. Hist. Ser., ch. 14; Koch, Rev. of Europe, period 5th, part of 6th.

§ 62. Hist. Ser., ch. 15, 16; Koch, ut sup.

§ 63. Hist. Ser., ch. 15, 16; Koch, ut sup.

§ 64. Hist. Ser., ch. 18.

§ 65, 66, 67. Hist. Ser., ch. 19.

§ 68, 69, 70, 71, 72. Hist. Ser., ch. 17.

§ 73. Hist. Ser., ch. 20; Hallam, ch. 9.

THE END.

English.

BOJESEN AND ARNOLD'S
MANUALS of GREEK and ROMAN ANTIQUITIES

I.

A MANUAL OF GRECIAN ANTIQUITIES.

BY DR. E. F. BOJESEN,

Professor of the Greek Language and Literature in the University of Soro.

Translated from the German.

EDITED, WITH NOTES AND A COMPLETE SERIES OF QUESTIONS, BY THE REV. THOMAS K. ARNOLD, M. A.

FIRST AMERICAN EDITION, REVISED WITH ADDITIONS AND CORRECTIONS

One neat volume, 12mo. Price 62½ cents.

II.

A MANUAL OF ROMAN ANTIQUITIES

WITH A SHORT

HISTORY OF ROMAN LITERATURE.

BY DR. E. F. BOJESEN.

EDITED BY THOMAS K. ARNOLD, M. A.

One neat volume. 12mo. Price 62½ cents.

*** THE ABOVE TWO VOLUMES BOUND IN ONE. PRICE $1.

The present manuals of Greek and Roman Antiquities are far superior to any thing on the same topics as yet offered to the American public. A principal Review of Germany says of the Roman Manual :—" Small as the compass of it is, we may confidently affirm that it is a great improvement on all preceding works of the kind. We no longer meet with the wretched old method, in which subjects essentially distinct are herded together, and connected subjects disconnected, but have a simple, systematic arrangement, by which the reader easily receives a clear representation of Roman life. We no longer stumble against countless errors in detail, which, though long ago assailed and extirpated by Niebuhr and others, have found their last place of refuge in our Manuals. The recent investigations of Philologists and jurists have been extensively, but carefully and circumspectly used. The conciseness and precision which the author has every where prescribed to himself prevents the superficial observer from perceiving the essential superiority of the book to its predecessors, but whoever subjects it to a careful examination will discover this on every page."

The Editor says :—" I fully believe that the pupil will receive from these little works a correct and tolerably complete picture of Grecian and Roman life ; what I may call the POLITICAL portions—the account of the national constitutions and their effects—appear to me to be of great value ; and the very moderate extent of each volume admits of its being thoroughly mastered—of being GOT UP and RETAINED."

From Professor Lincoln, of Brown University.

I found on my table after a short absence from home, your edition of Bojesen's Greek and Roman Antiquities. Pray accept my acknowledgments for it. I am agreeably surprised to find on examining it, that within so very narrow a compass for so comprehensive a subject. the book contains so much valuable matter, and indeed so far as I see, omits noticing no topics essential It will be a very useful book in Schools and Colleges, and it is far superior to any thing that I know of the same kind. Besides being cheap and accessible to all students it has the great merit of discussing its topics in a consecutive and connected manner."

English.

A MANUAL OF ANCIENT AND MODERN HISTORY,

COMPRISING:

I. ANCIENT HISTORY, containing the Political History, Geographical Position, and Social State of the Principal Nations of Antiquity, carefully digested from the Ancient Writers, and illustrated by the discoveries of Modern Travellers and Scholars.

II. MODERN HISTORY, containing the Rise and Progress of the principal European Nations, their Political History, and the changes in their Social Condition: with a History of the Colonies Founded by Europeans. By W. COOKE TAYLOR, LL.D., of Trinity College, Dublin. Revised, with Additions on American History, by C. S. Henry, D. D., Professor of History in the University of N. Y., and Questions adapted for the Use of Schools and Colleges. One handsome vol., 8vo. of 800 pages, $2,25; Ancient History in 1 vol. $1,25, Modern History in 1 vol., $1,50.

The ANCIENT HISTORY division comprises Eighteen Chapters, which include the general outlines of the History of Egypt—the Ethiopians—Babylonia and Assyria—Western Asia—Palestine—the Empire of the Medes and Persians—Phœnician Colonies in Northern Africa—Foundation and History of the Grecian States—Greece—the Macedonian Kingdom and Empire—the States that arose from the dismemberment of the Macedonian Kingdom and Empire—Ancient Italy—Sicily—the Roman Republic—Geographical and Political Condition of the Roman Empire—History of the Roman Empire—and India—with an Appendix of important illustrative articles

This portion is one of the best Compends of Ancient History that ever yet has appeared. It contains a complete text for the collegiate lecturer; and is an essential hand-book for the student who is desirous to become acquainted with all that is memorable in general secular archæology.

The MODERN HISTORY portion is divided into Fourteen Chapters, on the following general subjects:—Consequences of the Fall of the Western Empire—Rise and Establishment of the Saracenic Power—Restoration of the Western Empire—Growth of the Papal Power—Revival of Literature—Progress of Civilization and Invention—Reformation, and Commencement of the States System in Europe—Augustan Ages of England and France—Mercantile and Colonial System—Age of Revolutions—French Empire—History of the Peace—Colonization—China—the Jews—with Chronological and Historical Tables and other Indexes. Dr. Henry has appended a new chapter on the History of the United States.

This Manual of Modern History, by Mr. Taylor, is the most valuable and instructive work concerning the general subjects which it comprehends, that can be found in the whole department of historical literature. Mr. Taylor's book is fast superseding all other compends, and is already adopted as a text-book in Harvard, Columbia, Yale, New-York, Pennsylvania and Brown Universities, and several leading Academies.

MANUAL
OF
ANCIENT GEOGRAPHY AND HISTORY.

BY WILHELM PÜTZ,

PRINCIPAL TUTOR IN THE GYMNASIUM OF DUREN.

Translated from the German.

EDITED BY THE REV. THOMAS K. ARNOLD, M. A.

Author of a Series of "Greek and Latin Text-Books."

One volume, 12mo. $1.

☞ This work supplies a desideratum in our classical Schools.

"At no period has History presented such strong claims upon the attention of the learned, as at the present day; and to no people were its lessons of such value as to those of the United States. With no past of our own to revert to, the great masses of our better educated are tempted to overlook a science, which comprehends all others in its grasp. To prepare a text-book, which shall present a full, clear, and accurate view of the ancient world, its geography, its political, civil, social, religions state, must be the result only of vast industry and learning. Our examination of the present volume leads us to believe, that as a text-book on Ancient History, for Colleges and Academies, it is the best compend yet published. It bears marks in its methodical arrangement, and condensation of materials, of the untiring patience of German scholarship; and in its progress through the English and American press, has been adapted for acceptable use in our best institutions. A noticeable feature of the book, is its pretty complete list of "sources of information" upon the nations which it describes. This will be an invaluable aid to the student in his future course of reading"

English.

THE SHAKSPEARIAN READER:

A COLLECTION OF THE MOST APPROVED PLAYS OF

SHAKSPEARE.

Carefully Revised, with Introductory and Explanatory Notes, and a Memoir of the Author. Prepared expressly for the use of Classes, and the Family Reading Circle.

BY JOHN W. S. HOWS,

Professor of Elocution in Columbia College.

——The MAN, whom *Nature's* self hath made
To mock herself, and TRUTH to imitate.—*Spenser.*

One Volume, 12mo, $1 25.

At a period when the fame of Shakspeare is "striding the world like a colossus," and editions of his works are multiplied with a profusion that testifies the desire awakened in all classes of society to read and study his imperishable compositions,—there needs, perhaps, but little apology for the following selection of his works, prepared expressly to render them unexceptionable for the use of Schools, and acceptable for Family reading. Apart from the fact, that Shakspeare is the "well-spring" from which may be traced the origin of the purest poetry in our language,—a long course of professional experience has satisfied me that a necessity exists for the addition of a work like the present, to our stock of Educational Literature. His writings are peculiarly adapted for the purposes of Elocutionary exercise, when the system of instruction pursued by the Teacher is based upon the true principle of the art, viz.—a careful analysis of the structure and meaning of language, rather than a servile adherence to the arbitrary and mechanical rules of Elocution.

To impress upon the mind of the pupil that words are the exposition of thought, and that in reading, or speaking, every shade of thought and feeling has its appropriate shade of modulated tone, ought to be the especial aim of every Teacher; and an author like Shakspeare, whose every line embodies a volume of meaning, should surely form one of our Elocutionary Text Books. * * * Still, in preparing a selection of his works for the express purpose contemplated in my design, I have not hesitated to exercise a severe revision of his language, beyond that adopted in any similar undertaking—"Bowdler's Family Shakspeare" not even excepted;—and simply, because I practically know the impossibility of introducing Shakspeare as a Class Book, or as a satisfactory Reading Book for Families without this precautionary revision.—*Extract from the Preface.*

Professor Greene's Historical Series.

(NEARLY READY.)

MANUAL OF THE GEOGRAPHY AND HISTORY
OF THE
MIDDLE AGES.

Translated from the French of M. DES MICHELS, Rector of the College of Rouen, with Additions and Corrections.

BY G. W. GREENE,

Professor of Modern Languages in Brown University.

Accompanied with Numerous Engravings and Maps. One Volume, 12mo.

TO BE FOLLOWED BY

A Manual of Modern History, down to the French Revolution.
A Manual of Ancient History.
A History of Rome.

. Great pains will be taken to adapt these books to the practical purposes of the Class Room, and for the guidance of private students.

HISTORICAL

AND

MISCELLANEOUS QUESTIONS.

BY RICHMALL MANGNALL.

First American, from the Eighty-fourth London Edition. With large Additions Embracing the Elements of Mythology, Astronomy, Architecture, Heraldry, &c. Adapted for Schools in the United States

BY MRS. JULIA LAWRENCE.

Illustrated with numerous Engravings. One Volume, 12mo. $1.

CONTENTS.

A Short View of Scripture History, from the Creation to the Return of the Jews—Questions from the Early Ages to the time of Julius Cæsar—Miscellaneous Questions in Grecian History—Miscellaneous Questions in General History, chiefly Ancient—Questions containing a Sketch of the most remarkable Events from the Christian Era to the close of the Eighteenth Century—Miscellaneous Questions in Roman History—Questions in English History, from the Invasion of Cæsar to the Reformation—Continuation of Questions in English History, from the Reformation to the Present Time—Abstract of Early British History—Abstract of English Reigns from the Conquest—Abstract of the Scottish Reigns—Abstract of the French Reigns, from Pharamond to Philip I—Continuation of the French Reigns, from Louis VI to Louis Phillippe—Questions Relating to the History of America, from its Discovery to the Present Time—Abstract of Roman Kings and most distinguished Heroes—Abstract of the most celebrated Grecians—Of Heathen Mythology in general—Abstract of Heathen Mythology—The Elements of Astronomy—Explanation of a few Astronomical Terms—List of Constellations—Questions on Common Subjects—Questions on Architecture—Questions on Heraldry—Explanations of such Latin Words and Phrases as are seldom Englished—Questions on the History of the Middle Ages.

"This is an admirable work to aid both teachers and parents in instructing children and youth, and there is no work of the kind that we have seen that is so well calculated "to awaken a spirit of laudable curiosity in young minds," and to satisfy that curiosity when awakened."

HISTORY OF ENGLAND,

From the Invasion of Julius Cæsar to the Reign of Queen Victoria.

BY MRS. MARKHAM.

A new Edition, with Questions, adapted for Schools in the United States.

BY ELIZA ROBBINS,

Author of "American Popular Lessons," "Poetry for Schools," &c.

One Volume, 12mo. Price 75 cents.

There is nothing more needed in our schools than good histories; not the dry compends in present use, but elementary works that shall suggest the moral uses of history, and the providence of God, manifest in the affairs of men.

Mr. Markham's history was used by that model for all teachers, the late Dr. Arnold, master of the great English school at Rugby, and agrees in its character with his enlightened and pious views of teaching history. It is now several years since I adapted this history to the form and price acceptable in the schools in the United States. I have recently revised it, and trust that it may be extensively serviceable in education.

The principal alterations from the original are a new and more convenient division of paragraphs, and entire omission of the conversations annexed to the chapters. In the place of these I have affixed questions to every page that may at once facilitate the work of the teacher and the pupil. The rational and moral features of this book first commended it to me, and I have used it successfully with my own scholars.—*Extract from the American Editor's Preface*

French, German, Spanish, and English Dictionaries.

I.

A DICTIONARY OF THE GERMAN AND ENGLISH LANGUAGES,

Indicating the Accentuation of every German Word, containing several hundred German Synonyms, together with a Classification and Alphabetical List of the Irregular Verbs, and a List of German Abbreviations. Compiled from the Works of HILPERT, FLÜGEL, GREIB, HEYSE, and others.

IN TWO PARTS: I. GERMAN AND ENGLISH. II. ENGLISH AND GERMAN.

By G. J. ADLER, A. M.,

Professor of the German Language and Literature in the University of the City of New-York. One large volume, 8vo., of 1400 pages. Price $5. Strongly and neatly bound.

II.

THE STANDARD PRONOUNCING DICTIONARY OF THE FRENCH AND ENGLISH LANGUAGES.

IN TWO PARTS: I. FRENCH AND ENGLISH. II. ENGLISH AND FRENCH.

The FIRST PART comprehending words in common use—Terms connected with Science—Terms belonging to the Fine Arts—4000 Historical Names—4000 Geographical Names—1100 terms lately published, with the PRONUNCIATION OF EVERY WORD, according to the French Academy and the most eminent Lexicographers and Grammarians; together with 750 *Critical Remarks*, in which the various methods of pronouncing employed by different authors are investigated and compared with each other.

The SECOND PART containing a copious Vocabulary of English words and expressions, with the Pronunciation according to Walker.

The whole preceded by a practical and comprehensive System of French Pronunciation.

By GABRIEL SURENNE, F. A. S. E.,

French Teacher in Edinburgh; Corresponding Member of the French Grammatical Society of Paris, &c., &c. Reprinted from a duplicate cast of the stereotype plates of the last Edinburgh edition. One stout volume, 12mo., of nearly 900 pages. Price $1 50.

III.

A DICTIONARY of the ENGLISH LANGUAGE,

CONTAINING THE PRONUNCIATION, ETYMOLOGY, AND EXPLANATION OF ALL WORDS AUTHORIZED BY EMINENT WRITERS;

To which are added, a Vocabulary of the Roots of English Words, and an Accented List of Greek, Latin, and Scripture Proper Names.

By ALEXANDER REID, A. M.,

Rector of the Circus School, Edinburgh. With a Critical Preface, by HENRY REED, Professor of English Literature in the University of Pennsylvania, and an Appendix, showing the pronunciation of nearly 3000 of the most important Geographical Names. One volume, 12mo., of nearly 600 pages, bound in leather. Price $1

IV.

In preparation,

A DICTIONARY OF THE SPANISH AND ENGLISH LANGUAGES.

IN TWO PARTS: I. SPANISH AND ENGLISH. II. ENGLISH AND SPANISH.

By MARIANO VELAZQUEZ DE LA CADENA,

Editor of Ollendorff's Spanish Grammar, and

M. SEOANE, M. D.

In one large 8vo. volume, uniform with "Adler's German Lexicon."

French.

OLLENDORFF'S NEW METHOD
OF
LEARNING TO READ, WRITE, AND SPEAK
THE FRENCH LANGUAGE,

With an Appendix, containing the Cardinal and Ordinal Numbers, and full Paradigms of the Regular and Irregular, Auxiliary, Reflective, and Impersonal Verbs

By J. L. Jewett. One volume, 12mo. $1.

' New Method of Learning the French Language.—This grammar must supersede all others now used for instruction in the French language. Its conception and arrangement are admirable,—the work evidently of a mind familiar with the deficiencies of the systems, the place of which it is designed to supply. In all the works of the kind that have fallen under our notice, there has been so much left unexplained or obscure, and so many things have been omitted—trifles, perhaps, in the estimation of the author, but the cause of great embarrassment to the learner—that they have been comparatively valueless as self-instructors. The student, deceived by their specious pretensions, has not proceeded far before he has felt himself in a condition similar to that of a mariner who should put out to sea without a compass to direct him. He has encountered difficulty after difficulty, to which his grammar afforded no clue; when, disappointed and discouraged, he has either abandoned the study in disgust, or if his means permitted, has resorted to a teacher to accomplish what it was not in his power to effect by the aid of his 'self-instructor.'

"Ollendorff has passed his roller over the whole field of French instruction, and the rugged inequalities formerly to be encountered, no longer discourage the learner. What were the difficulties of the language, are here mastered in succession; and the only surprise of the student, as he passes from lesson to lesson, is, that he meets none of these 'lions in the way.'

"The value of the work has been greatly enhanced by a careful revision, and the addition of an appendix containing matter essential to its compeleteness either as a book for the use of teachers or for self-instruction."—*New-York Commercial Advertiser.*

OLLENDORFF'S
FIRST LESSONS IN FRENCH,
OR
ELEMENTARY FRENCH GRAMMAR,
INTRODUCTORY TO OLLENDORFF'S LARGER GRAMMAR,

BY G. W. GREENE,

Instructor of Modern Languages in Brown University.

One volume, 16mo. 38 cents.; with a Key, 50 cents.

This volume is intended as an introduction to "Ollendorff's complete French Method," and is published in accordance with a very general demand made for a more elementary work than the larger Grammar.

"It is believed that the student who shall take the pains to go carefully through this volume, in the manner suggested in the Directions for studying it, will come to the study of the 'Complete Method' with a degree of praparation which will render his subsequent progress easy and agreeable."

OLLENDORFF'S NEW METHOD
OF LEARNING TO READ, TRANSLATE, WRITE, AND SPEAK
THE FRENCH LANGUAGE.

Preceded by a Treatise on French Pronunciation, by which that difficult part of a spoken language can be easily acquired in 12 Lessons.

Together with a Commercial Correspondence, a Complete Grammatical Synopsis, and a Correct Index.

BY V. VALUE,

Professor of the French Language.

One vol. 12mo.

OLLENDORFF'S NEW METHOD

OF

LEARNING TO READ, WRITE, AND SPEAK

THE ITALIAN LANGUAGE.

With Additions and Corrections by FELIX FORESTI, Prof. of the Italian Language in Columbia College, New-York City. One volume, 12mo. $1 50.

KEY TO THE EXERCISES.

One vol. 12mo. 75 cts.

United States' Gazette.

"OLLENDORFF'S ITALIAN GRAMMAR.—The system of learning and teaching the living languages by Ollendorff is so superior to all other modes, that in England and on the continent of Europe, scarcely any other is in use, in well-directed academies and other institutions of learning. To those who feel disposed to cultivate an acquaintance with Italian literature, this work will prove invaluable, abridging, by an immense deal, the period commonly employed in studying the language."

ACCOMPANIMENT TO OLLENDORFF'S ITALIAN GRAMMAR.

CRESTOMAZIA ITALIANA:

A COLLECTION OF

SELECTED PIECES IN ITALIAN PROSE,

DESIGNED AS A

CLASS READING BOOK FOR BEGINNERS

IN THE STUDY OF

THE ITALIAN LANGUAGE.

BY E. FELIX FORESTI, LL. D.,

PROFESSOR OF THE ITALIAN LANGUAGE AND LITERATURE IN COLUMBIA COLLEGE AND IN THE UNIVERSITY OF THE CITY OF NEW-YORK.

One volume, 12mo. Price $1.

"The *Italian Reader* is compiled by Mr. Foresti, Professor of the Italian Language in the Columbia College and the University of New-York. It appears to be designed to follow the study of Ollendorff's Italian Grammar, on which work many correct judges have pronounced that no important improvement can well be made. In making selections for the book before us, Mr. Foresti has preferred modern Italian writers to the old school of novelists, historians, and poets. In this he has done a good thing; for the Italian Reader contains the modern language. True, there are some innovations, some changes which many would deem a departure from original purity, but nevertheless it is *the* language which one finds and hears spoken in Italy. These changes have gone on under the eye and against the stern authority of the Academy *della Crusca*, and in their magnificent new dictionary, new in process of publication, they have found themselves compelled to insert many words which are the growth not only of modern necessity, but of caprice.

"The selections in the Italian Reader are from popular authors, such as Botta, Manzoni, Machiavelli, Villani, and others. They are so made as not to constitute mere exercises, but contain distinct relations so complete as to gratify the reader and engage his attention while they instruct. This is a marked improvement on that old system which exacted much labor without enlisting the sympathies of the student. The selections from Manzoni, for example, are from the "*Promessi Sposi*," one of the noblest works of fiction ever issued from the press—a work so popular as to have gone through an incredible number of editions in Italy, while it has been translated into every language of Europe. There have been, we believe, no less than three distinct English translations made, two of which were done in this country. The Reader contains six extracts from this novel, among which are the beautiful episodes of Father Cristoforo and the Nun of Monza, and a description of the famine and plague of Milan in the year 1630. The account of the plague rivals the celebrated one of Boccacio in his Decameron. The idioms that occur in the selections are explained by a glossary appended to each. The Italian Reader can with confidence be recommended to students in the language as a safe and sure guide. After mastering it, the Italian poets and other classicists may be approached with confidence."—*Savannah Republican.*

OLLENDORFF'S NEW METHOD OF LEARNING TO READ, WRITE, AND SPEAK THE GERMAN LANGUAGE.

Reprinted from the Frankfort edition, to which is added a Systematic Outline of the different Parts of Speech, their Inflection and Use, with full Paradigms, and a complete List of the Irregular Verbs.

BY GEORGE J. ADLER, A. B.,

Professor of German in the University of the City of New-York. One volume, 12mo. **$1 50.**

☞ A KEY TO THE EXERCISES, in a separate volume. 75 cts.

"OLLENDORFF'S *new method of Learning to Read, Write, and Speak the German Language*, with a systematic outline of German Grammar, by George J. Adler, is one of those rare works which leave nothing to be desired on the subjects of which they treat. The learner's difficulties are so fully and exactly provided for, that a constant sense of satisfaction and progress is felt from the beginning to the end of the book. A bare inspection of one of the lessons will satisfy any one acquainted with the elements of German grammar, that it adapts itself perfectly to his wants. With the systematic outline of grammar by Prof. Adler, the new method is substantially perfect, and it is probably second in its advantages only to residence and intercourse with educated Germans."

"The study of the German is becoming so essential a part of an ordinary education, that every work tending to facilitate the acquisition of the language should be welcomed. An American edition of Ollendorff has been much wanted. His system is based upon *natural* principles. He teaches by leading the student to the acquisition of phrases, from which he deduces the rules of the language. The *idioms* are also carefully taught, and the entire construction of the system is such that, if adhered to with fidelity and perseverance, it will secure such a practical knowledge of the German as can be acquired by no other mode, so rapidly and thoroughly. We heartily commend the book to all who really wish to understand a tongue which contains so many treasures.

A PROGRESSIVE GERMAN READER,

PREPARED WITH REFERENCE TO

OLLENDORFF'S GERMAN GRAMMAR,

WITH COPIOUS NOTES AND A VOCABULARY,

BY G. J. ADLER,

Professor of the German Language and Literature in the University of the City of N. Y.

One volume, 12mo. $1.

The favorable reception which Ollendorff's German Grammar has received from the American public, has induced the Publishers and the Editor to comply with the very general demand for a *German Reader*.

The plan of this Reader is as follows, viz.:

1. The pieces are both prose and poetry, selected from the best authors, and are so arranged as to present sufficient variety to keep alive the interest of the scholar.
2. It is progressive in its nature, the pieces being at first very short and easy, and increasing in difficulty and length as the learner advances.
3. At the bottom of the page constant references to the Grammar are made, the difficult passages are explained and rendered. To encourage the first attempt of the learner as much as possible, the twenty-one pieces of the first section are analyzed, and all the necessary words given at the bottom of the page. The notes, which at first are very abundant, diminish as the learner advances.
4. It contains *five* sections. The *first* contains easy pieces, chiefly in prose, with all the words necessary for translating them; the *second*, short pieces in prose and poetry alternately, with copious notes and renderings; the *third*, short popular tales of GRIMM and others; the *fourth* select ballads and other poems from BUERGER, GOETHE, SCHILLER, UHLAND, SCHWEB, CHAMISSO, &c.; the *fifth*, prose extracts from the first classics.
5. At the end is added a VOCABULARY of all the words occurring in the book.

JUST READY,

THE PRACTICAL GERMAN GRAMMAR;

OR, A NATURAL METHOD OF LEARNING TO READ, WRITE, AND SPEAK

THE GERMAN LANGUAGE.

By CHARLES EICHHORN. One vol. 12mo, $1.

THE HISTORIES
OF
CAIUS CORNELIUS TACITUS.
WITH NOTES FOR COLLEGES

BY W. S. TYLER,

Professor of Languages in Amherst College.

One volume, 12mo. $1,00.

The text of this edition follows, for the most part, Orelli's, Zurich, 1848, which, being based on a new and most faithful recension of the Medicean MS., by his friend Baiter, may justly be considered as marking a new era in the history of the text of Tacitus. In several passages, however, where he has needlessly departed from the MS., I have not hesitated to adhere to it in company with other editors, believing, that not unfrequently "the most corrected copies are the less correct." The various readings have been carefully compared throughout, and, if important, are referred to in the notes.

The editions which have been most consulted, whether in the criticism of the text or in the preparation of the notes, are, besides Orelli's, those of Walther, Halle, 1831; Ruperti, Hanover, 1839; and Döderlein, Halle, 1847. * * * *

It will be seen, that there are not unfrequent references to my edition of the Germania and Agricola. These are not of such a nature, as to render this incomplete without that, or essentially dependent upon it. Still, if both editions are used, it will be found advantageous to read the Germania and Agricola first. The Treatises were written in that order, and in that order they best illustrate the history of the author's mind. The editor has found in his experience as a teacher, that students generally read them in that way with more facility and pleasure, and he has constructed his notes accordingly. It is hoped, that the notes will be found to contain not only the grammatical, but likewise all the geographical, archæological and historical illustrations, that are necessary to render the author intelligible. The editor has at least endeavored to avoid the fault, which Lord Bacon says "is over usual in annotations and commentaries, viz., to blanch the obscure places, and discourse upon the plain." But it has been his constant, not to say his chief aim, to carry students beyond the dry details of grammar and lexicography, and introduce them into a familiar acquaintance and lively sympathy with the author and his times, and with that great empire, of whose degeneracy and decline in its beginnings he has bequeathed to us so profound and instructive a history. The Indexes have been prepared with much labor and care, and, it is believed, will add materially to the value of the work.—*Extract from Preface.*

THE GERMANIA AND AGRICOLA
OF
CAIUS CORNELIUS TACITUS.
WITH NOTES FOR COLLEGES.

BY W. S. TYLER,

Professor of the Greek and Latin Languages in Amherst College.

One very neat volume, 12mo. 62½ cents.

"We welcome the book as a useful addition to the classical literature of our country. It is very correctly and elegantly prepared and printed. Thirteen pages are occupied by a well-written Life of Tacitus, in which not merely outward events are narrated, but the character of the historian, both as a man and a writer, is minutely and faithfully drawn. The notes to each of the treatises are introduced by a general *critique* upon the merits and matter of the work. The body of the notes is drawn up with care, learning, and judgment. Points of style and grammatical constructions, and historical references, are ably illustrated. We have been struck with the elegant precision which marks these notes; they hit the happy medium between the too much of some commentators, and the too little of others."—*North American Review.*

Among the numerous classical Professors who have highly commended and introduced this volume, are Felton of Howard, Lincoln of Brown University, Crosby of Dartmouth, Coleman of Princeton, North of Hamilton, Packard of Bowdoin, Owen of New-York, Champlin of Waterville, &c., &c

TITUS LIVIUS.

CHIEFLY FROM THE TEXT OF ALSCHEFSKI.

WITH

ENGLISH NOTES, GRAMMATICAL AND EXPLANATORY.

TOGETHER

WITH A GEOGRAPHICAL AND HISTORICAL INDEX.

BY J. L. LINCOLN,

Professor of Latin in Brown University.

WITH AN ACCOMPANYING PLAN OF ROME, AND A MAP OF THE PASSAGE OF HANNIBAL.

One volume, 12mo. Price $1.

The publishers believe that, in the edition of Livy herewith announced, a want is supplied which has been universally felt; there being previous to this no American edition furnished with the requisite apparatus for the successful prosecution of the study of this Latin author.

OPINIONS OF CLASSICAL PROFESSORS.

From Professor Kingsley, of Yale College.

"I have not yet been able to read the whole of your work, but have examined it enough to be satisfied that it is judiciously prepared, and well adapted to the purpose intended. We use it for the present year, in connection with the edition that has been used for several years. Most of the class, however, have procured your edition; and it is probable that next year it will be used by all."

From Professor Tyler, of Amherst College.

"The notes seem to me to be prepared with much care, learning, and taste; the grammatical illustrations are unusually full, faithful, and able. The book has been used by our Freshman Class, and will I doubt not come into general use in our colleges.

From Professor Packard, of Bowdoin College.

"I have recommended your edition to our Freshman Class. I have no doubt that your labors will give a new impulse to the study of this charming classic.

From Professor Anderson, of Waterville College.

"A careful examination of several portions of your work has convinced me that, for the use of students it is altogether superior to any edition of Livy with which I am acquainted. Among its excellences you will permit me to name, the close attention given to particles—to the subjunctive mood—the constant references to the grammars—the discrimination of words nearly synonymous, and the care in giving the localities mentioned in the text. The book will be hereafter used in our college."

From Professor Johnson, of New-York University.

"I can at present only say that your edition pleases me much. I shall give it to one of my classes next week. I am prepared to find it just what was wanted."

NEARLY READY.

WORKS OF HORACE.

WITH ENGLISH NOTES, CRITICAL AND EXPLANATORY.

BY J. L. LINCOLN,

Professor of Latin in Brown University.

WITH MAPS AND ILLUSTRATIONS.

One volume, 12mo.

The text of this edition will be chiefly that of Orelli; and the Notes, besides embodying whatever is valuable in the most recent and approved German editions of Horace, will contain the results of the Editor's studies and experience as a College Professor, which he has been gathering and maturing for several years with a view to publication. It will be the aim of both the Publishers and the Editor to make this edition in all respects suitable to the wants of American schools and colleges.

C. JULIUS CÆSAR'S COMMENTARIES

ON THE

GALLIC WAR.

With English Notes, Critical and Explanatory; A Lexicon, Geographical and Historical Indexes, &c.

BY REV. J. A. SPENCER, A. M.,

Editor of "Arnold's Series of Greek and Latin Books," etc.

One handsome vol. 12mo, with Map. Price $1.

The press of Messrs. Appleton is becoming prolific of superior editions of the classics used in schools, and the volume now before us we are disposed to regard as one of the most beautiful and highly finished among them all, both in its editing and its execution. The classic Latin in which the greatest general and the greatest writer of his age recorded his achievements, has been sadly corrupted in the lapse of centuries, and its restoration to a pure and perfect text is a work requiring nice discrimination and sound learning. The text which Mr. Spencer has adopted is that of Oudendorp, with such variations as were suggested by a careful collation of the leading critics of Germany. The notes are as they should be, designed to aid the labors of the student, not to supersede them. In addition to these, the volume contains a sketch of the life of Cæsar, a brief Lexicon of Latin words, a Historical and a Geographical Index, together with a map of the country in which the great Roman conqueror conducted the campaigns he so graphically describes. The volume, as a whole, however, appears to be admirably suited to the purpose for which it was designed. Its style of editing and its typographical execution reminds us of Prof. Lincoln's excellent edition of Livy—a work which some months since had already passed to a second impression, and has now been adopted in most of the leading schools and colleges of the country.—*Providence Journal.*

CICERO DE OFFICIIS.

WITH CRITICAL AND PHILOLOGICAL NOTES, INDEXES, &c

BY PROFESSOR THATCHER,

Of Yale College, New Haven.

One Volume, 12mo. (Just ready.)

CICERO'S ORATIONS.

WITH CRITICAL AND PHILOLOGICAL NOTES, INDEXES, &c

BY E. A. JOHNSON,

Professor of Latin in the University of the City of New-York.

One Volume, 12mo. (Nearly ready.)

EXERCISES IN GREEK PROSE COMPOSITION,

ADAPTED TO THE

FIRST BOOK OF XENOPHON'S ANABASIS.

BY JAMES R. BOISE,

Professor in Brown University.

One Volume, 12mo. Price Seventy-five Cents

For the convenience of the learner, an English-Greek Vocabulary, a Catalogue of the Irregular Verbs, and an Index to the principal Grammatical Notes, have been appended

French, German, Italian, and Spanish Reading Books.

I.

NEW ELEMENTARY FRENCH READER.

AN INTRODUCTION TO THE FRENCH LANGUAGE.

Containing Fables, Select Tales, Remarkable Facts, Amusing Anecdotes, &c. With a Dictionary of all the Words, translated into English. By M. De Fivas, Member of Several Literary Societies.

One neat volume, 16mo. Price 50 cents.

II.

NEW MODERN FRENCH READER.

MORCEAUX CHOISIES DES AUTEURS MODERNES,

A LA USAGE DE LA JEUNESSE;

With a Vocabulary of the New and Difficult Words and Idiomatic Phrases adopted in Modern French Literature. By F. Rowan. Edited by J. L. Jewett, Editor of Ollendorff's French Grammar.

One volume, 12mo. 75 cents.

III.

NEW DRAMATIC FRENCH READER.

CHEFS-D'ŒUVRES DRAMATIQUES DE LA LANGUE FRANCAISE.

Mis en Ordre Progressif, et Annotés, pour en faciliter L'Intelligence. Par A. G. Collot, Professor de Langues et de Litterature.

One volume, 12mo, of 520 pages. Price $1.

IV.

A PROGRESSIVE GERMAN READER,

Prepared with reference to Ollendorff's German Grammar, with copious Notes and a Vocabulary. By G J. Adler, Professor of the German Language and Literature in the University of the City of New-York.

One neat volume, 12mo. $1.

V.

NEW ITALIAN READER.

CRESTOMAZIA ITALIANA:

A Collection of Selected Pieces in Italian Prose, designed as a Class Reading-Book for Beginners in the Study of the Italian Language. By E. Felix Foresti, LL. D., Professor of the Italian Language and Literature in Columbia College and in the University of the City of New-York.

One neat volume, 12mo. Price $1.

VI.

A NEW SPANISH READER.

Consisting of Passages from the most approved Authors in Prose and Verse arranged in Progressive Order;

For the use of those who wish to obtain easily a Practical Knowledge of the Castilian Language; with Plain Rules for its Pronunciation, Notes Explanatory of the Idioms and Difficult Constructions, and a Copious Vocabulary.

BEING A SEQUEL TO OLLENDORFF'S METHOD OF LEARNING TO READ, WRITE, AND SPEAK THE SPANISH LANGUAGE.

By MARIANO VELAZQUEZ DE LA CADENA,

Editor of Ollendorff's Spanish Grammar. One neat volume 12mo. Price $1.25

A DICTIONARY OF THE ENGLISH LANGUAGE,

CONTAINING THE PRONUNCIATION, ETYMOLOGY, AND EXPLANATION OF ALL WORDS AUTHORIZED BY EMINENT WRITERS;

To which are added, a Vocabulary of the Roots of English Words, and an Accented List of Greek, Latin, and Scripture Proper Names

BY ALEXANDER REID, A. M.,
Rector of the Circus School, Edinburgh.

With a Critical Preface, by Henry Reed, Professor of English Literature in the University of Pennsylvania, and an Appendix, showing the Pronunciation of nearly 3000 of the most important Geographical Names. One volume, 12mo of nearly 600 pages, bound in Leather. Price $1

Among the wants of our time was a good dictionary of our own language, especially adapted for academies and schools. The books which have long been in use were of little value to the junior students, being too concise in the definitions, and immethodical in the arrangement Reid's English Dictionary was compiled expressly to develop the precise analogies and various properties of the authorized words in general use, by the standard authors and orators who use our vernacular tongue.

Exclusive of the large number of proper names which are appended, this Dictionary includes four especial improvements—and when their essential value to the student is considered, the sterling character of the work as a hand-book of our language will be instantly perceived.

The primitive word is distinguished by a larger type; and when there are any derivatives from it, they follow in alphabetical order, and the part of speech is appended, thus furnishing a complete classification of all the connected analogous words of the same species.

With this facility to comprehend accurately the determinate meaning of the English word, is conjoined a rich illustration for the linguist. The derivation of all the primitive words is distinctly given, and the phrases of the languages whence they are deduced, whether composite or simple; so that the student of foreign languages, both ancient and modern, by a reference to any word, can ascertain the source whence it has been adopted into our own form of speech. This is a great acquisition to the person who is anxious to use words in their utmost clearness of meaning.

To these advantages is subjoined a Vocabulary of the Roots of English Words, which is of peculiar value to the collegian. The fifty pages which it includes, furnish the linguist with a wide-spread field of research, equally amusing and instructive. There is also added an Accented List, to the number of fifteen thousand, of Greek, Latin, and Scripture Proper Names.

BURNHAM'S SERIES OF ARITHMETICS
FOR
COMMON SCHOOLS AND ACADEMIES.

PART FIRST is a work on Mental Arithmetic. The philosophy of the mode of teaching adopted in this work, is: commence where the child commences, and proceed as the child proceeds: fall in with his own mode of arriving at truth; aid him to think for himself, and do not the thinking for him. Hence a series of exercises are given, by which the child is made familiar with the process, which he has already gone through with in acquiring his present knowledge. These exercises interest the child, and prepare him for future rapid progress. The plan is so clearly unfolded by illustration and example, that he who follows it can scarcely fail to secure on the part of his pupils, a thorough knowledge of the subject.

PART SECOND is a work on Written Arithmetic. It is the result of a long experience in teaching, and contains sufficient of Arithmetic for the practical business purposes of life. It illustrates more fully and applies more extendedly and practically the principle of Cancellation than any other Arithmetical treatise. This method as here employed in connection with the ordinary, furnishes a variety of illustrations, which cannot fail to interest and instruct the scholar. It is a prominent idea throughout, to impress upon the mind of the scholar the truth that he will never discover, nor need a new principle beyond the simple rules. The pupil is shown, by a variety of new modes of illustration, that new names and new positions introduce no new principle, but that they are merely matters of convenience. Fractions are treated and explained the same as whole numbers. Formulas are also given for drilling the scholar upon the *Blackboard*, which will be found of service to many teachers of Common Schools.

PROF. MANDEVILLE'S READING BOOKS.

I. PRIMARY, OR FIRST READER. Price 10 cents.

II. SECOND READER. Price 16 cents.

These two Readers are formed substantially on the same plan; and the second is a continuation of the first. The design of both is, to combine a knowledge of the meaning and pronunciation of words, with a knowledge of their grammatical functions. The parts of speech are introduced successively, beginning with the articles, these are followed by the demonstrative pronouns; and these again by others, class after class, until all that are requisite to form a sentence have been separately considered; when the common reading lessons begin.

The Second Reader reviews the ground passed over in the Primary, but adds largely to th amount of information. The child is here also taught to read writing as well as printed matter; and in the reading lessons, attention is constantly directed to the different ways in which sentences are formed and connected, and of the peculiar manner in which each of them is delivered. All who have examined these books, have pronounced them a decided and important advance on every other of the same class in use.

III. THIRD READER. Price 25 cents.

IV. FOURTH READER. Price 38 cents.

In the first two Readers, the main object is to make the pupil acquainted with the meaning and functions of words, and to impart facility in pronouncing them in sentential connection: the leading design of these, is to form a natural, flexible, and varied delivery. Accordingly, the Third Reader opens with a series of exercises on articulation and modulation, containing numerous examples for practice on the elementary sounds (including errors to be corrected) and on the different movements of the voice, produced by sentential structure, by emphasis, and by the passions. The habits formed by these exercises, which should be thoroughly, as they can be easily mastered, under intelligent instruction, find scope for improvement and confirmation in the reading lessons which follow, in the same book and that which succeeds.

These lessons have been selected with special reference to the following peculiarities: 1st. Colloquial character; 2d, Variety of sentential structure; 3d, Variety of subject matter; 4th Adaptation to the progressive development of the pupil's mind; and, as far as possible, 5th, Tendency to excite moral and religious emotions. Great pains have been taken to make the books in these respects, which are, in fact, characteristic of the whole series, superior to any others in use; with what success, a brief comparison will readily show.

V. THE FIFTH READER; OR, COURSE OF READING. Price 75 cents.

VI. THE ELEMENTS OF READING AND ORATORY. Price $1.

These books are designed to cultivate the literary taste, as well as the understanding and vocal powers of the pupil.

THE COURSE OF READING comprises three parts; the *first part* containing a more elaborate description of elementary sounds and the parts of speech grammatically considered than was deemed necessary in the preceding works; here indispensable: *part second*, a complete classification and description of every sentence to be found in the English, or any other language; examples of which in every degree of expansion, from a few words to the half of an octavo page in length, are adduced, and arranged to be read; and as each species has its peculiar delivery as well as structure, both are learned at the same time; *part third*, paragraphs; or sentences in their connection unfolding general thoughts, as in the common reading books. It may be observed that the selections of sentences in part second, and of paragraphs in part third, comprise some of the finest gems in the language: distinguished alike for beauty of thought and facility of diction. If not found in a school book, they might be appropriately called "elegant extracts."

The ELEMENTS OF READING AND ORATORY closes the series with an exhibition of the whole theory and art of Elocution exclusive of gesture. It contains, besides the classification of sentences already referred to, but here presented with fuller statement and illustration, the laws of punctuation and delivery deduced from it: the whole followed by carefully selected pieces for sentential analysis and vocal practice.

THE RESULT.—The student who acquaints himself thoroughly with the contents of this book, will, as numerous experiments have proved; 1st, Acquire complete knowledge of the structure of the language; 2d, Be able to designate any sentence of any book by name at a glance; 3d, Be able to declare with equal rapidity its proper punctuation; 4th, Be able to delare, and with sufficient practice to give its proper delivery. Such are a few of the general characteristics of the series of school books which the publishers now offer to the friends and patrons of a sound common school and academic education. For more particular information, reference is respectfully made to the "Hints," which may be found at the beginning of each volume.

N. B. The punctuation in all these books conforms, in the main, to the sense and proper delivery of every sentence, and is a guide to both. When a departure from the proper punctuation occurs, the proper delivery is indicated. As reading books are usually punctuated, it is a matter of surprise that children should learn to read at all.

*** The above series of Reading Books are already very extensively introduced and commended by the most experienced Teachers in the country. "Prof. Mandeville's system is eminently original, scientific and practical, and destined wherever it is introduced to supersede at once all others."

ARNOLD'S CLASSICAL SERIES.

I.

A FIRST AND SECOND LATIN BOOK

AND PRACTICAL GRAMMAR. By THOMAS K. ARNOLD, A. M. Revised and carefully Corrected, by J. A. Spencer, A. M. One vol. 12mo., 75 cts.

II.

LATIN PROSE COMPOSITION:

A Practical Introduction to Latin Prose Composition. By THOMAS K. ARNOLD, A. M. Revised and Corrected by J. A. Spencer, A. M. 12mo., $1.

III.

FIRST GREEK BOOK;

With Easy Exercises and Vocabulary. By THOMAS K. ARNOLD, A. M. Revised and Corrected by J. A. Spencer, A. M. 12mo., 63 cts.

IV.

GREEK PROSE COMPOSITION:

A Practical Introduction to Greek Prose Composition. By THOMAS K. ARNOLD, A. M. Revised and Corrected by J. A. Spencer, A. M. One vol. 12mo., 75 cts.

V.

GREEK READING BOOK,

For the Use of Schools; containing the substance of the Practical Introduction to Greek Construing, and a Treatise on the Greek Particles, by the Rev. THOMAS K. ARNOLD, A. M., and also a Copious Selection from Greek Authors, with English Notes, Critical and Explanatory, and a Lexicon, by J. A. Spencer, A. M. 12mo., $1 50

VI.

CORNELIUS NEPOS;

With Practical Questions and Answers, and an Imitative Exercise on each Chapter. By THOMAS K. ARNOLD, A. M. Revised, with Additional Notes, by Prof. Johnson, Professor of the Latin Language in the University of the City of New-York. 12mo. A new, enlarged edition, with Lexicon, Index, &c., $1.

"ARNOLD'S GREEK AND LATIN SERIES.—The publication of this valuable collection of classical school books may be regarded as the presage of better things in respect to the mode of teaching and acquiring languages. Heretofore boys have been condemned to the drudgery of going over Latin and Greek Grammar without the remotest conception of the value of what they were learning, and every day becoming more and more disgusted with the dry and unmeaning task; but now, by Mr. Arnold's admirable method—substantially the same with that of Ollendorff—the moment they take up the study of Latin or Greek, they begin to learn sentences, to acquire ideas, to see how the Romans and Greeks expressed themselves, how their mode of expression differed from ours, and by degrees they lay up a stock of knowledge which is utterly astonishing to those who have dragged on month after month in the old-fashioned, dry, and tedious way of learning languages.

"Mr. Arnold, in fact, has had the good sense to adopt the system of nature. A child learns his own language by *imitating* what he hears, and constantly *repeating* it till it is fastened in the memory; in the same way Mr. A. puts the pupil immediately to work at Exercises in Latin and Greek, involving the elementary principles of the language—words are supplied—the mode of putting them together is told the pupil—he is shown how the ancients expressed their ideas; and then, by repeating these things again and again—*iterum iterumque*—the docile pupil has them indelibly impressed upon his memory and rooted in his understanding.

"The American Editor is a thorough classical scholar, and has been a practical teacher for years in this city. He has devoted the utmost care to a complete revision of Mr. Arnold's works, has corrected several errors of inadvertence or otherwise, has rearranged and improved various matters in the early volumes of the series, and has attended most diligently to the accurate printing and mechanical execution of the whole. We anticipate most confidently the speedy adoption of these works in our schools and colleges."

⁂ Arnold's Series of Classical Works has attained a circulation almost unparalleled, being introduced into nearly all the Colleges and leading Educational Institutions in the United States.

www.ingramcontent.com/pod-product-compliance
Lightning Source LLC
LaVergne TN
LVHW050518100826
845148LV00002B/374

* 9 7 8 1 4 2 5 5 2 0 8 0 9 *